● "EACH OF THESE PAGES . . . IS MORE THRILLING THAN ANY FICTION. NO ONE CAN READ THIS—SO SIMPLE YET SO DRAMATIC—WITHOUT REALIZING ONCE AGAIN WHAT THE WORLD LOST BY THE DEATH OF THESE TWO BROTHERS."

—Harold Macmillan

"The general feeling, at this stage, was that an air strike against the missile sites could be the only course. Listening to the proposals, I passed a note to the President: 'I now know how Tojo felt when he was planning Pearl Harbor.'"

—Robert F. Kennedy

"Everything was going to work out satisfactorily . . . I went back to the White House and talked to the President for a long time. As I was leaving, he said, making reference to Abraham Lincoln, 'This is the night I should go to the theatre.' I said, 'If you go, I want to go with you.'"

—Robert F. Kennedy

Other MENTOR and SIGNET Books
of Special Interest

☐ **NIXON AGONISTES by Garry Wills.** In this rich study of Richard Nixon, Garry Wills presents an exciting new combination of on-the-spot reporting and political analysis for anyone who hopes to understand one of the most complex American Presidents. "One is tempted to quote constantly from NIXON AGONISTES because Mr. Wills writes with a scalpel . . . an astonishing book."—*New York Times*
(#ME1750—$2.50)

☐ **THE MAKING OF THE PRESIDENT® 1960 by Theodore H. White.** The masterful Pulitzer Prize-winning account of the 1960 campaign and election of John F. Kennedy. A hardcover bestseller for 49 weeks. (#MJ1598—$1.95)

☐ **THE TWILIGHT OF THE PRESIDENCY by George E. Reedy.** Here is a candid and disturbing evaluation of the presidency by a uniquely qualified observer. In THE TWILIGHT OF THE PRESIDENCY, George Reedy subjects the highest office in the land to long overdue scrutiny. (#ME1733—$1.75)

☐ **MARATHON: The Pursuit of the Presidency 1972-1976 by Jules Witcover.** "A masterful handling . . . Witcover, one of the ablest and most expert political reporters, writes with deep sure knowledge of the real kingmakers in America at election time and often long afterwards."—*The New York Times Book Review* A Book-of-the-Month Club Main Selection
(#E8034—$2.95)

Thirteen Days

A MEMOIR OF THE CUBAN MISSILE CRISIS

BY *Robert F. Kennedy*

With Introductions by
Robert S. McNamara and Harold Macmillan

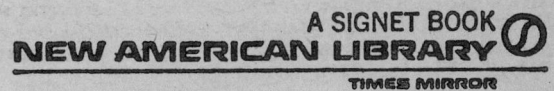

A SIGNET BOOK
NEW AMERICAN LIBRARY
TIMES MIRROR

"Who feel the giant agony of the world,
  And more, like slaves to poor humanity,
  Labor for mortal good . . ."

Contents

Photographs

following page 96

MEN AND EVENTS

President John F. Kennedy with his brother, Attorney General Robert F. Kennedy.

THE NEW YORK TIMES

October 18, 1962. President Kennedy meets with Soviet Foreign Minister Andrei Gromyko. At this meeting, the President did not reveal U.S. awareness of Cuban missiles.

UNITED PRESS INTERNATIONAL

Soviet Ambassador Anatoly Dobrynin leaves the State Department October 22 with U.S. diplomatic note for Moscow.

WIDE WORLD

Ex Comm meets in the White House.

CECIL STOUGHTON

The man who bore the burden, John F. Kennedy, photographed signing the U.S. Proclamation on Interdiction of Offensive Weapons, October 23, 1962.

CECIL STOUGHTON

Fidel Castro in a typical pose.

MAGNUM

Nikita Khrushchev photographed at the opera on the evening of the thirteenth day.

WIDE WORLD

Secretary of State Dean Rusk leaving the White House on October 22.

WIDE WORLD

Secretary of Defense Robert S. McNamara announcing the extension of Navy and Marine Corps duty on October 23.

WIDE WORLD

October 24. Attorney General Robert Kennedy leaves the White House after conferring with President Kennedy on the crisis.

WIDE WORLD

General Maxwell D. Taylor, Chairman of the Joint Chiefs of Staff, at the time of the crisis.

UNITED PRESS INTERNATIONAL

Theodore C. Sorensen, Special Counsel to President Kennedy.

UNITED PRESS INTERNATIONAL

McGeorge Bundy, National Security Assistant.

MAGNUM

George Ball, Undersecretary of State.

UNITED PRESS INTERNATIONAL

sition, and a missile container observed between two of the buildings, among other ready developments.

U.S. AIR FORCE

October 23. A low-level photograph showing specifics of the development at San Cristobal.

U.S. AIR FORCE

Later details of San Cristobal site.

U.S. AIR FORCE

San Julian airfield photographed on October 27.

U.S. AIR FORCE

October 24. Soviet ship laden with jet-bomber crates photographed by U.S. reconnaissance aircraft.

UNITED PRESS INTERNATIONAL FROM THE U.S. DEFENSE DEPT.

A Soviet ship with fuselage crates on deck inbound to Cuba.

U.S. AIR FORCE

Another inbound Soviet ship with miscellaneous cargo.

U.S. AIR FORCE

One of the first outbound Soviet vessels.

U.S. AIR FORCE

San Cristobal site No. 4 on October 29, apparently photographed before the beginnings of Soviet withdrawal there.

U.S. AIR FORCE

A chart indicating the Soviet military build-up in Cuba.

U.S. AIR FORCE

October 25. Adlai Stevenson describes aerial photos of launching sites as Soviet Delegate Valerian Zorin listens.

WIDE WORLD

Adlai Stevenson, seated next to British Delegate Sir Patrick Dean, reads reply from President Kennedy to message from Acting UN Secretary-General U Thant.

WIDE WORLD

THE BUILD-UP AND WITHDRAWAL

Two U.S. low-altitude reconnaissance planes: Air Force RF 101 and Navy F8U.

U.S. AIR FORCE

The photo of a ballistic-missile launch site at San Cristobal which provided the first photographic evidence of Soviet offensive-missile deployment in Cuba, October 14, 1962.

U.S. AIR FORCE

October 15. Further evidence: a ballistic-missile site at Guanajay showing extensive construction scarring and activity.

U.S. AIR FORCE

October 17. A later view of a site at Guanajay.

U.S. AIR FORCE

October 17. A later view of a site at San Cristobal.

U.S. AIR FORCE

October 17. A view of a missile site at Sagua showing completed service roads and launch pads, missile erectors in po-

Photograph of San Cristobal site No. 2 on October 29 showing evidence of the start of dismantling, despite some continued construction.

U.S. AIR FORCE

November 1. Dismantling proceeds rapidly at Guanajay.

U.S. AIR FORCE

November 1. Further evidence of dismantling at San Cristobal.

U.S. AIR FORCE

The missile-laden Soviet ship *Volgoles* leaving Cuba, November 9, with U.S. Navy radar picket ship *Vesole* alongside.

U.S. NAVY

Major Rudolf Anderson, Jr., U-2 pilot shot down by the Communists on October 27.

U.S. AIR FORCE

●   ●   ●

Front end papers: Facsimile of Robert Kennedy's longhand first draft of opening paragraphs of the manuscript.

Back end papers: Facsimile of Robert Kennedy's longhand first draft of the portion of manuscript that appears on page 106 in this edition.

Introduction by Robert S. McNamara

*E*XPOSURE TO DANGER strips away the protective covering with which each of us guards his inner thoughts—it quickly and dramatically displays a man's character. And common exposure to danger forges bonds and understanding between men stronger than those formed by decades of close association. So it was that I came to know, admire, and love Robert F. Kennedy by his behavior during the Cuban missile crisis.

A few weeks before his death, he asked me to write a few words of my recollection of that period. This is what I wrote:

You will recall that in the fall of 1962, the Soviets moved offensive weapons, including ballistic missiles, into Cuba. The world was faced with what many of us felt then, and what since has been generally agreed, was the greatest danger of a catastrophic war since the advent of the nuclear age. Prime Minister Macmillan has said that the weeks of the crisis represented the greatest period of strain which he faced in several decades of public service, including the whole of World War II.

The performance of the U.S. Government during that critical period was more effective than at any other time during my seven years' service as Secretary of Defense. The agencies of the Government: the State Department, the civilian and military leaders of the Defense Department, the CIA, the White House staff, the UN Mission, worked together smoothly and harmoniously. That they did so was in large part a result of the efforts of Robert Kennedy. It was he, acting with his brother's consent, who did so much to organize the effort, monitor the results, and assure the completion of the work on which the recommendations to the President were to be based.

But his contribution was far more than administrative. On the basic policy question of whether to force the missiles out by massive air and ground attack or by the far less risky application of a maritime quarantine, he strongly supported the quarantine.

He did so because he saw that the air and ground strikes favored by so many would have brought death to thousands of innocent Cuban civilians and to thousands of U.S. military personnel. He saw, too, that such attacks ran the risk of triggering the launch of nuclear weapons from Cuba against the U.S. and the risk of Soviet retaliatory attacks on Berlin or other vulnerable points on the periphery of NATO.

And he opposed a massive surprise attack by a large country on a small country because he believed such an attack to be inhuman, contrary to our traditions and ideals, and an act of brutality for which the world would never forgive us.

He understood then as now that above all else a U.S. President must, while defending our vital interests, prevent the confrontations between nuclear powers which can lead to nuclear holocaust.

His objective was to force the missiles out of Cuba without war. That objective was accomplished. It was accomplished by a strategy which he helped to shape and which his brother directed—a strategy which applied pressure against the Soviets without ever pushing them to the point where they were forced to an irrational, suicidal, spasm response.

He showed a shrewd sense of diplomacy both in the concept and in the application of the strategy. As a matter of fact, it was Robert Kennedy's suggestion, when we had received two contradictory messages from Khrushchev, the first favorable and the second unfavorable, that we reply to the first and not the second. He actually drafted the reply, stating the terms we were willing to accept, plucking them from the several often disparate Soviet messages. They were the terms on which the settlement ultimately was based.

Throughout the entire period of the crisis—a period of the most intense strain I have ever operated under—he remained calm and cool; firm but restrained; never nettled and never rattled.

And he demonstrated then, as I have seen him do on so many other occasions before and since, a most extraordinary combination of energy and courage, compassion and wisdom.

At the time I wrote those lines I was unaware that he, himself, had written a report of those days of crisis. After reading his manuscript, a moving, sensitive document, I can only repeat, in words now dampened by tears, what I wrote before: "He demonstrated then, as I have seen him do on so many other occasions before and since, a most extraordinary combination of energy and courage, compassion and wisdom."

Introduction by Harold Macmillan

I<small>T IS IMPOSSIBLE</small> to take up this book without a renewed sense of loss. The inner story of the masterly handling of the Cuba missile crisis by one brother is told us by another. Both these men who played leading parts in this drama, one as principal, the other as adjutant, have been struck down in the prime of life. We can only speculate as to what might have been their fuller achievements, singly or jointly, had they been spared. Each has his place in history. Meanwhile we must be grateful for this simple yet enthralling account by his closest and most intimate colleague of the President's thoughts and actions throughout the most dangerous issue which the world has had to face since the end of the Second War.

What President John Kennedy thought and did during these fateful hours, Senator Robert Kennedy has here faithfully recorded.

Many thousands of words were written at the time and have been published since concerning this strange and still scarcely explicable affair. In this book we have the story as it appeared to one brother presented through the eyes of the other. It is a clear and simple record. Yet each of these few pages of soberly reported fact is more thrilling than any fiction.

The crisis was short. It lasted from October 16, when irrefutable evidence became known in Washington of the Russian deployment of nuclear missiles in Cuba, till October 28, when the news came of Khrushchev's compliance with the American demands. In these few days, in Secretary Rusk's words, "We looked into the mouth of the cannon; the Russians flinched." Perhaps it was not quite so simple as that. Nevertheless, the President's will prevailed. Throughout all the pressures, internal and external, to which he was subjected, President Kennedy remained calm and firm.

Apart from the various diplomatic weapons which were used with consummate skill, the President's decision to adopt the method of the blockade gave an opportunity both for the Americans to prepare and to the Soviet Government to recede. Yet they would not have done so had they not been assured of his determination not to flinch from the ultimate recourse to other and more decisive measures. Indeed, the Russian retreat came only just in time.

There are many questions which still remain unanswered. Why did the Russians risk so much? What was their ultimate purpose? Why did they withdraw? Why did they not retaliate at other, but equally sensitive, points? This account does not seek to solve or even to pose these problems. Its value is twofold. First, it is a historical record of a unique kind, written with clarity and succinctness, and written with equal accuracy and objectiveness. Secondly, it gives a remarkable picture of the President's combination of flexibility and determination in a position in which scarcely any statesman in history has ever been placed. In addition, although we know the end of the story, it holds the reader in a mood of intense excitement as the tale unfolds. I have referred to some of my own records of these tense days and the many conversations which I had with the President by our secret telephone. In due course I shall tell the story of my own part; now it is enough to say that it was one of complete support for the President at every stage. Perhaps his most difficult decision was the refusal, against the advice of weaker brethren in America and elsewhere, to bargain the security of the Western world by yielding to the specious Russian offers of a face-saving accommodation at the expense of America's allies.

Apart from its intrinsic value as a historical document, this book lifts the veil on the President's methods. Always ready to listen to advice, generous in giving due weight to opinions however diverse, careful and even cautious before reaching final conclusions on any problem, he had the supreme quality, shared by only very great men, of refusing to evade or cushion his final responsibility by an attempt to spread it out upon the backs of his colleagues. He was ready to carry the burden of responsibility himself.

While boldly facing the ultimate resort to force, his tactics and his sense of timing were perfect. He was at the same time ready to act, and to allow his adversary the opportunity of retreat. When we recall the many occasions in history where hesitation and self-deception have led to war, our admiration is correspondingly increased. For President Kennedy really did preserve both Peace and Honour.

No one can read this little book, so simple yet so dramatic, without realising once again what the world has lost by the death of these two brothers.

Thirteen Days

A MEMOIR OF THE CUBAN MISSILE CRISIS

"Tuesday morning, October 16, 1962..."

ON TUESDAY MORNING, OCTOBER 16, 1962, shortly after 9:00 o'clock, President Kennedy called and asked me to come to the White House. He said only that we were facing great trouble. Shortly afterward, in his office, he told me that a U-2 had just finished a photographic mission and that the Intelligence Community had become convinced that Russia was placing missiles and atomic weapons in Cuba.

That was the beginning of the Cuban missile crisis—a confrontation between the two giant atomic nations, the U.S. and the U.S.S.R., which brought the world to the abyss of nuclear destruction and the end of mankind. From that moment in President Kennedy's office until Sunday morning, October 28, that was my life—and for Americans and Russians, for the whole world, it was their life as well.

At 11:45 that same morning, in the Cabinet Room, a formal presentation was made by the Central Intelligence Agency to a number of high officials of the government. Photographs were shown to us. Experts arrived with their charts and their pointers and told us that if we looked carefully, we could see there was a missile base being constructed in a field near San Cristobal, Cuba. I, for one, had to take their word for it. I examined the pictures carefully, and what I saw appeared to be no more than the clearing of a field for a farm or the basement of a house. I was relieved to hear later that this was the same reaction of virtually everyone at the meeting, including President Kennedy. Even a few days later, when more work had taken place on the site, he remarked that it looked like a football field.

The dominant feeling at the meeting was stunned surprise. No one had expected or anticipated that the Russians would deploy surface-to-surface ballistic missiles in Cuba. I thought back to my meeting with Soviet Ambassador Anatoly Dobrynin in my office some weeks before. He came to tell me that the Russians were prepared to sign an atmospheric-test-ban treaty if we could make certain agreements on underground testing. I told him I would transmit this message and the accompanying documents to President Kennedy.

I told him we were deeply concerned within the Administration about the amount of military equipment being sent to Cuba. That very morning, I had met on this subject with the President and the Secretaries of

State and Defense. There was some evidence that, in addition to the surface-to-air-missile (SAM) sites that were being erected, the Russians, under the guise of a fishing village, were constructing a large naval shipyard and a base for submarines. This was all being watched carefully—through agents within Cuba who were reporting the military buildup in a limited but frequently important way, through the questioning of refugees who were screened and processed as they arrived in Florida, and through U-2 flights.

It was election time. The autumn days of September and October were filled with charges and countercharges. Republicans "viewing with alarm" were claiming the U.S. was not taking the necessary steps to protect our security. Some, such as Senator Homer E. Capehart of Indiana, were suggesting that we take military action against Cuba.

I told Ambassador Dobrynin of President Kennedy's deep concern about what was happening. He told me I should not be concerned, for he was instructed by Soviet Chairman Nikita S. Khrushchev to assure President Kennedy that there would be no ground-to-ground missiles or offensive weapons placed in Cuba. Further, he said, I could assure the President that this military buildup was not of any significance and that

Khrushchev would do nothing to disrupt the relationship of our two countries during this period prior to the election. Chairman Khrushchev, he said, liked President Kennedy and did not wish to embarrass him.

I pointed out that I felt he had a very strange way of showing his admiration; that what the Russians had been doing in Cuba was a matter of the deepest concern to the United States; and that his protestations of friendship meant little alongside the military activities in the Caribbean. I told him we were watching the buildup carefully and that he should know it would be of the gravest consequence if the Soviet Union placed missiles in Cuba. That would never happen, he assured me, and left.

I reported the conversation to President Kennedy, Secretary of State Dean Rusk, and Secretary of Defense Robert McNamara, and relayed my own skepticism, and suggested that it might be advisable to issue a statement making it unequivocally clear that the U.S. would not tolerate the introduction of offensive surface-to-surface missiles, or offensive weapons of any kind, into Cuba.

That same afternoon, September 4, from a draft prepared by Nicholas Katzenbach, the Deputy Attorney General, and myself, the President issued exactly this kind of warning and pointed out the serious consequences that would result from such a step.

A week later, on September 11, Moscow disclaimed publicly any intention of taking such action and stated that there was no need for nuclear missiles to be transferred to any country outside the Soviet Union, including Cuba.

During this same period of time, an important official in the Soviet Embassy, returning from Moscow, brought me a personal message from Khrushchev to President Kennedy, stating that he wanted the President to be assured that under no circumstances would surface-to-surface missiles be sent to Cuba.

Now, as the representatives of the CIA explained the U-2 photographs that morning, Tuesday, October 16, we realized that it had all been lies, one gigantic fabric of lies. The Russians were putting missiles in Cuba, and they had been shipping them there and beginning the construction of the sites at the same time those various private and public assurances were being forwarded by Chairman Khrushchev to President Kennedy.

Thus the dominant feeling was one of shocked incredulity. We had been deceived by Khrushchev, but we had also fooled ourselves. No official within the government had ever suggested to President Kennedy that the Russian buildup in Cuba would include missiles. On a number of occasions, the President had asked for a specific evaluation on what the Intelligence Community felt to be the implications for the U.S. of that buildup. The Intelligence Community, in its National Estimate of the future course of events, had advised him—on each of the four occasions in 1962 when they furnished him with official reports on Cuba and the Caribbean—that the Russians would not make offensive weapons available to Cuba. The last estimate before our meeting of the 16th of October was dated the 19th of September, and it advised the President that without reservation the United States Intelligence Board, after considerable discussion and examination, had concluded that the Soviet Union would not make Cuba a strategic base. It pointed out that the Soviet Union had not taken this kind of step with any of its satellites in the past and would feel the risk of retaliation from the United States to be too great to take the risk in this case.

We heard later, in a postmortem study, that reports had come from agents within Cuba indicating the presence of missiles in September of 1962. Most of the reports were false; some were the result of confusion by untrained observers between surface-to-air missiles and surface-to-surface missiles. Several reports, however, turned out to be accurate—one from a former employee at the Hilton Hotel in Havana, who believed a-missile installation was being constructed near San Cristobal, and another from someone who overheard Premier Fidel Castro's pilot talking in a boastful and intoxicated way one evening about the nuclear missiles that were going to be furnished Cuba by Russia.

But before these reports were given substance, they had to be checked and rechecked. They were not even considered substantial enough to pass on to the President or other high officials within the government. In retrospect, this was perhaps a mistake. But the same postmortem study also stated that there was no action the U.S. could have taken before the time we actually did act, on the grounds that even the films available on October 16 would not have been substantial enough to convince the governments and peoples of the world of the presence of offensive missiles in Cuba. Certainly, unsubstantiated refugee reports would not have been sufficient.

The important fact, of course, is that the missiles were uncovered and the information was made available to the government and the people before the missiles became operative and in time for the U.S. to act.

The same group that met that first morning in the Cabinet Room met almost continuously through the next twelve days and almost daily for some six weeks thereafter. Others in the group, which was later to be called the "Ex Comm" (the Executive Committee of the National Security Council), included Secretary of State Dean Rusk; Secretary of Defense Robert McNamara; Director of the Central Intelligence Agency John McCone; Secretary of the Treasury Douglas Dillon; President Kennedy's adviser on national-security affairs, McGeorge Bundy; Presidential Counsel Ted Sorensen; Under Secretary of State George Ball; Deputy Under Secretary of State U. Alexis Johnson; General Maxwell Taylor, Chairman of the Joint Chiefs of Staff; Edward Martin, Assistant Secretary of State for Latin America; originally, Chip Bohlen, who, after the first day, left to become Ambassador to France and was succeeded by Llewellyn Thompson as the adviser on Russian affairs; Roswell Gilpatric, Deputy Secretary of Defense; Paul Nitze, Assistant Secretary of Defense; and, intermittently at various meetings, Vice-President Lyndon B. Johnson; Adlai Stevenson, Ambassador to the United Nations; Ken O'Donnell, Special Assistant to the President; and Don Wilson, who was Deputy Director of the United States Information Agency. This was the group that met, talked, argued, and fought together during that crucial period of time. From this group came the recommendations from which President Kennedy was ultimately to select his course of action.

They were men of the highest intelligence, industrious, courageous, and dedicated to their country's well-being. It is no reflection on them that none was consistent in his opinion from the very beginning to the very end. That kind of open, unfettered mind was essential. For some there were only small changes, perhaps varieties of a single idea. For others there were continuous changes of opinion each day; some, because of the pressure of events, even appeared to lose their judgment and stability.

The general feeling in the beginning was that some form of action was required. There were those, although they were a small minority, who felt the missiles did not alter the balance of power and therefore necessitated no action. Most felt, at that stage, that an air strike against the missile sites could be the only course. Listening to the proposals, I passed a note to the President: "I now know how Tojo felt when he was planning Pearl Harbor."

"The President . . . knew he would have to act."

*A*FTER THE MEETING in the Cabinet Room, I walked back to the Mansion with the President. It would be difficult; the stakes were high—of the highest and most substantial kind—but he knew he would have to act. The U.S. could not accept what the Russians had done. What that action would be was still to be determined. But he was convinced from the beginning that he would have to do something. To keep the discussions from being inhibited and because he did not want to arouse attention, he decided not to attend all the meetings of our committee. This was wise. Personalities change when the President is present, and frequently even strong men make recommendations on the basis of what they believe the President wishes to hear. He instructed our group to come forward with recommendations for one course or possibly several alternative courses of action.

It was during the afternoon and evening of that

first day, Tuesday, that we began to discuss the idea of a quarantine or blockade. Secretary McNamara, by Wednesday, became the blockade's strongest advocate. He argued that it was limited pressure, which could be increased as the circumstances warranted. Further, it was dramatic and forceful pressure, which would be understood yet, most importantly, still leave us in control of events. Later he reinforced his position by reporting that a surprise air strike against the missile bases alone —a surgical air strike, as it came to be called—was militarily impractical in the view of the Joint Chiefs of Staff, that any such military action would have to include all military installations in Cuba, eventually leading to an invasion. Perhaps we would come to that, he argued. Perhaps that course of action would turn out to be inevitable. "But let's not start with that course," if by chance that kind of confrontation with Cuba, and of necessity with the Soviet Union, could be avoided.

Those who argued for the military strike instead of a blockade pointed out that a blockade would not in fact remove the missiles and would not even stop the work from going ahead on the missile sites themselves. The missiles were already in Cuba, and all we would be doing with a blockade would be "closing the door after the horse had left the barn." Further, they argued, we would be bringing about a confrontation with the Soviet Union by stopping their ships, when we should be concentrating on Cuba and Castro.

Their most forceful argument was that our installation of a blockade around Cuba invited the Russians to do the same to Berlin. If we demanded the removal of missiles from Cuba as the price for lifting our blockade, they would demand the removal of missiles surrounding the Soviet Union as the reciprocal act.

And so we argued, and so we disagreed—all dedicated, intelligent men, disagreeing and fighting about the future of their country, and of mankind. Meanwhile, time was slowly running out.

An examination of photography taken on Wednesday, the 17th of October, showed several other installations, with at least sixteen and possibly thirty-two missiles of over a thousand-mile range. Our military experts advised that these missiles could be in operation within a week. The next day, Thursday, estimates by our Intelligence Community placed in Cuba missiles with an atomic-warhead potential of about one half the current ICBM capacity of the entire Soviet Union. The photography having indicated that the missiles were being directed at certain American cities, the estimate was that within a few minutes of their being fired eighty million Americans would be dead.

The members of the Joint Chiefs of Staff were unanimous in calling for immediate military action. They forcefully presented their view that the blockade would not be effective. General Curtis LeMay, Air Force Chief of Staff, argued strongly with the President that a military attack was essential. When the President questioned what the response of the Russians might be, General LeMay assured him there would be no reaction. President Kennedy was skeptical. "They, no more than we, can let these things go by without doing something. They can't, after all their statements, permit us to take out their missiles, kill a lot of Russians, and then do nothing. If they don't take action in Cuba, they certainly will in Berlin."

The President went on to say that he recognized the validity of the arguments made by the Joint Chiefs, the danger that more and more missiles would be placed in Cuba, and the likelihood, if we did nothing, that the Russians would move on Berlin and in other areas of the world, feeling the U.S. was completely impotent. Then it would be too late to do anything in Cuba, for by that time all their missiles would be operational.

General David M. Shoup, Commandant of the Marine Corps, summed up everyone's feelings: "You are in a pretty bad fix, Mr. President." The President answered quickly, "You are in it with me." Everyone laughed, and, with no final decision, the meeting adjourned.

Later, Secretary McNamara, although he told the President he disagreed with the Joint Chiefs and favored a blockade rather than an attack, informed him that the necessary planes, men, and ammunition were being deployed and that we could be ready to move with the necessary air bombardments on Tuesday, October 23, if that was to be the decision. The plans called for an initial attack, consisting of five hundred sorties, striking all military targets, including the missile sites, airfields, ports, and gun emplacements.

I supported McNamara's position in favor of a blockade. This was not from a deep conviction that it would be a successful course of action, but a feeling that it had more flexibility and fewer liabilities than a military attack. Most importantly, like others, I could not accept the idea that the United States would rain bombs on Cuba, killing thousands and thousands of civilians in a surprise attack. Maybe the alternatives were not very palatable, but I simply did not see how we could accept that course of action for our country.

Former Secretary of State Dean Acheson began

attending our meetings, and he was strongly in favor of an air attack. I was a great admirer of his. In 1961, President Kennedy asked him to prepare a report for the National Security Council recommending a course of action to deal with the Russian threat to Berlin. Listening to his presentation then, I had thought to myself that I had never heard anyone so lucid and convincing and would never wish to be on the other side of an argument with him. Now he made his arguments that an air attack and invasion represented our only alternative in the same clear and brilliant way. He said that the President of the United States had the responsibility for the security of the people of the United States and of the whole free world, that it was his obligation to take the only action which could protect that security, and that that meant destroying the missiles.

With some trepidation, I argued that, whatever validity the military and political arguments were for an attack in preference to a blockade, America's traditions and history would not permit such a course of action. Whatever military reasons he and others could marshal, they were nevertheless, in the last analysis, advocating a surprise attack by a very large nation against a very small one. This, I said, could not be undertaken by the U.S. if we were to maintain our moral position at home and around the globe. Our struggle against Communism throughout the world was far more than physical survival—it had as its essence our heritage and our ideals, and these we must not destroy.

We spent more time on this moral question during the first five days than on any other single matter. At various times, it was proposed that we send a letter to Khrushchev twenty-four hours before the bombardment was to begin, that we send a letter to Castro, that leaflets and pamphlets listing the targets be dropped over Cuba before the attack—all these ideas and more were abandoned for military or other reasons. We struggled and fought with one another and with our consciences, for it was a question that deeply troubled us all.

In the midst of all these discussions, Andrei Gromyko came to see the President. It was an appointment made long before the missiles were uncovered, and the President felt it would be awkward to cancel it. He debated whether he should confront the Soviet Foreign Minister with our knowledge of the missiles' presence and finally decided that, as he had not yet determined a final course of action and the disclosure of our knowledge might give the Russians the initiative, he would simply listen to Gromyko.

They met late Wednesday afternoon in the President's office in the White House. Gromyko began the conversation by saying the United States should stop threatening Cuba. All Cuba wanted was peaceful coexistence, he said; she was not interested in exporting her system to other Latin American countries. Cuba, like the Soviet Union, wanted only peace. Premíer Khrushchev had instructed him, Gromyko said, to tell President Kennedy that the only assistance being furnished Cuba was for agriculture and land development, so the people could feed themselves, plus a small amount of defensive arms. In view of all the publicity in the American press, he said, he wanted to emphasize that the Soviet Union would never become involved in the furnishing of offensive weapons to Cuba.

Gromyko said he wished to appeal to the U.S. and to President Kennedy on behalf of Premier Khrushchev and the Soviet Union to lessen the tensions that existed with regard to Cuba.

President Kennedy listened, astonished, but also with some admiration for the boldness of Gromyko's position. Firmly, but with great restraint considering the provocation, he told Gromyko that it was not the United States which was fomenting discord, but the Soviet Union. The U.S.S.R.'s supplying of arms to Cuba was having a profound effect on the people of the United

States and was a source of great concern to him. Because of the personal assurances he had received from Khrushchev, he had been taking the public position that no action was required against Cuba, and yet the situation was becoming steadily more dangerous.

Gromyko repeated that the sole objective of the U.S.S.R. was to "give bread to Cuba in order to prevent hunger in that country." As far as arms were concerned the Soviet Union had simply sent some specialists to train Cubans to handle certain kinds of armament, which were only "defensive." He then said he wished to emphasize the word "defensive" and that none of these weapons could ever constitute a threat to the United States.

The President replied that there should be no misunderstanding of the position of the United States—that that position had been made clear to the Soviet Union in meetings between the Attorney General and Ambassador Dobrynin and in his own public statements. To avoid any misunderstanding, he read aloud his statement of September 4, which pointed out the serious consequences that would arise if the Soviet Union placed missiles or offensive weapons within Cuba.

Gromyko assured him this would never be done, that the United States should not be concerned. After touching briefly on some other matters, he said good-by.

I came by shortly after Gromyko left the White House. The President of the United States, it can be said, was displeased with the spokesman of the Soviet Union. . . .

"A majority opinion ... for a blockade ..."

*B*Y THURSDAY NIGHT, there was a majority opinion in our group for a blockade. Our committee went from the State Department to the White House around 9:15 that night. In order to avoid the suspicion that would have ensued from the presence of a long line of limousines, we all went in my car—John McCone, Maxwell Taylor, the driver, and myself all crowded together in the front seat, and six others sitting in back.

We explained our recommendations to the President. At the beginning, the meeting seemed to proceed in an orderly and satisfactory way. However, as people talked, as the President raised probing questions, minds and opinions began to change again, and not only on small points. For some, it was from one extreme to another—supporting an air attack at the beginning of the meeting and, by the time we left the White House, supporting no action at all.

The President, not at all satisfied, sent us back to

our deliberations. Because any other step would arouse suspicion, he returned to his regular schedule and his campaign speaking engagements.

The next morning, at our meeting at the State Department, there were sharp disagreements again. The strain and the hours without sleep were beginning to take their toll. However, even many years later, those human weaknesses—impatience, fits of anger—are understandable. Each one of us was being asked to make a recommendation which would affect the future of all mankind, a recommendation which, if wrong and if accepted, could mean the destruction of the human race. That kind of pressure does strange things to a human being, even to brilliant, self-confident, mature, experienced men. For some it brings out characteristics and strengths that perhaps even they never knew they had, and for others the pressure is too overwhelming.

Our situation was made more difficult by the fact that there was no obvious or simple solution. A dogmatism, a certainty of viewpoint, was simply not possible. For every position there were inherent weaknesses; and those opposed would point them out, often with devastating effects.

Finally, we agreed on a procedure by which we felt we could give some intelligent recommendations to the President. We knew that time was running out and that delay was not possible. We split into groups to write up our respective recommendations, beginning with an outline of the President's speech to the nation and the whole course of action thereafter, trying to anticipate all possible contingencies and setting forth recommendations as to how to react to them.

In the early afternoon, we exchanged papers, each group dissected and criticized the other, and then the papers were returned to the original group to develop further answers. Gradually from all this came the outline of definitive plans. For the group that advocated the blockade, it was an outline of the legal basis for our action, an agenda for a meeting of the Organization of American States, recommendations for the role of the United Nations, the military procedures for stopping ships, and, finally, the circumstances under which military force might be used. For the group that advocated immediate military action, it was an outline of the areas to be attacked, a defense of our position in the United Nations, suggestions as to how to obtain support from Latin American countries, and a proposed communication to Khrushchev to convince him of the inadvisability of moving militarily against us in the Caribbean, Berlin, or elsewhere in the world.

During all these deliberations, we all spoke as equals. There was no rank, and, in fact, we did not even have a chairman. Dean Rusk—who, as Secretary of State, might have assumed that position—had other duties during this period of time and frequently could not attend our meetings. As a result, with the encouragement of McNamara, Bundy, and Ball, the conversations were completely uninhibited and unrestricted. Everyone had an equal opportunity to express himself and to be heard directly. It was a tremendously advantageous procedure that does not frequently occur within the executive branch of the government, where rank is often so important.

"It was now up to one single man."

We met all day Friday and Friday night. Then again early Saturday morning we were back at the State Department. I talked to the President several times on Friday. He was hoping to be able to meet with us early enough to decide on a course of action and then broadcast it to the nation Sunday night. Saturday morning at 10:00 o'clock I called the President at the Blackstone Hotel in Chicago and told him we were ready to meet with him. It was now up to one single man. No committee was going to make this decision. He canceled his trip and returned to Washington.

As he was returning to Washington, our armed forces across the world were put on alert. Telephoning from our meeting in the State Department, Secretary McNamara ordered four tactical air squadrons placed at readiness for an air strike, in case the President decided to accept that recommendation.

The President arrived back at the White House at 1:40 P.M. and went for a swim. I sat on the side of the pool, and we talked. At 2:30 we walked up to the Oval

Room.

The meeting went on until ten minutes after five. Convened as a formal meeting of the National Security Council, it was a larger group of people who met, some of whom had not participated in the deliberations up to that time. Bob McNamara presented the arguments for the blockade; others presented the arguments for the military attack.

The discussion, for the most part, was able and organized, although, like all meetings of this kind, certain statements were made as accepted truisms, which I, at least, thought were of questionable validity. One member of the Joint Chiefs of Staff, for example, argued that we could use nuclear weapons, on the basis that our adversaries would use theirs against us in an attack. I thought, as I listened, of the many times that I had heard the military take positions which, if wrong, had the advantage that no one would be around at the end to know.

The President made his decision that afternoon in favor of the blockade. There was one final meeting the next morning, with General Walter C. Sweeney, Jr., Commander in Chief of the Tactical Air Command, who told the President that even a major surprise air attack could not be certain of destroying all the missile sites and nuclear weapons in Cuba. That ended the small, lingering doubt that might still have remained in his mind. It had worried him that a blockade would not remove the missiles—now it was clear that an attack could not accomplish that task completely, either.

The strongest argument against the all-out military attack, and one no one could answer to his satisfaction, was that a surprise attack would erode if not destroy the moral position of the United States throughout the world.

Adlai Stevenson had come from New York to attend the meeting Saturday afternoon, as he had attended several of the Ex Comm meetings. He had always been dubious about the air strike, but at the Saturday meeting he strongly advocated what he had only tentatively suggested to me a few days before—namely, that we make it clear to the Soviet Union that if it withdrew its missiles from Cuba, we would be willing to withdraw our missiles from Turkey and Italy and give up our naval base at Guantanamo Bay.

There was an extremely strong reaction from some of the participants to his suggestion, and several sharp exchanges followed. The President, although he rejected Stevenson's suggestion, pointed out that he had for a long period held reservations about the value of

Jupiter missiles in Turkey and Italy and some time ago had asked the State Department to conduct negotiations for their removal; but now, he said, was not the appropriate time to suggest this action, and we could not abandon Guantanamo Bay under threat from the Russians.

Stevenson has since been criticized publicly for the position he took at this meeting. I think it should be emphasized that he was presenting a point of view from a different perspective than the others, one which was therefore important for the President to consider. Although I disagreed strongly with his recommendations, I thought he was courageous to make them, and I might add they made as much sense as some others considered during that period of time.

The President's speech was now scheduled for Monday evening. Under the direction of George Ball, Alex Johnson, and Ed Martin, a detailed hour-to-hour program was arranged, to inform our allies, prepare for the meeting of the OAS, inform the ambassadors stationed in Washington, and prepare for them and others, in written form, the legal justification on which our action was predicated. More and more government officials were brought into the discussions, and finally word began to seep through to the press that a serious crisis was imminent. Through the personal intervention of the President with several newspapers, the only stories written Monday morning were reports that a major speech was to be given by the President and that the country faced a serious crisis.

The diplomatic effort was of great significance. We were able to establish a firm legal foundation for our action under the OAS Charter, and our position around the world was greatly strengthened when the Organization of American States unanimously supported the recommendation for a quarantine. Thus the Soviet Union and Cuba faced the united action of the whole Western Hemisphere. Further, with the support of detailed photographs, Dean Acheson—who obliged the President by once again being willing to help—was able to quickly convince French President Charles de Gaulle of the correctness of our response and later to reassure Chancellor Adenauer. Macmillan made it clear the U.S. would have his country's support. And in these present days of strain, it is well to remember that no country's leader supported the U.S. more forcefully than did France. General de Gaulle said, "It is exactly what I would have done," adding that it was not necessary to see the photographs, as "a great government such as yours does not act without evidence." Chancellor Konrad Adenauer of West Germany voiced his support as well, and the Soviet Union was prevented from separating the U.S. from Europe. (John Diefenbaker, Prime Minister of Canada, was greatly concerned with how to convince the rest of the world.)

All this was done simultaneously with the President's speech and made possible only by the immense work and painstaking planning which preceded it. During this same period, military preparations went forward. Missile crews were placed on maximum alert. Troops were moved into Florida and the southeastern part of the United States. Late Saturday night, the First Armored Division began to move out of Texas into Georgia, and five more divisions were placed on alert. The base at Guantanamo Bay was strengthened.

The Navy deployed one hundred eighty ships into the Caribbean. The Strategic Air Command was dispersed to civilian landing fields around the country, to lessen its vulnerability in case of attack. The B-52 bomber force was ordered into the air fully loaded with atomic weapons. As one came down to land, another immediately took its place in the air.

An hour before the President's speech, Secretary Rusk called in Ambassador Dobrynin and told him of the speech. The newspapers reported that Dobrynin left the Secretary's office looking considerably shaken.

On that Monday afternoon, before his speech and after lunch with Jackie, the President held several meetings. At the first, he formally constituted our committee—which up until that time had been called "the group" or "war council"—under National Security Council Action Memorandum Number 196 as the Executive Committee of the National Security Council, "for the purpose of effective conduct of the operations of the executive branch in the current crisis." The President became the official chairman, and until further notice we were to meet with him every morning at 10:00 A.M.

Shortly thereafter, the President met with the members of the Cabinet and informed them for the first time of the crisis. Then, not long before the broadcast, he met with the leaders of Congress. This was the most difficult meeting. I did not attend, but I know from seeing him afterward that it was a tremendous strain.

Many Congressional leaders were sharp in their criticism. They felt that the President should take more forceful action, a military attack or invasion, and that the blockade was far too weak a response. Senator Richard B. Russell of Georgia said he could not live with himself if he did not say in the strongest possible terms how important it was that we act with greater strength than the President was contemplating.

Senator J. William Fulbright of Arkansas also strongly advised military action rather than such a weak step as the blockade. Others said they were skeptical but would remain publicly silent, only because it was such a dangerous hour for the country.

The President, after listening to the frequently emotional criticism, explained that he would take whatever steps were necessary to protect the security of the United States, but that he did not feel greater military action was warranted initially. Because it was possible that the matter could be resolved without a devastating war, he had decided on the course he had outlined. Perhaps in the end, he said, direct military action would be necessary, but that course should not be followed lightly. In the meantime, he assured them, he had taken measures to prepare our military forces and place them in a position to move.

He reminded them that once an attack began our adversaries could respond with a missile barrage from which many millions of Americans would be killed. That was a gamble he was not willing to take until he had finally and forcefully exhausted all other possibilities. He told them this was an extremely hazardous undertaking and that everyone should understand the risks involved.

He was upset by the time the meeting ended. When we discussed it later he was more philosophical, pointing out that the Congressional leaders' reaction to what we should do, although more militant than his, was much the same as our first reaction when we first heard about the missiles the previous Tuesday.

At 7:00 o'clock, he went on television to the nation to explain the situation in Cuba and the reasons for the quarantine. He was calm and confident that he had selected the right course.

In his speech, he emphasized that the blockade was the *initial* step. He had ordered the Pentagon to make all the preparations necessary for further military action. Secretary McNamara, in a confidential report, had listed the requirements: 250,000 men, 2,000 air sorties against the various targets in Cuba, and 90,000 Marines and Airborne in the invasion force. One estimate of American casualties put the expected figure over 25,000. The President gave his approval for these preparations, and the plans moved ahead. Troops were rapidly moving into the southeastern part of the U.S., equipped and prepared. Arrangements were begun to gather the over a hundred vessels that would be needed for an invasion.

We went to bed that night filled with concern

and trepidation, but filled also with a sense of pride in the strength, the purposefulness, and the courage of the President of the United States. No one could predict what was in store in the days ahead, but we all felt that the President, because of his own wisdom and personal dignity, would have the support of a unified country.

"The important meeting of the OAS..."

THE NEXT DAY, Tuesday, was the important meeting of the OAS previously mentioned. It was anticipated that we might have difficulty obtaining the two thirds vote of support necessary for the ordering of a quarantine. But the Latin American countries, demonstrating a unique sense of unity, unanimously supported the recommendations of the United States. In fact, a number contributed men, supplies, and ships during the several weeks that followed.

Our group met with the President at 10:00 in the morning at the White House. There was a certain spirit of lightness—not gaiety certainly, but a feeling of relaxation, perhaps. We had taken the first step, it wasn't so bad, and we were still alive.

There was much to report. John McCloy, formerly High Commissioner to Germany and an adviser to President Kennedy on European and security matters, had been located in Germany and asked to return and join with Adlai Stevenson in presenting our case to the United Nations. As a Republican, he made our efforts there bipartisan, and as a counterbalance to Stevenson's point of view, he had initially favored a military attack and invasion of Cuba.

John McCone reported to our committee that as yet there had been no general alert of the Soviet forces in Cuba or around the globe. No extraordinary military action of any kind had been reported. In Cuba, the Russians were not permitting anyone other than Russian technical and military personnel to enter the missile bases. He also reported that they were beginning to camouflage the missile sites. It was never clear why they waited until that late date to do so.

The President ordered preparations to proceed for a possible blockade of Berlin. We also discussed in detail what would be done if a U-2 plane were to be shot down, agreeing that—after obtaining specific permission from the President—bomber and fighter planes would destroy a surface-to-air-missile site. Secretary McNamara said that such an attack could take place within two hours after notification of the firing on one of our planes.

By this time, the relaxed, lighter mood had completely disappeared. It had taken only a few minutes.

President Kennedy expressed his deep concern that no error should occur, and that any attack against one of our planes be verified before we return the attack. He asked about the fate of pilots who might be shot down. He then asked Secretary McNamara to put into effect a rescue mission to supplement our U-2 flights. He agreed with Secretary McNamara on extending certain military-personnel tours of duty and on placing the 101st Airborne in readiness for early action. He wanted to make certain that we would have taken all the necessary steps, in case of a military reaction by the Soviets.

"Now, the only thing I say once again is that if the Russians' response makes a military action or invasion inevitable, I want to be able to feel that we will not have to waste any days having to get ready," he said.

At the end of the meeting, the President pointed out that an attack on one of their installations might very well bring an attack against our airfields. He asked for a report from the military as to whether our own planes had been dispersed. When it was reported to him that our photography showed that the Russians and Cubans had inexplicably lined up their planes wing tip to wing tip on Cuban airfields, making them perfect targets, he requested General Taylor to have a U-2 fly a photographic mission over our fields in Florida. "It would be interesting if we have done the same thing," he remarked. We had. He examined the pictures the next day and ordered the Air Force to disperse our planes.

Finally, he made arrangements for regular meetings with ambassadors from the European countries, to prepare for a blockade of Berlin, as well as other contingencies elsewhere. Nothing, whether a weighty matter or small detail, was overlooked.

We came back about 6:00 o'clock that evening. The OAS had announced its support, and the President prepared the proclamation which would put the quarantine into effect at 10:00 o'clock the next morning.

During the course of this meeting, we learned that an extraordinary number of coded messages had been sent to all the Russian ships on their way to Cuba. What they said we did not know then, nor do we know now, but it was clear that the ships as of that moment were still straight on course.

The President composed a letter to Khrushchev, asking him to observe the quarantine legally established by a vote of the OAS, making it clear that the U.S. did not wish to fire on any ships of the Soviet Union, and adding at the end: "I am concerned that we both show prudence and do nothing to allow events to make the situation more difficult to control than it is."

We then discussed in detail the rules that were to be given to the Navy intercepting a merchant vessel in the quarantine zone. To avoid a major military confrontation if a vessel refused to stop, the Navy was to shoot at its rudders and propellers, disabling the vessel but, hopefully, avoiding any loss of life or the sinking of the ship. The President then expressed concern about the boarding of these vessels if the Russians decided to resist. We could anticipate a rough, fierce fight and many casualties, he said. Secretary McNamara felt the vessel might not have to be boarded but would, within a reasonably short period of time, have to be towed into Jacksonville or Charleston.

"What would you do then," the President said, "if we go through all of this effort and then find out there's baby food on it?" Everyone agreed that we should try to intercept the vessels on which there was quite clearly military equipment, but the treatment of other vessels in the meantime posed a serious problem. What criteria could we use for letting some merchant ships through and stopping others? And then how could we be sure?

Our problems for that day were hardly over. John McCone reported that Russian submarines were beginning to move into the Caribbean. One had refueled the day before in the Azores and was headed now toward Cuba. The President ordered the Navy to give the highest priority to tracking the submarines and to put into effect the greatest possible safety measures to protect our own aircraft carriers and other vessels.

After the meeting, the President, Ted Sorensen, Kenny O'Donnell, and I sat in his office and talked. "The great danger and risk in all of this," he said, "is a miscalculation—a mistake in judgment." A short time before, he had read Barbara Tuchman's book *The Guns of August,* and he talked about the miscalculations of the Germans, the Russians, the Austrians, the French, and the British. They somehow seemed to tumble into war, he said, through stupidity, individual idiosyncrasies, misunderstandings, and personal complexes of inferiority and grandeur. We talked about the miscalculation of the Germans in 1939 and the still unfulfilled commitments and guarantees that the British had given to Poland.

Neither side wanted war over Cuba, we agreed, but it was possible that either side could take a step that —for reasons of "security" or "pride" or "face"—would require a response by the other side, which, in turn, for the same reasons of security, pride, or face, would bring about a counterresponse and eventually an escalation into armed conflict. That was what he wanted to avoid. He did not want anyone to be able to say that the U.S. had not done all it could to preserve the peace. We were not going to misjudge, or miscalculate, or challenge the other side needlessly, or precipitously push our adversaries into a course of action that was not intended or anticipated.

Afterward, the President and I talked for a little while alone. He suggested I might visit Ambassador Dobrynin and personally relate to him the serious implications of the Russians' duplicity and the crisis they had created through the presence of their missiles within Cuba.

"I met with Dobrynin . . ."

I CALLED Dobrynin and made arrangements to see him at 9:30 that same Tuesday night. I met with him in his office on the third floor of the Russian Embassy. I reviewed with him the circumstances of the past six weeks which had brought about this confrontation. I pointed out to him that when I had met with him in early September, he had told me that the Russians had not placed any long-range missiles in Cuba and had no intentions of doing so in the future.

He interrupted at that moment and said that was exactly what he had told me and that he had given me his word that the Soviet Union would not put missiles in Cuba that could reach the continental United States.

I said that, based on that statement and the subsequent statement by Tass, the Soviet news agency, the President had taken a less belligerent attitude toward the Soviet Union's actions than other political figures in the U.S. and assured the American people that military action was not necessary against Cuba. Now the President knew he had been deceived, and that had devastating implications for the peace of the world.

Dobrynin's only answer was that he told me there was no missiles in Cuba; that this was what Khrushchev had said, and, as far as he knew, there were still no missiles in Cuba. He then asked me why President Kennedy had not told Gromyko the facts when he had seen him the previous Thursday.

I replied by saying there was nothing the President could tell Gromyko that Gromyko didn't already know—and, after all, why didn't Gromyko tell the President? In fact, the President was shocked that Gromyko's statements even at that late date were so misleading. Dobrynin was extremely concerned. As I left, I asked him if the Soviet ships were going to go through to Cuba. He replied that that had been their instructions and he knew of no changes.

I left the Russian Embassy around 10:15 P.M. and went back to the White House. I found the President meeting Ambassador David Ormsby-Gore of Great Britain, an old friend whom he trusted implicitly. I related the conversation to both of them. The President talked about the possibility of arranging an immediate summit with Khrushchev, but finally dismissed the idea, concluding that such a meeting would be useless until Khrushchev first accepted, as a result of our deeds as well as our statements, the U.S. determination in this matter. Before a summit took place, and it should, the President wanted to have some cards in his own hands.

Ambassador Ormsby-Gore expressed concern that the line of interception for the quarantine had been extended 800 miles. This would mean a probable interception within a very few hours after it was put into effect. "Why not give them more time," he said, "to analyze their position?" The 800 miles had been fixed by the Navy to stay outside the range of some of the MIG fighters in Cuba. The President called McNamara and shortened it to five hundred miles.

The next morning, Wednesday, the quarantine went into effect, and the reports during the early hours told of the Russian ships coming steadily on toward Cuba. I talked with the President for a few moments before we went in to our regular meeting. He said, "It looks really mean, doesn't it? But then, really there was no other choice. If they get this mean on this one in our part of the world, what will they do on the next?" "I just don't think there was any choice," I said, "and not only that, if you hadn't acted, you would have been impeached." The President thought for a moment and said, "That's what I think—I would have been impeached."

The choice was to have gone in and taken steps

which were not necessary or to have acted as we did. At least we now had the support of the whole Western Hemisphere and all our allies around the world.

This Wednesday-morning meeting, along with that of the following Saturday, October 27, seemed the most trying, the most difficult, and the most filled with tension. The Russian ships were proceeding, they were nearing the five-hundred-mile barrier, and we either had to intercept them or announce we were withdrawing. I sat across the table from the President. This was the moment we had prepared for, which we hoped would never come. The danger and concern that we all felt hung like a cloud over us all and particularly over the President.

The U-2s and low-flying planes had returned the previous day with their film, and through the evening it was analyzed—by now in such volume that the film alone was more than twenty-five miles long. The results were presented to us at the meeting. The launching pads, the missiles, the concrete boxes, the nuclear storage bunkers, all the components were there, by now clearly defined and obvious. Comparisons with the pictures of a few days earlier made clear that the work on those sites was proceeding and that within a few days several of the launching pads would be ready for war.

It was now a few minutes after 10:00 o'clock. Secretary McNamara announced that two Russian ships, the *Gagarin* and the *Komiles*, were within a few miles of our quarantine barrier. The interception of both ships would probably be before noon Washington time. Indeed, the expectation was that at least one of the vessels would be stopped and boarded between 10:30 and 11:00 o'clock.

Then came the disturbing Navy report that a Russian submarine had moved into position between the two ships.

It had originally been planned to have a cruiser make the first interception, but, because of the increased danger, it was decided in the past few hours to send in an aircraft carrier supported by helicopters, carrying antisubmarine equipment, hovering overhead. The carrier *Essex* was to signal the submarine by sonar to surface and identify itself. If it refused, said Secretary McNamara, depth charges with a small explosive would be used until the submarine surfaced.

I think these few minutes were the time of gravest concern for the President. Was the world on the brink of a holocaust? Was it our error? A mistake? Was there something further that should have been done? Or not done? His hand went up to his face and covered his mouth. He opened and closed his fist. His face seemed drawn, his eyes pained, almost gray. We stared at each other across the table. For a few fleeting seconds, it was almost as though no one else was there and he was no longer the President.

Inexplicably, I thought of when he was ill and almost died; when he lost his child; when we learned that our oldest brother had been killed; of personal times of strain and hurt. The voices droned on, but I didn't seem to hear anything until I heard the President say: "Isn't there some way we can avoid having our first exchange with a Russian submarine—almost anything but that?" "No, there's too much danger to our ships. There is no alternative," said McNamara. "Our commanders have been instructed to avoid hostilities if at all possible, but this is what we must be prepared for, and this is what we must expect."

We had come to the time of final decision. "We must expect that they will close down Berlin—make the final preparations for that," the President said. I felt we were on the edge of a precipice with no way off. This time, the moment was now—not next week—not tomorrow, "so we can have another meeting and decide"; not in eight hours, "so we can send another message to Khrushchev and perhaps he will finally understand."

No, none of that was possible. One thousand miles away in the vast expanse of the Atlantic Ocean the final decisions were going to be made in the next few minutes. President Kennedy had initiated the course of events, but he no longer had control over them. He would have to wait—we would have to wait. The minutes in the Cabinet Room ticked slowly by. What could we say now —what could we do?

Then it was 10:25—a messenger brought in a note to John McCone. "Mr. President, we have a preliminary report which seems to indicate that some of the Russian ships have stopped dead in the water."

Stopped dead in the water? Which ships? Are they checking the accuracy of the report? Is it true? I looked at the clock. 10:32. "The report is accurate, Mr. President. Six ships previously on their way to Cuba at the edge of the quarantine line have stopped or have turned back toward the Soviet Union. A representative from the Office of Naval Intelligence is on his way over with the full report." A short time later, the report came that the twenty Russian ships closest to the barrier had stopped and were dead in the water or had turned around.

"So no ships will be stopped or intercepted," said the President. I said we should make sure the Navy knew nothing was to be done, that no ships were to be interfered with. Orders would go out to the Navy immediately. "If the ships have orders to turn around, we want to give them every opportunity to do so. Get in direct touch with the *Essex*, and tell them not to do anything, but give the Russian vessels an opportunity to turn back. We must move quickly because the time is expiring," said the President.

Then we were back to the details. The meeting droned on. But everyone looked like a different person. For a moment the world had stood still, and now it was going around again.

"The danger was anything but over."

DESPITE WHAT HAD HAPPENED, the danger was anything but over. We learned later in the day that fourteen of the ships had stopped or had turned back to Russia. Most of those continuing were tankers.

The ship that became the matter of greatest concern was a Russian tanker called the *Bucharest*. During the day, it had reached the barrier, identified itself to one of our naval ships, and, because it was a tanker, been allowed to pass. There was little likelihood that the *Bucharest* carried any missiles or any of the kinds of armament covered by the quarantine. Nevertheless, there were those in the Executive Committee who felt strongly that the *Bucharest* should be stopped and boarded, so that Khrushchev would make no mistake of our will or intent. The President himself emphasized that eventually we would have to stop and board one of the ships approaching Cuba. Those who favored letting the *Bucharest* pass argued that it probably carried no contraband and that Khrushchev needed more time to consider what he should do.

The President postponed a decision and ordered the *Bucharest* shadowed by American warships. At that time, it was proceeding toward Cuba at 17 knots, and a decision had to be made before nightfall.

Meanwhile, the whole world was becoming more and more alarmed. All kinds of people were, officially and unofficially, giving their advice and opinions. Bertrand Russell sent a message to Khrushchev praising him for his conciliatory position and a message to President Kennedy castigating the United States for its warlike attitude. The President took time out of his other deliberations personally to compose an answer: "I think your attention might well be directed to the burglar rather than to those who caught the burglar."

U Thant, Acting Secretary General of the United Nations, suggested that the quarantine be lifted for several weeks if in return the Russians agreed not to send missiles to Cuba. Khrushchev agreed and suggested a summit meeting. President Kennedy responded that the crisis was "created by the secret introduction of offensive weapons into Cuba and the answer lies in the removal of such weapons." He added that we would be happy to have any discussions leading to a satisfactory and peaceful solution, but the missiles in Cuba had to be removed.

Adlai Stevenson, at a meeting of the United Nations Security Council, publicly confronted Ambassador V. A. Zorin of the Soviet Union. President Kennedy had made arrangements for photographs of the missile sites to be furnished to Stevenson. Many newspapers around the world, and particularly in Great Britain, were openly skeptical of the U.S. position. At the urgings of Pierre Salinger, the President's Press Secretary, and of Don Wilson, representing the USIA, the President, on October 23, had released the pictures for use at the UN and for publication. Stevenson used them most skillfully in his dramatic televised confrontation with the Russians:

STEVENSON: "Well, let me say something to you, Mr. Ambassador, we do have the evidence. We have it, and it is clear and incontrovertible. And let me say something else. Those weapons must be taken out of Cuba. . . . You, the Soviet Union, have sent these weapons to Cuba. You, the Soviet Union, have created this new danger—not the United States. . . .

"Finally, Mr. Zorin, I remind you that the other day you did not deny the existence of these weapons. But today, again, if I heard you correctly, you now say that they do not exist, or that we haven't proved they exist.

"All right, sir, let me ask you one simple question. Do you, Ambassador Zorin, deny that the U.S.S.R. has placed and is placing medium- and intermediate-range missiles and sites in Cuba? Yes or no? Don't wait for the translation, yes or no?"

ZORIN: "I am not in an American courtroom, sir, and therefore I do not wish to answer a question that is put to me in the fashion in which a prosecutor puts questions. In due course, sir, you will have your answer."

STEVENSON: "You are in the courtroom of world opinion right now, and you can answer yes or no. You have denied that they exist, and I want to know whether I have understood you correctly."

ZORIN: "Continue with your statement. You will have your answer in due course."

STEVENSON: "I am prepared to wait for my answer until hell freezes over, if that's your decision. And I am also prepared to present the evidence in this room."

And with that Stevenson revealed the photographs of the Russian missiles and sites, with devastating effect.

That evening, the President, after further heated discussion, made the final decision permitting the *Bucharest* to go through to Cuba. Against the advice of many of his advisers and of the military, he decided to give Khrushchev more time. "We don't want to push him to a precipitous action—give him time to consider. I don't want to put him in a corner from which he cannot escape."

In the meantime, however, he increased the pressure in other ways. Low-flying flights of eight planes apiece flew over Cuba morning and afternoon, supplementing the photography of the U-2s. All six Russian submarines then in the area or moving toward Cuba from the Atlantic were followed and harassed and, at one time or another, forced to surface in the presence of U.S. military ships.

By now, in the Caribbean surrounding Cuba, we had twenty-five destroyers, two cruisers, several submarines, several carriers, and a large number of support ships.

On the night of Thursday, October 25, our aerial photography revealed that work on the missile sites was proceeding at an extraordinarily rapid pace. By the following evening, October 26, it was clear that the IL-28 bombers were also being rapidly uncrated and assembled.

By this time, an East German passenger ship, carrying some fifteen hundred people, had reached the barrier. Another decision had to be made. Again, there were strong arguments within our group as to what should be done. Again, there were those who urged that the ship be stopped; that it would not directly involve the prestige of the Russians, as it was not a ship of Soviet registry and stopping it would not violate U Thant's request that we not interfere with Russian vessels. The President ultimately decided that the risk of life was so great—with so many people aboard the ship, and so high a possibility of something going seriously wrong—that he would let the vessel through.

"There were almost daily communications with Khrushchev."

THERE WERE almost daily communications with Khrushchev. On Monday, October 22, the day of his speech to the nation, President Kennedy sent a long letter and a copy of his statement directly to the Soviet Chairman. In the course of the letter he said:

"In our discussions and exchanges on Berlin and other international questions, the one thing that has most concerned me has been the possibility that your Government would not correctly understand the will and determination of the United States in any given situation, since I have not assumed that you or any other sane man would, in this nuclear age, deliberately plunge the world into war which it is crystal clear no country could win and which could only result in catastrophic consequences to the whole world, including the aggressor."

Khrushchev, in a letter received October 23, had accused the President of threatening him and the Soviet

Union with the blockade and asserted that it was not going to be observed by the Soviet Union. "The actions of the USA with regard to Cuba are outright banditry or, if you like, the folly of degenerate imperialism." The U.S., he said, was pushing mankind "to the abyss of a world missile-nuclear war," and the Soviet Union would not give instructions to the captains of Soviet vessels bound for Cuba to obey the orders of American naval forces. If any effort to interfere with Soviet ships were to be made, "we would then be forced for our part to take the measures which we deem necessary and adequate in order to protect our rights. For this we have all that is necessary."

The President replied on Thursday, October 25, restating again what had occurred and stressing that—despite private and public assurances that missiles would not be placed in Cuba—that very step had been taken by the Soviet Union.

"In early September I indicated very plainly that the United States would regard any shipment of offensive weapons as presenting the gravest issues. After that time, this Government received the most explicit assurances from your Government and its representatives, both publicly and privately, that no offensive weapons were being sent to Cuba. If you will review the statement issued by Tass in September, you will see how clearly this assurance was given.

"In reliance on these solemn assurances I urged restraint upon those in this country who were urging action in this matter at that time. And then I learned beyond doubt what you have not denied—namely, that all these public assurances were false and that your military people had set out recently to establish a set of missile bases in Cuba. I ask you to recognize clearly, Mr. Chairman, that it was not I who issued the first challenge in this case, and that in the light of this record these activities in Cuba required the responses I have announced.

"I repeat my regret that these events should cause a deterioration in our relations."

And then he added, very simply: "I hope that your Government will take the necessary action to permit a restoration of the earlier situation."

All our efforts and letters, however, seemed to be having little effect. On the contrary, as we waited for the reply to President Kennedy's latest communication with Khrushchev, reports came in that a greater number of Russian personnel were working to expedite the construction of the missile sites and to assemble the IL-28s.

At 7:00 o'clock Friday morning, October 26, the

first vessel was stopped and boarded. She was surely an international ship. It was the *Marucla*, an American-built Liberty ship, Panamanian-owned, registered from Lebanon, and bound for Cuba under a Soviet charter from the Baltic port of Riga. The *Marucla* had been sighted the night before and followed by two destroyers: the *John Pierce* and—a surprise to President Kennedy —the *Joseph P. Kennedy, Jr.*, the destroyer named after the oldest member of our family, who was a Navy pilot and was killed in the Second World War. The *Marucla* had been carefully and personally selected by President Kennedy to be the first ship stopped and boarded. He was demonstrating to Khrushchev that we were going to enforce the quarantine and yet, because it was not a Soviet-owned vessel, it did not represent a direct affront to the Soviets, requiring a response from them. It gave them more time, but simultaneously demonstrated that the U.S. meant business.

At 7:24 A.M., an armed boarding party from both destroyers went alongside the *Marucla* and by 8:00 was aboard and had started the inspection. There were no incidents. The vessel was found to contain no weapons and was allowed to sail on.

The fact that this inspection had been successfully accomplished, however, did not lift the feeling of gloom that was settling over our committee and its deliberations. The Soviet Union had been adamant in its refusal to recognize the quarantine. At the same time, it was obviously preparing its missiles in Cuba for possible use. The President in response ordered a gradual increase in pressure, still attempting to avoid the alternative of direct military action. He increased the number of low-level flights over Cuba from twice a day to once every two hours. Preparations went ahead for night flights, which would take pictures of the missile sites with bright flares that would be dropped across the island. The State Department and the Defense Department were asked to prepare to add petroleum oil and lubricants to the embargo list.

But privately the President was not sanguine about the results of even these efforts. Each hour the situation grew steadily more serious. The feeling grew that this cup was not going to pass and that a direct military confrontation between the two great nuclear powers was inevitable. Both "hawks" and "doves" sensed that our combination of limited force and diplomatic efforts had been unsuccessful. If the Russians continued to be adamant and continued to build up their missile strength, military force would be the only alternative.

"Expect very heavy casualties in an invasion."

FRIDAY MORNING President Kennedy ordered the State Department to proceed with preparations for a crash program on civil government in Cuba to be established after the invasion and occupation of that country. Secretary McNamara reported the conclusion of the military that we should expect very heavy casualties in an invasion.

The President turned to us all: "We are going to have to face the fact that, if we do invade, by the time we get to these sites, after a very bloody fight, they will be pointed at us. And we must further accept the possibility that when military hostilities first begin, those missiles will be fired."

John McCone said everyone should understand that an invasion was going to be a much more serious undertaking than most people had previously realized. "They have a hell of a lot of equipment," he said. "And it will be damn tough to shoot them out of those hills, as we learned so clearly in Korea."

Despite the heavy pressure on the big decisions, President Kennedy followed every detail. He requested, for instance, the names of all the Cuban doctors in the Miami area, should their services be required in Cuba. Learning that a U.S. military ship with extremely sensitive equipment (similar to the *Liberty*, which was struck by Israel during the Israeli-Arab war) was very close to the coast of Cuba, he ordered it farther out to sea, where it would be less vulnerable to attack. He supervised everything, from the contents of leaflets to be dropped over Cuba to the assembling of ships for the invasion.

In the meantime, we awaited Khrushchev's answer.

At 6:00 o'clock that night the message came.

A great deal has been written about this message, including the allegation that at the time Khrushchev wrote it he must have been so unstable or emotional that he had become incoherent. There was no question that the letter had been written by him personally. It was very long and emotional. But it was not incoherent, and the emotion was directed at the death, destruction, and anarchy that nuclear war would bring to his people and all mankind. That, he said again and again and in many different ways, must be avoided.

We must not succumb to "petty passions" or to "transient things," he wrote, but should realize that "if indeed war should break out, then it would not be in our power to stop it, for such is the logic of war. I have participated in two wars and know that war ends when it has rolled through cities and villages, everywhere sowing death and destruction." The United States, he went on to say, should not be concerned about the missiles in Cuba; they would never be used to attack the United States and were there for defensive purposes only. "You can be calm in this regard, that we are of sound mind and understand perfectly well that if we attack you, you will respond the same way. But you too will receive the same that you hurl against us. And I think that you also understand this. . . . This indicates that we are normal people, that we correctly understand and correctly evaluate the situation. Consequently, how can we permit the incorrect actions which you ascribe to us? Only lunatics or suicides, who themselves want to perish and to destroy the whole world before they die, could do this."

But he went on: "We want something quite different . . . not to destroy your country . . . but despite our ideological differences, to compete peacefully, not by military means."

There was no purpose, he said, for us to interfere with any of his ships now bound for Cuba, for they contained no weapons. He then explained why they carried no missiles: all the shipments of weapons were already within Cuba. This was the first time he had acknowledged the presence of missiles in Cuba. He made reference to the landing at the Bay of Pigs and the fact that President Kennedy had told him in Vienna that this was a mistake. He valued such frankness, wrote Khrushchev, and he, too, had similar courage, for he had acknowledged "those mistakes which had been committed during the history of our state and I not only acknowledge but sharply condemned them." (President Kennedy had told him in Vienna that he was quick to acknowledge and condemn the mistakes of Stalin and others, but he never acknowledged any mistakes of his own.)

The reason he had sent these weapons to Cuba was because the U.S. was interested in overthrowing the Cuban government, as the U.S. had actively attempted to overthrow the Communist government in the Soviet Union after their revolution. Khrushchev and the Soviet people wished to help Cuba protect herself.

But then he went on: "If assurances were given that the President of the United States would not participate in an attack on Cuba and the blockade lifted, then the question of the removal or the destruction of the missile sites in Cuba would then be an entirely different question. Armaments bring only disasters. When one accumulates them, this damages the economy, and if one puts them to use, then they destroy people on both sides. Consequently, only a madman can believe that armaments are the principal means in the life of society. No, they are an enforced loss of human energy, and what is more are for the destruction of man himself. If people do not show wisdom, then in the final analysis they will come to a clash, like blind moles, and then reciprocal extermination will begin."

This is my proposal, he said. No more weapons to Cuba and those within Cuba withdrawn or destroyed, and you reciprocate by withdrawing your blockade and also agree not to invade Cuba. Don't interfere, he said, in a piratical way with Russian ships. "If you have not lost your self-control and sensibly conceive what this might lead to, then, Mr. President, we and you ought not to pull on the ends of the rope in which you have tied the knot of war, because the more the two of us pull, the tighter the knot will be tied. And a moment may come when that knot will be tied so tight that even he who tied it will not have the strength to untie it, and then it will be necessary to cut that knot, and what that would mean is not for me to explain to you, because you yourself understand perfectly of what terrible forces our countries dispose. Consequently, if there is no intention to tighten that knot, and thereby to doom the world to the catastrophe of thermonuclear war, then let us not only relax the forces pulling on the ends of the rope, let us take measures to untie that knot. We are ready for this."

The message was examined and re-examined at a meeting we held late Friday night. As the hours went on into the morning, it was finally decided that the State Department would come forward with an analysis and some recommendations on how it should be answered; that we would meet again early Saturday morning, October 27.

I had a slight feeling of optimism as I drove home from the State Department that night. The letter, with all its rhetoric, had the beginnings perhaps of some accommodation, some agreement. The feeling was strengthened by the fact that John Scali, a very able and experienced reporter for ABC, had been approached by an important official of the Soviet Embassy with a proposal that the Soviet Union would remove the missiles under United Nations supervision and inspection and the U.S. would lift the blockade and give a pledge not to invade Cuba as its part of the understanding. He was asked to transmit this message to the United States government, which he had immediately done.

Why they selected this means of communication was not clear, but an unorthodox procedure of this kind was not unusual for the Soviet Union.

I was also slightly more optimistic because when I left the President that night, he too was for the first time hopeful that our efforts might possibly be successful.

"This would mean war."

ON SATURDAY MORNING, October 27, I received a memorandum from J. Edgar Hoover, Director of the Federal Bureau of Investigation, that gave me a feeling of considerable disquiet. He had received information the night before that certain Soviet personnel in New York were apparently preparing to destroy all sensitive documents on the basis that the U.S. would probably be taking military action against Cuba or Soviet ships, and this would mean war. I asked myself as I drove to the White House: If the Soviets were anxious to find an answer to the crisis, why this conduct on the part of Soviet personnel? Did the Khrushchev letter really indicate a solution could be found?

It was therefore with some sense of foreboding that I went to the meeting of our Ex Comm. My concern was justified. A new, this time very formal, letter had arrived from Khrushchev to President Kennedy. It was obviously no longer Mr. Khrushchev personally who was writing, but the Foreign Office of the Kremlin. The letter was quite different from the letter received twelve hours before. "We will remove our missiles from Cuba, you will remove yours from Turkey. . . . The Soviet Union will pledge not to invade or interfere with the internal affairs of Turkey; the U.S. to make the same pledge regarding Cuba."

To add to the feeling of foreboding and gloom, Secretary McNamara reported increased evidence that the Russians in Cuba were now working day and night, intensifying their efforts on all the missile sites and on the IL-28s. Thus began the most difficult twenty-four hours of the missile crisis.

The fact was that the proposal the Russians made was not unreasonable and did not amount to a loss to the U.S. or to our NATO allies. On several occasions over the period of the past eighteen months, the President had asked the State Department to reach an agreement with Turkey for the withdrawal of Jupiter missiles in that country. They were clearly obsolete, and our Polaris submarines in the Mediterranean would give Turkey far greater protection.

At the President's insistence, Secretary Rusk had raised the question with the representatives of Turkey following a NATO meeting in the spring of 1962. The Turks objected, and the matter was permitted to drop. In the summer of 1962, when Rusk was in Europe, President Kennedy raised the question again. He was told by the State Department that they felt it unwise to press the matter with Turkey. But the President disagreed. He wanted the missiles removed even if it would cause political problems for our government. The State Department representatives discussed it again with the Turks and, finding they still objected, did not pursue the matter.

The President believed he was President and that, his wishes having been made clear, they would be followed and the missiles removed. He therefore dismissed the matter from his mind. Now he learned that the failure to follow up on this matter had permitted the same obsolete Turkish missiles to become hostages of the Soviet Union.

He was angry. He obviously did not wish to order the withdrawal of the missiles from Turkey under threat from the Soviet Union. On the other hand, he did not want to involve the U.S. and mankind in a catastrophic war over missile sites in Turkey that were antiquated and useless. He pointed out to the State Department and the others that, to reasonable people, a trade of this kind might look like a very fair suggestion, that our position had become extremely vulnerable, and that it was our own fault.

The change in the language and tenor of the letters from Khrushchev indicated confusion within the Soviet Union; but there was confusion among us as well. At that moment, not knowing exactly what to suggest, some recommended writing to Khrushchev and asking him to clarify his two letters. There was no clear course of action. Yet we realized that, as we sat there, the work was proceeding on the missile sites in Cuba, and we now had the additional consideration that if we destroyed these sites and began an invasion, the door was clearly open for the Soviet Union to take reciprocal action against Turkey.

The NATO countries were supporting our position and recommending that the U.S. be firm; but, President Kennedy said, they did not realize the full implications for them. If we carried out an air strike against Cuba and the Soviet Union answered by attacking Turkey, all NATO was going to be involved. Then, immediately, the President would have to decide whether he would use nuclear weapons against the Soviet Union, and all mankind would be threatened.

The Joint Chiefs of Staff joined the meeting and recommended their solution. It had the attraction of being a very simple next step—an air strike on Monday, followed shortly afterward by an invasion. They pointed

Photographs

MEN AND EVENTS

President John F. Kennedy with his brother, Attorney General Robert F. Kennedy.

October 18, 1962. President Kennedy meets with Soviet Foreign Minister Andrei Gromyko. At this meeting the President did not reveal that the U.S. was aware of the Cuban missile build-up.

The Soviet Ambassador Anatoly Dobrynin leaves the State Department October 22 with U.S. diplomatic note for Moscow.

Ex Comm meets in the White House. Robert F. Kennedy is at far left. Other participants—identified clockwise from President Kennedy, bending over table at right—are Dean Rusk, Robert McNamara, Roswell Gilpatric, General Maxwell Taylor, Paul Nitze, Don Wilson (hidden), Theodore Sorensen, Bromley Smith (seated by bookcase), McGeorge Bundy, Douglas Dillon, Vice-President Johnson, Llewellyn Thompson, William C. Foster, and (hidden) John McCone and George Ball.

The man who bore the burden, John F. Kennedy, photographed signing the U.S. Proclamation on Interdiction of Offensive Weapons, October 23, 1962.

The challengers:
Fidel Castro in a typi-
cal pose; Nikita Khru-
shchev at the opera
on the evening of the
thirteenth day.

The Secretaries of State and Defense: Dean Rusk leaving the White House on October 22; Robert S. McNamara announcing the extension of Navy and Marine Corps duty on October 23.

October 24. Attorney General Robert Kennedy leaves the White House after conferring with President Kennedy on the crisis.

General Maxwell D. Taylor, Chairman of the Joint Chiefs of Staff, at the time of the crisis. Right, Theodore C. Sorensen, Special Counsel to President Kennedy.

Two members of the Ex Comm: left, McGeorge Bundy, National Security Assistant; right, George Ball, Undersecretary of State.

October 25. Adlai Stevenson turns to describe aerial photos of launching sites. Soviet Delegate Valerian Zorin listens at left.

Adlai Stevenson, seated next to British Delegate Sir Patrick Dean, reads reply from President Kennedy to message from Acting UN Secretary-General U Thant.

THE BUILD-UP AND WITHDRAWAL

U.S. low-altitude reconnaissance planes.

This photo of a ballistic-missile launch site at San Cristobal provided the first photographic evidence of Soviet offensive-missile deployment in Cuba, October 14, 1962.

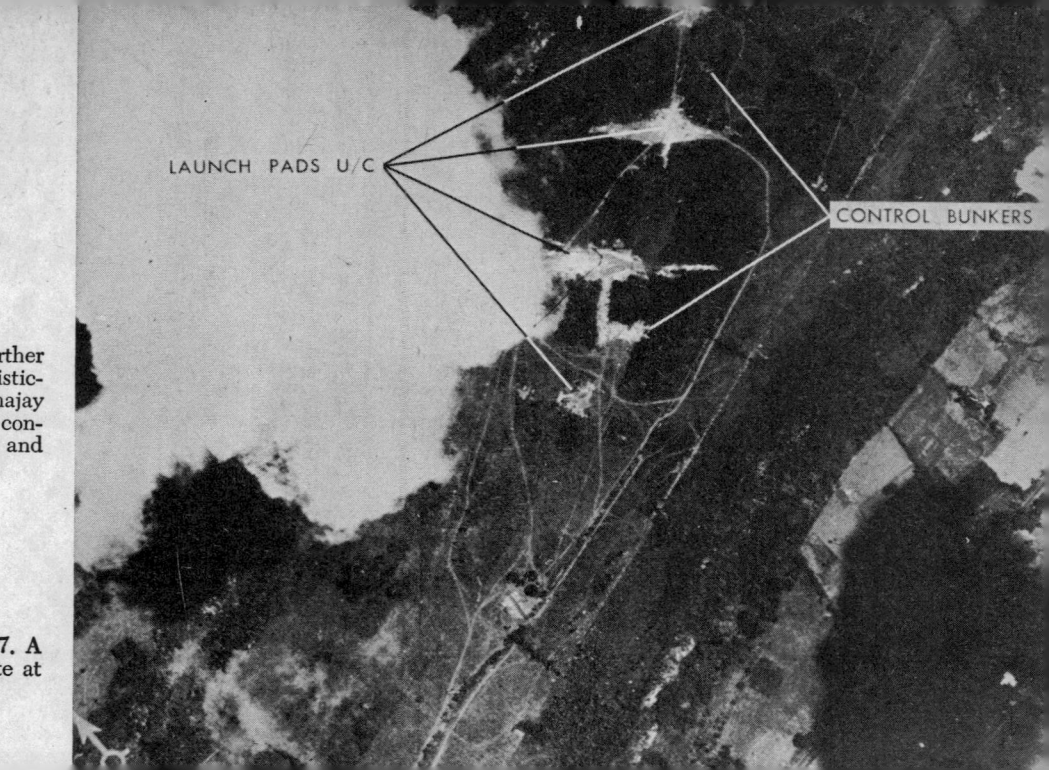

LAUNCH PADS U/C

CONTROL BUNKERS

October 15. Further evidence: a ballistic-missile site at Guanajay showing extensive construction scarring and activity.

Below, October 17. A later view of a site at Guanajay.

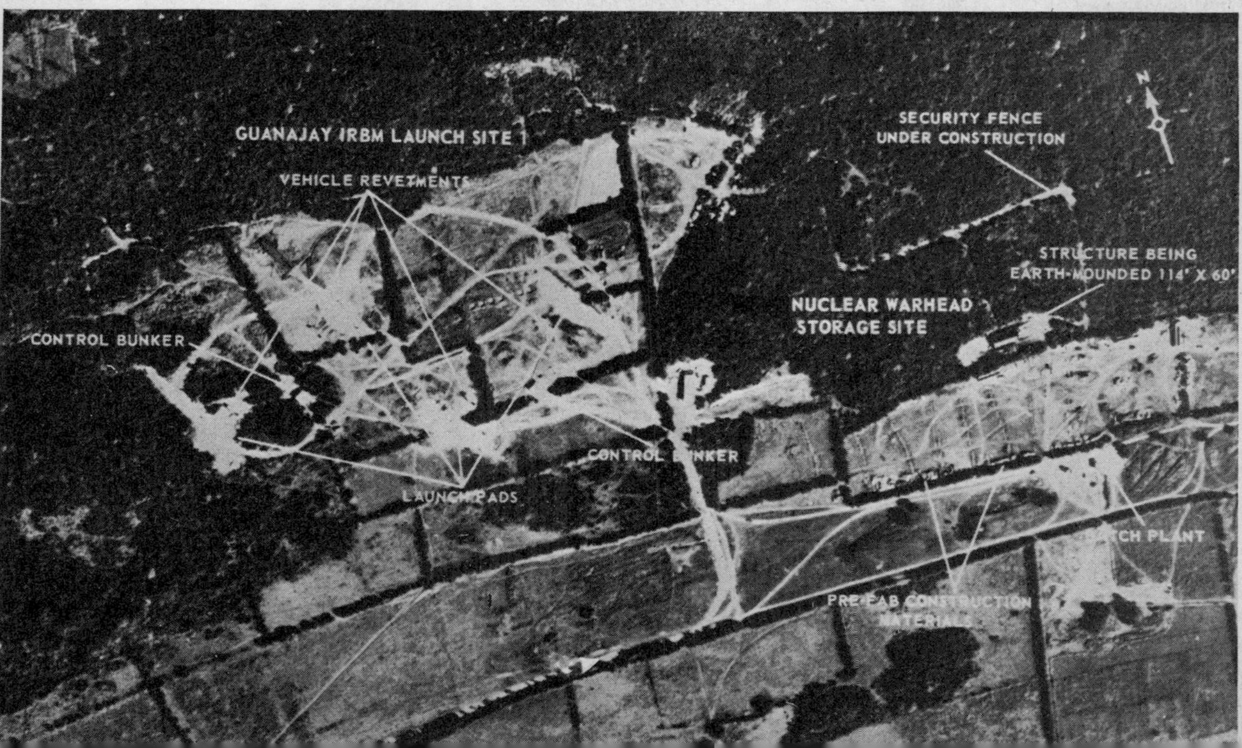

N
GUANAJAY IRBM LAUNCH SITE 1
VEHICLE REVETMENTS
CONTROL BUNKER
LAUNCH PADS
CONTROL BUNKER
SECURITY FENCE
UNDER CONSTRUCTION
STRUCTURE BEING
EARTH-MOUNDED 114' X 60'
NUCLEAR WARHEAD
STORAGE SITE
PRE-FAB

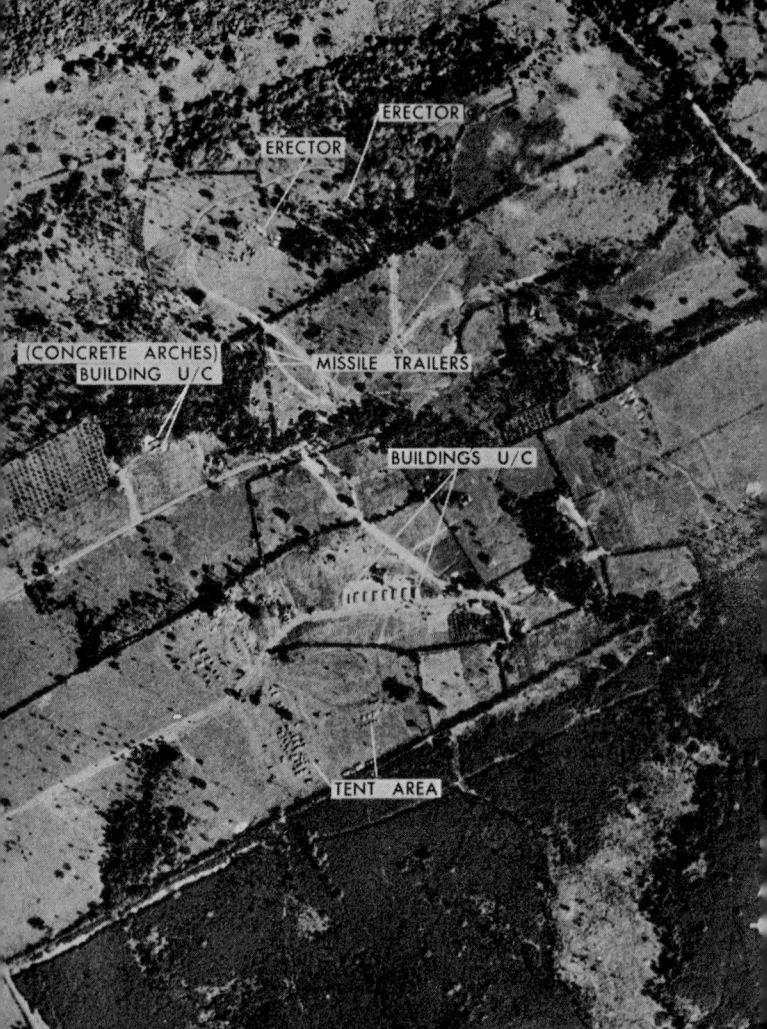

October 17. A later view of a site at San Cristobal.

October 17. A view of a missile site at Sagua showing completed service roads and launch pads, missile erectors in position, and a missile container observed between two of the buildings, among other ready developments.

MOTOR POOL

TENT AREA

MOTOR POOL

ERECTORS

3 MISSILE READY BLDGS AND MISSILE CONTAINER 63 LONG

LAUNCH PADS WITH ERECTORS

LAUNCH PADS

October 23. A low-level photograph showing specifics of the development at San Cristobal. On the next two pages, later details of this site.

MRBM LAUNCH SITE 1
SAN CRISTOBAL, CUBA
22-40N 83-18W

ERECTOR

HARDSTAND FOR ERECTOR

FIRING TABLE

TRACKED PRIME MOVER

MISSILE SHELTER TENTS

MISSILE TRANSPORTERS

NUCLEAR WARHEAD BUNKER UNDER CONSTRUCTION
SAN CRISTOBAL SITE 1

PREFABRICATION MATERIALS

UNCRATED FUSELAGE AND TAIL SECTION

BEAGLES BEING ASSEMBLED

San Julian airfield photographed on October 27.

Inbound and outbound Soviet ships carrying bomber crates or missiles. Above, October 24, Soviet ship laden with jet-bomber crates photographed by U.S. reconnaissance aircraft. Below, another Soviet ship with fuselage crates on deck inbound to Cuba. On the next page, above, an inbound ship with miscellaneous cargo. Below, one of the first outbound Soviet vessels.

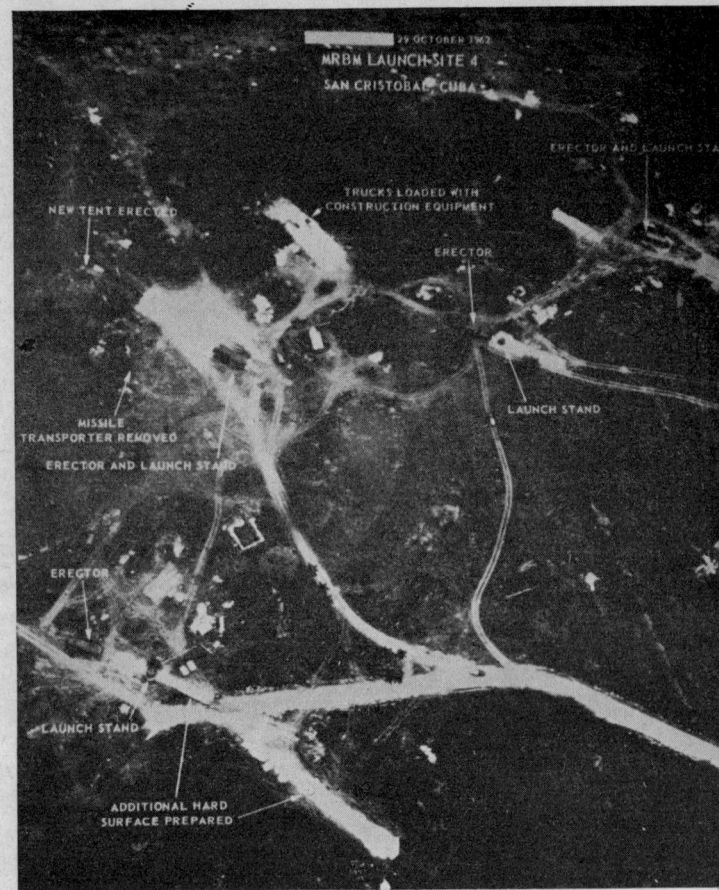

San Cristobal site No. 4 on October 29, apparently photographed before the beginnings of a Soviet withdrawal there.

On the next page is a chart indicating the Soviet military build-up in Cuba.

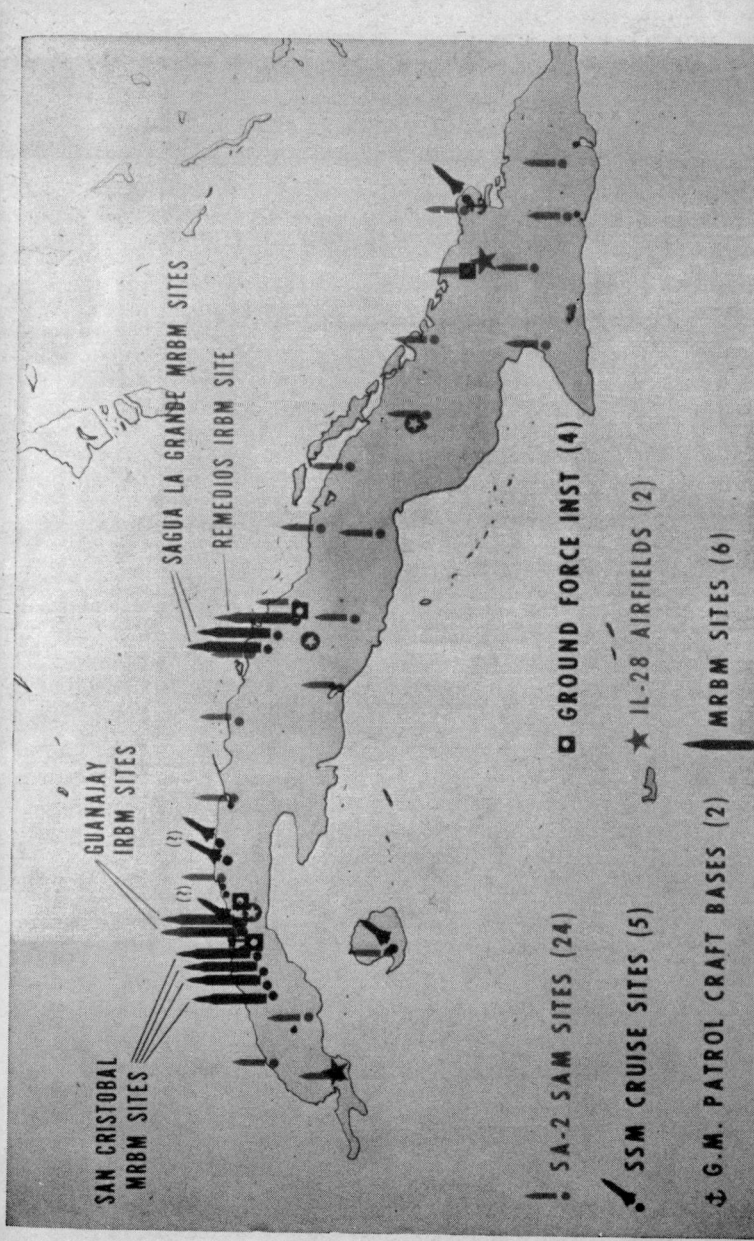

ERECTORS REMOVED FROM LAUNCH POSITIONS

CAMOUFLAGED MISSILE TRANSPORTER REMOVED

LAUNCH STANDS REMAINING

CONTINUED CONSTRUCTION

Photograph of San Cristobal site No. 2 on October 29 showing evidence of the start of dismantling, despite some continued construction. Below, November 1, dismantling proceeds rapidly at Guanajay.

MISSILE READY TENT FOUNDATIONS (TENTS REMOVED)

ABANDONED LAUNCH POSITION

November 1. Further evidence of dismantling at San Cristobal.

VOLGOLES ENR USSR 9 NOVEMBER

A U.S. Navy photograph of Soviet missile-laden ship *Volgoles* leaving Cuba, November 9, with U.S. Navy radar picket ship *Vesole* alongside. Wing of U.S. Navy patrol plane is overhead.

Major Rudolf Anderson, Jr., U-2 pilot shot down by the Communists on October 27.

"It is always the brave and the best who die."

out to the President that they had always felt the blockade to be far too weak a course and that military steps were the only ones the Soviet Union would understand. They were not at all surprised that nothing had been achieved by limited force, for this is exactly what they had predicted.

In the midst of these deliberations, another message came, to change the whole course of events and alter history. Major Rudolf Anderson, Jr., from South Carolina, one of the two Air Force pilots who had carried out the original U-2 reconnaissance that uncovered the presence of missiles in Cuba, had since flown several other photo-reconnaissance missions and was flying one that Saturday morning, October 27. Our meeting was interrupted by the report that his plane had been hit by a SAM missile, that it had crashed in Cuba, and that he had been killed.

There was sympathy for Major Anderson and his family. There was the knowledge that we had to take military action to protect our pilots. There was the realization that the Soviet Union and Cuba apparently were preparing to do battle. And there was the feeling that the noose was tightening on all of us, on Americans, on mankind, and that the bridges to escape were crumbling.

"How can we send any more U-2 pilots into this area tomorrow unless we take out all of the SAM sites?" the President asked. "We are now in an entirely new ball game."

At first, there was almost unanimous agreement that we had to attack early the next morning with bombers and fighters and destroy the SAM sites. But again the President pulled everyone back. "It isn't the first step that concerns me," he said, "but both sides escalating to the fourth and fifth step—and we don't go to the sixth because there is no one around to do so. We must remind ourselves we are embarking on a very hazardous course."

He asked for absolute verification that the U-2 was shot down and did not crash accidentally, and for a careful review, "before we decide finally what we shall do," of the implications of all possible courses of action. His mind went to other areas of the world. What was going to occur in Berlin, in Turkey? If we attacked Cuba, and the Russians reciprocated with an attack on Turkey, would or should the Turkish missiles be fired? He ordered preparations taken to defuse missiles with atomic warheads, so that he personally would have to give permission before they were used. What role should Turkey and the rest of NATO have in determining our response? Within a very short time, they might be faced with decisions of life and death. Before that happened, should they not have a right to learn, if not pass on, what we were deciding to do, particularly if that was likely to affect them in such a rapid and possibly devastating way?

Again and again he emphasized that we must understand the implications of every step. What response could we anticipate? What were the implications for us? He stressed again our responsibility to consider the effect our actions would have on others. NATO was supporting the United States, but were these countries truly and completely aware of the dangers for them? These hourly decisions, necessarily made with such rapidity, could be made only by the President of the United States, but any one of them might close and lock doors for peoples and governments in many other lands. We had to be aware of this responsibility at all times, he said, aware that we were deciding, the President was deciding, for the U.S., the Soviet Union, Turkey, NATO, and really for all mankind. . . .

"Those hours in the Cabinet Room . . ."

THOSE HOURS in the Cabinet Room that Saturday afternoon in October could never be erased from the minds of any of us. We saw as never before the meaning and responsibility involved in the power of the United States, the power of the President, the responsibility we had to people around the globe who had never heard of us, who had never heard of our country or the men sitting in that room determining their fate, making a decision which would influence whether they would live or die.

We won't attack tomorrow, the President said. We shall try again.

The State Department submitted a draft of a letter for response from President Kennedy to Khrushchev. It answered the arguments made in Khrushchev's latest letter, maintaining that we could not remove the missiles from Turkey and that no trade could be made.

I disagreed with the content and tenor of the letter. I suggested, and was supported by Ted Sorensen and others, that we ignore the latest Khrushchev letter and respond to his earlier letter's proposal, as refined in the offer made to John Scali, that the Soviet missiles and offensive weapons would be removed from Cuba under UN inspection and verification if, on its side, the United States would agree with the rest of the Western Hemisphere not to invade Cuba.

There were arguments back and forth. There were sharp disagreements. Everyone was tense; some were already near exhaustion; all were weighted down with concern and worry. President Kennedy was by far the calmest. Finally, when we almost seemed unable to communicate with one another, he suggested with a note of some exasperation that—inasmuch as I felt so strongly that the State Department's various efforts to respond were not satisfactory—Ted Sorensen and I should leave the meeting and go into his office and compose an alternative response, so he could then decide between the two. The two of us left and, sitting in the President's office, wrote a draft. Forty-five minutes later, we took it to him and to the whole group. He worked on it, refined it, had it typed, and signed it.

It accepted Khrushchev's "offer":

"Dear Mr. Chairman:

"I have read your letter of October 26th with great care and welcomed the statement of your desire to seek a prompt solution to the problem. The first thing that needs to be done, however, is for work to cease on offensive missile bases in Cuba and for all weapons systems in Cuba capable of offensive use to be rendered inoperable, under effective United Nations arrangements.

"Assuming this is done promptly, I have given my representatives in New York instructions that will permit them to work out this weekend—in cooperation with the Acting Secretary General and your representative—an arrangement for a permanent solution to the Cuban problem along the lines suggested in your letter of October 26th. As I read your letter, the key elements of your proposals—which seem generally acceptable as I understand them—are as follows:

"1. You would agree to remove these weapons systems from Cuba under appropriate United Nations observation and supervision; and undertake, with suitable safeguards, to halt the further introduction of such weapons systems into Cuba.

"2. We, on our part, would agree—upon the establishment of adequate arrangements through the United Nations to ensure the carrying out and continuation of these commitments—(a) to remove promptly the quarantine measures now in effect, and (b) to give assurances against an invasion of Cuba. I am confident that other nations of the Western Hemisphere would be prepared to do likewise.

"If you will give your representative similar instructions, there is no reason why we should not be able to complete these arrangements and announce them to the world within a couple of days. The effect of such a settlement on easing world tensions would enable us to work toward a more general arrangement regarding 'other armaments,' as proposed in your second letter, which you made public. I would like to say again that the United States is very much interested in reducing tensions and halting the arms race; and if your letter signifies that you are prepared to discuss a detente affecting NATO and the Warsaw Pact, we are quite prepared to consider with our allies any useful proposals.

"But the first ingredient, let me emphasize, is the cessation of work on missile sites in Cuba and measures to render such weapons inoperable, under effective international guarantees. The continuation of this threat, or a prolonging of this discussion concerning Cuba by linking these problems to the broader questions of European and world security, would surely lead to an intensification of the Cuban crisis and a grave risk to the peace of the world. For this reason, I hope we can quickly agree along the lines outlined in this letter and in your letter of October 26th.

"John F. Kennedy"

"The President ordered the Ex Comm . . ."

THE PRESIDENT ordered the Ex Comm to meet again at 9:00 P.M. in the White House. While the letter was being typed and prepared for transmission, he and I sat in his office. He talked about Major Anderson and how it is always the brave and the best who die. The politicians and officials sit home pontificating about great principles and issues, make the decisions, and dine with their wives and families, while the brave and the young die. He talked about the miscalculations that lead to war. War is rarely intentional. The Russians don't wish to fight any more than we do. They do not want to war with us nor we with them. And yet if events continue as they have in the last several days, that struggle—which no one wishes, which will accomplish nothing—will engulf and destroy all mankind.

He wanted to make sure that he had done everything in his power, everything conceivable, to prevent such a catastrophe. Every opportunity was to be given to the Russians to find a peaceful settlement which would not diminish their national security or be a public humiliation. It was not only for Americans that he was concerned, or primarily the older generation of any land. The thought that disturbed him the most, and that made the prospect of war much more fearful than it would otherwise have been, was the specter of the death of the children of this country and all the world—the young people who had no role, who had no say, who knew nothing even of the confrontation, but whose lives would be snuffed out like everyone else's. They would never have a chance to make a decision, to vote in an election, to run for office, to lead a revolution, to determine their own destinies.

Our generation had. But the great tragedy was that, if we erred, we erred not only for ourselves, our futures, our hopes, and our country, but for the lives, futures, hopes, and countries of those who had never been given an opportunity to play a role, to vote aye or nay, to make themselves felt.

It was this that troubled him most, that gave him such pain. And it was then that he and Secretary Rusk decided that I should visit with Ambassador Dobrynin and personally convey the President's great concern.

I telephoned Ambassador Dobrynin about 7:15 P.M. and asked him to come to the Department of Justice. We met in my office at 7:45. I told him first that we knew that work was continuing on the missile bases in Cuba and that in the last few days it had been expedited. I said that in the last few hours we had learned that our reconnaissance planes flying over Cuba had been fired upon and that one of our U-2s had been shot down and the pilot killed. That for us was a most serious turn of events.

President Kennedy did not want a military conflict. He had done everything possible to avoid a military engagement with Cuba and with the Soviet Union, but now they had forced our hand. Because of the deception of the Soviet Union, our photographic reconnaissance planes would have to continue to fly over Cuba, and if the Cubans or Soviets shot at these planes, then we would have to shoot back. This would inevitably lead to further incidents and to escalation of the conflict, the implications of which were very grave indeed.

He said the Cubans resented the fact that we were violating Cuban air space. I replied that if we had not violated Cuban air space, we would still be believing what Khrushchev had said—that there would be no missiles placed in Cuba. In any case, I said, this matter was far more serious than the air space of Cuba—it involved the peoples of both of our countries and, in fact, people all over the globe.

The Soviet Union had secretly established missile bases in Cuba while at the same time proclaiming privately and publicly that this would never be done. We had to have a commitment by tomorrow that those bases would be removed. I was not giving them an ultimatum but a statement of fact. He should understand that if they did not remove those bases, we would remove them. President Kennedy had great respect for the Ambassador's country and the courage of its people. Perhaps his country might feel it necessary to take retaliatory action; but before that was over, there would be not only dead Americans but dead Russians as well.

He asked me what offer the United States was making, and I told him of the letter that President Kennedy had just transmitted to Khrushchev. He raised the question of our removing the missiles from Turkey. I said that there could be no quid pro quo or any arrangement made under this kind of threat or pressure, and that in the last analysis this was a decision that would have to be made by NATO. However, I said, President Kennedy had been anxious to remove those missiles from Turkey and Italy for a long period of time. He had ordered their removal some time ago, and it was our judgment that, within a short time after this crisis was over, those missiles would be gone.

I said President Kennedy wished to have peaceful relations between our two countries. He wished to resolve the problems that confronted us in Europe and Southeast Asia. He wished to move forward on the control of nuclear weapons. However, we could make progress on these matters only when the crisis was behind us. Time was running out. We had only a few more hours—we needed an answer immediately from the Soviet Union. I said we must have it the next day.

I returned to the White House. The President was not optimistic, nor was I. He ordered twenty-four troop-carrier squadrons of the Air Force Reserve to active duty. They would be necessary for an invasion. He had not abandoned hope, but what hope there was now rested with Khrushchev's revising his course within the next few hours. It was a hope, not an expectation. The expectation was a military confrontation by Tuesday and possibly tomorrow. . . .

I had promised my daughters for a long time that I would take them to the Horse Show, and early Sunday morning I went to the Washington Armory to watch the horses jump. In any case, there was nothing I could do but wait. Around 10:00 o'clock, I received a call at the Horse Show. It was Secretary Rusk. He said he had just received word from the Russians that they had agreed to withdraw the missiles from Cuba.

I went immediately to the White House, and there I received a call from Ambassador Dobrynin, saying he would like to visit with me. I met him in my office at 11:00 A.M.

He told me that the message was coming through that Khrushchev had agreed to dismantle and withdraw the missiles under adequate supervision and inspection; that everything was going to work out satisfactorily; and that Mr. Khrushchev wanted to send his best wishes to the President and to me.

It was quite a different meeting from the night before. I went back to the White House and talked to the President for a long time. While I was there, he placed telephone calls to former Presidents Truman and Eisenhower. As I was leaving, he said, making reference to Abraham Lincoln, "This is the night I should go to the theater." I said, "If you go, I want to go with you." As I closed the door, he was seated at the desk writing a letter to Mrs. Anderson. . . .

"Some of the things we learned . . ."

I OFTEN THOUGHT afterward of some of the things we learned from this confrontation. The time that was available to the President and his advisers to work secretly, quietly, privately, developing a course of action and recommendations for the President, was essential. If our deliberations had been publicized, if we had had to make a decision in twenty-four hours, I believe the course that we ultimately would have taken would have been quite different and filled with far greater risks. The fact that we were able to talk, debate, argue, disagree, and then debate some more was essential in choosing our ultimate course. Such time is not always present, although, perhaps surprisingly, on most occasions of great crisis it is; but when it is, it should be utilized.

But more than time is necessary. I believe our deliberations proved conclusively how important it is that the President have the recommendations and opinions of more than one individual, of more than one department, and of more than one point of view. Opinion, even fact itself, can best be judged by conflict, by debate. There is an important element missing when there is unanimity of viewpoint. Yet that not only can happen; it frequently does when the recommendations are being given to the President of the United States. His office creates such respect and awe that it has almost a cowering effect on men. Frequently I saw advisers adapt their opinions to what they believed President Kennedy and, later, President Johnson wished to hear.

I once attended a preliminary meeting with a Cabinet officer, where we agreed on a recommendation to be made to the President. It came as a slight surprise to me when, a few minutes later, in the meeting with the President himself, the Cabinet officer vigorously and fervently expressed the opposite point of view, which, from the discussion, he quite accurately learned would be more sympathetically received by the President.

We had virtual unanimity at the time of the Bay of Pigs. At least, if any officials in the highest ranks of government were opposed, they did not speak out. Thereafter, I suggested there be a devil's advocate to give an opposite opinion if none was pressed. At the time of the Cuban missile crisis, this was obviously not needed.

It is also important that different departments of

government be represented. Thirty years ago, the world was a far, far different place. The Secretary of State and his department could handle all international problems. Perhaps they were not always handled correctly, but at least this handling by one department was manageable. Our commitments were few—we were not as widely involved as we are today—but we were nevertheless a very powerful nation. We could and did, in places we felt our national interests were involved (such as Latin America), impose our will by force if we believed it necessary. The Secretary of State dealt with all the responsibilities without great difficulty, giving foreign-policy advice to the President, administering the department, directing our relationships with that handful of countries which were considered significant, and protecting the financial interests of our citizens around the world.

But that position has very little relationship with that of the Secretary of State today. The title is the same; it still deals with foreign affairs; but there the similarity virtually disappears. Today, the Secretary of State's position is at least five jobs, five different areas of responsibility, all of which could properly require his full time.

The Secretary of State must deal with more than one hundred twenty countries, attend to the affairs of the United Nations, and travel to numerous countries.

He must receive ambassadors, attend dinners, and handle other protocol and social affairs (and lest anyone believe this to be unimportant, we might remember that Secretary Rusk missed President Kennedy's extremely important meeting with Prime Minister Macmillan in Nassau because of a diplomatic dinner he felt he should attend). The Secretary of State must deal with a dozen crises of various significance that arise every week all over the globe, in the Congo, Nigeria, Indonesia, Aden, or elsewhere. He must deal with the one or two major crises that seem to be always with us, such as Berlin in 1961, Cuba in 1962, and now Vietnam. Finally, he must administer one of the largest and most complicated of all departments.

Beyond the time and energy that are required in administering the office, there is another major difference in foreign affairs. Thirty years ago, only the State Department was involved in international matters. But that is no longer true. A number of other agencies and departments have primary responsibilities and power in the foreign-relations field, including the Pentagon, the CIA, the Agency for International Development, and, to a lesser degree, the USIA and other independent or semi-independent departments.

In some countries of the world, the most powerful single voice is that of the AID administrator, with the Ambassador—even though he is representing the State Department and is ostensibly the chief spokesman for the United States and its President—having relatively little power. In some countries that I visited, the dominant U.S. figure was the representative of the CIA; in several of the Latin American countries, it was the head of our military mission. In all these countries, an important role was played by the USIA and, to a lesser degree, the Peace Corps, the Export-Import Bank, the American business community in general, and, in certain countries, particular businessmen.

Individual representatives of at least the Pentagon, the CIA, and AID must be heard and listened to by the President of the United States in addition to the State Department. They have information, intelligence, opinions, and judgments which may be invaluable and which may be quite different from those of the State Department.

It is also true that because of the heavy responsibility of the Secretary of State, he cannot possibly keep himself advised on the details of every crisis with which his department has to deal. There is also the risk that as information is sifted through a number of different hands up to him or to the President, vital facts may be eliminated or distorted through an error of judgment. Thus it is essential for a President to have personal access to those within the department who have expertise and knowledge. He can in this way have available unfiltered information to as great a degree as is practical and possible.

During the Cuban missile crisis, the President not only received information from all the significant departments, but went to considerable lengths to ensure that he was not insulated from individuals or points of view because of rank or position. He wanted the advice of his Cabinet officers, but he also wanted the opinion of those who were connected with the situation itself. He wanted to hear from Secretary Rusk, but he also wished to hear from Tommy Thompson, former (and now again) Ambassador to the Soviet Union, whose advice on the Russians and predictions as to what they would do were uncannily accurate and whose advice and recommendations were surpassed by none; from Ed Martin, Assistant Secretary for Latin America, who organized our effort to secure the backing of the Latin American countries; also from George Ball, the Under Secretary of State, whose advice and judgment were invaluable. He wanted to hear from Secretary McNamara, but he wanted to hear also from Under Secretary Gilpatric, whose ability, knowledge, and judgment he sought in every serious crisis.

On other occasions, I had frequently observed efforts being made to exclude certain individuals from participating in a meeting with the President because they held a different point of view. Often, the President would become aware of this fact and enlarge the meetings to include other opinions. At the missile-crisis conferences he made certain there were experts and representatives of different points of view. President Kennedy wanted people who raised questions, who criticized, on whose judgment he could rely, who presented an intelligent point of view, regardless of their rank or viewpoint.

He wanted to hear presented and challenged all the possible consequences of a particular course of action. The first step might appear sensible, but what would be the reaction of our adversaries and would we actually stand to gain? I remember an earlier meeting on Laos, in 1961, when the military unanimously recommended sending in substantial numbers of U.S. troops to stabilize the country. They were to be brought in through two airports with limited capability. Someone questioned what we would do if only a limited number landed and then the Communist Pathet Lao knocked out the airports and proceeded to attack our troops, limited in number and not completely equipped. The representatives of the military said we would then have to destroy Hanoi and possibly use nuclear weapons. President Kennedy did not send in the troops and concentrated on diplomatic steps to protect our interests.

It was to obtain an unfettered and objective analysis that he frequently, and in critical times, invited Secretary of the Treasury Douglas Dillon, for whose wisdom he had such respect; Kenny O'Donnell, his appointment secretary; Ted Sorensen; and, at times, former Secretary of State Dean Acheson, former Secretary of Defense Robert Lovett, former High Commissioner of Germany John McCloy, and others. They asked the difficult questions; they made others defend their position; they presented a different point of view; and they were skeptical.

I think this was more necessary in the military field than any other. President Kennedy was impressed with the effort and dedicated manner in which the military responded—the Navy deploying its vessels into the Caribbean; the Air Force going on continuous alert; the Army and the Marines moving their soldiers and equipment into the southeastern part of the U.S.; and all of them alert and ready for combat.

But he was distressed that the representatives with whom he met, with the notable exception of General Taylor, seemed to give so little consideration to the implications of steps they suggested. They seemed always to assume that if the Russians and the Cubans would not respond or, if they did, that a war was in our national interest. One of the Joint Chiefs of Staff once said to me he believed in a preventive attack against the Soviet Union. On that fateful Sunday morning when the Russians answered they were withdrawing their missiles, it was suggested by one high military adviser that we attack Monday in any case. Another felt that we had in some way been betrayed.

President Kennedy was disturbed by this inability to look beyond the limited military field. When we talked about this later, he said we had to remember that they were trained to fight and to wage war—that was their life. Perhaps we would feel even more concerned if they were always opposed to using arms or military means—for if they would not be willing, who would be? But this experience pointed out for us all the importance of civilian direction and control and the importance of raising probing questions to military recommendations.

It was for these reasons, and many more, that

President Kennedy regarded Secretary McNamara as the most valuable public servant in his Administration and in the government.

From all this probing and examination—of the military, State Department, and their recommendations —President Kennedy hoped that he would at least be prepared for the foreseeable contingencies and know that—although no course of action is ever completely satisfactory—he had made his decision based on the best possible information. His conduct of the missile crisis showed how important this kind of skeptical probing and questioning could be.

It also showed how important it was to be respected around the world, how vital it was to have allies and friends. Now, five years later, I discern a feeling of isolationism in Congress and through the country, a feeling that we are too involved with other nations, a resentment of the fact that we do not have greater support in Vietnam, an impression that our AID program is useless and our alliances dangerous. I think it would be well to think back to those days in October 1962.

We have not always had the support of Latin American countries in everything we have done. Frequently, our patience has been sorely tried by the opposition of some of the larger South American countries to measures we felt to be in our common interest and worthy of their support. During the Cuban missile crisis, however, when it was an issue of the greatest importance, when the United States was being sorely tried, those countries came unanimously to our support, and that support was essential.

It was the vote of the Organization of American States that gave a legal basis for the quarantine. Their willingness to follow the leadership of the United States was a heavy and unexpected blow to Khrushchev. It had a major psychological and practical effect on the Russians and changed our position from that of an outlaw acting in violation of international law into a country acting in accordance with twenty allies legally protecting their position.

Similarly, the support of our NATO allies—the rapid public acceptance of our position by Adenauer, de Gaulle, and Macmillan—was of great importance. They accepted our recitation of the facts without question and publicly supported our position without reservation. Had our relationship of trust and mutual respect not been present, had our NATO allies been skeptical about what we were doing and its implications for them, and had Khrushchev thus been able to split off the NATO countries or even one of our chief allies, our position would have been seriously undermined.

Even in Africa, support from a number of countries that had been considered antagonistic toward the United States was of great significance. With a naval quarantine around Cuba, our military reported, Soviet planes could still fly atomic warheads into Cuba. To do so they had to refuel in West Africa, and the critical countries with sufficiently large airports and the necessary refueling facilities were Guinea and Senegal. President Kennedy sent our two Ambassadors to see the Presidents of those two countries.

Sekou Touré of Guinea had been the subject of great criticism in the United States because of his friendship with the Communist nations; but he also admired President Kennedy. When our Ambassador visited him, he immediately accepted as true President Kennedy's description of what was happening in Cuba; said Guinea was not going to assist any country in constructing a military base on foreign soil; and announced that Russian planes would not be permitted to refuel in Conakry.

In Dakar, Ambassador Philip M. Kaiser had a close personal relationship with President Leopold Senghor, who a short time before had had a very successful visit to Washington. He, too, quickly perceived the danger and agreed not to permit Russian planes to land or refuel in Dakar.

In short, our friends, our allies, and, as Thomas Jefferson said, a respect for the opinions of mankind, are all vitally important. We cannot be an island even if we wished; nor can we successfully separate ourselves from the rest of the world.

Exasperation over our struggle in Vietnam should not close our eyes to the fact that we could have other missile crises in the future—different kinds, no doubt, and under different circumstances. But if we are to be successful then, if we are going to preserve our own national security, we will need friends, we will need supporters, we will need countries that believe and respect us and will follow our leadership.

"The importance of placing ourselves in the other country's shoes."

THE FINAL LESSON of the Cuban missile crisis is the importance of placing ourselves in the other country's shoes. During the crisis, President Kennedy spent more time trying to determine the effect of a particular course of action on Khrushchev or the Russians than on any other phase of what he was doing. What guided all his deliberations was an effort not to disgrace Khrushchev, not to humiliate the Soviet Union, not to have them feel they would have to escalate their response because their national security or national interests so committed them.

This was why he was so reluctant to stop and search a Russian ship; this was why he was so opposed to attacking the missile sites. The Russians, he felt, would have to react militarily to such actions on our part.

Thus the initial decision to impose a quarantine rather than to attack; our decision to permit the *Bu-*

charest to pass; our decision to board a non-Russian vessel first; all these and many more were taken with a view to putting pressure on the Soviet Union but not causing a public humiliation.

Miscalculation and misunderstanding and escalation on one side bring a counterresponse. No action is taken against a powerful adversary in a vacuum. A government or people will fail to understand this only at their great peril. For that is how wars begin—wars that no one wants, no one intends, and no one wins.

Each decision that President Kennedy made kept this in mind. Always he asked himself: Can we be sure that Khrushchev understands what we feel to be our vital national interest? Has the Soviet Union had sufficient time to react soberly to a particular step we have taken? All action was judged against that standard—stopping a particular ship, sending low-flying planes, making a public statement.

President Kennedy understood that the Soviet Union did not want war, and they understood that we wished to avoid armed conflict. Thus, if hostilities were to come, it would be either because our national interests collided—which, because of their limited interests and our purposely limited objectives, seemed unlikely —or because of our failure or their failure to understand the other's objectives.

President Kennedy dedicated himself to making it clear to Khrushchev by word and deed—for both are important—that the U.S. had limited objectives and that we had no interest in accomplishing those objectives by adversely affecting the national security of the Soviet Union or by humiliating her.

Later, he was to say in his speech at American University in June of 1963: "Above all, while defending our own vital interests, nuclear powers must avert those confrontations which bring an adversary to the choice of either a humiliating defeat or a nuclear war."

During our crisis talks, he kept stressing the fact that we would indeed have war if we placed the Soviet Union in a position she believed would adversely affect her national security or such public humiliation that she lost the respect of her own people and countries around the globe. The missiles in Cuba, we felt, vitally concerned our national security, but not that of the Soviet Union.

This fact was ultimately recognized by Khrushchev, and this recognition, I believe, brought about his change in what, up to that time, had been a very adamant position. The President believed from the start that the Soviet Chairman was a rational, intelligent man who, if given sufficient time and shown our determination, would alter his position. But there was always the chance of error, of mistake, miscalculation, or misunderstanding, and President Kennedy was committed to doing everything possible to lessen that chance on our side.

The possibility of the destruction of mankind was always in his mind. Someone once said that World War Three would be fought with atomic weapons and the next war with sticks and stones.

As mentioned before, Barbara Tuchman's *The Guns of August* had made a great impression on the President. "I am not going to follow a course which will allow anyone to write a comparable book about this time, *The Missiles of October*," he said to me that Saturday night, October 26. "If anybody is around to write after this, they are going to understand that we made every effort to find peace and every effort to give our adversary room to move. I am not going to push the Russians an inch beyond what is necessary."

After it was finished, he made no statement attempting to take credit for himself or for the Administration for what had occurred. He instructed all members of the Ex Comm and government that no interview should be given, no statement made, which would claim any kind of victory. He respected Khrushchev for properly determining what was in his own country's interest and what was in the interest of mankind. If it was a triumph, it was a triumph for the next generation and not for any particular government or people.

At the outbreak of the First World War the ex-Chancellor of Germany, Prince von Bülow, said to his successor, "How did it all happen?" "Ah, if only we knew," was the reply.

NOTE

It was Senator Kennedy's intention to add a discussion of the basic ethical question involved: what, if any, circumstance or justification gives this government or any government the moral right to bring its people and possibly all people under the shadow of nuclear destruction? He wrote this book in the summer and fall of 1967 on the basis of his personal diaries and recollections, but never had an opportunity to rewrite or complete it.

THEODORE C. SORENSEN

Documents

ADDRESS BY PRESIDENT KENNEDY
OCTOBER 22, 1962

Good evening, my fellow citizens. This Government, as promised, has maintained the closest surveillance of the Soviet military build-up on the island of Cuba. Within the past week unmistakable evidence has established the fact that a series of offensive missile sites is now in preparation on that imprisoned island. The purposes of these bases can be none other than to provide a nuclear strike capability against the Western Hemisphere.

Upon receiving the first preliminary hard information of this nature last Tuesday morning (October 16) at 9:00 A.M., I directed that our surveillance be stepped up. And having now confirmed and completed our evaluation of the evidence and our decision on a course of action, this Government feels obliged to report this new crisis to you in fullest detail.

The characteristics of these new missile sites indicate two distinct types of installations. Several of them include medium-range ballistic missiles capable of carrying a nuclear warhead for a distance of more than 1,000 nautical miles. Each of these missiles, in short, is capable of striking Washington, D.C., the Panama Canal, Cape Canaveral, Mexico City, or any other city in the southeastern part of the United States, in Central America, or in the Caribbean area.

Additional sites not yet completed appear to be designed for intermediate-range ballistic missiles capable of traveling more than twice as far—and thus capable of striking most of the major cities in the Western Hemisphere, ranging as far north as Hudson Bay, Canada, and as far south as Lima, Peru. In addition, jet bombers, capable of carrying nuclear weapons, are now being uncrated and assembled in Cuba, while the necessary air bases are being prepared.

This urgent transformation of Cuba into an important strategic base—by the presence of these large, long-range, and clearly offensive weapons of sudden mass destruction—constitutes an explicit threat to the peace and security of all the Americas, in flagrant and deliberate defiance of the Rio Pact of 1947, the traditions of this nation and Hemisphere, the Joint Resolution of the 87th Congress, the Charter of the United Nations, and my own public warnings to the Soviets on September 4 and 13.

This action also contradicts the repeated assurances of Soviet spokesmen, both publicly and privately delivered, that the arms build-up in Cuba would retain its original defensive character and that the Soviet Union had no need or desire to station strategic missiles on the territory of any other nation.

The size of this undertaking makes clear that it has been planned for some months. Yet only last month, after I had made clear the distinction between any introduction of ground-to-ground missiles and the existence of defensive antiaircraft missiles, the Soviet Government publicly stated on September 11 that, and I quote, "The armaments and military equipment sent to Cuba are designed exclusively for defensive purposes," and, and I quote the Soviet Government, "There is no need for the Soviet Government to shift its weapons for a retaliatory blow to any other country, for instance Cuba," and that, and I quote the Government, "The Soviet Union has so powerful rockets to carry these nuclear warheads that there is no need to search for sites for them beyond the boundaries of the Soviet Union." That statement was false.

Only last Thursday, as evidence of this rapid offensive build-up was already in my hand, Soviet Foreign Minister Gromyko told me in my office that he was instructed to make it clear once again, as he said his Government had already done, that Soviet assistance to Cuba, and I quote, "pursued solely the purpose of contributing to the defense capabilities of Cuba," that, and I quote him, "training by Soviet specialists of Cuban nationals in handling defensive armaments was by no means offensive," and that "if it were otherwise," Mr. Gromyko went on, "the Soviet Government would never become involved in rendering such assistance." That statement also was false.

Neither the United States of America nor the world community of nations can tolerate deliberate deception and offensive threats on the part of any nation, large or small. We no longer live in a world where only the actual firing of weapons represents a sufficient challenge to a nation's security to constitute maximum peril. Nuclear weapons are so destructive and ballistic missiles are so swift that any substantially increased possibility of their use or any sudden change in their deployment may well be regarded as a definite threat to peace.

For many years both the Soviet Union and the United States, recognizing this fact, have deployed strategic nuclear weapons with great care, never upsetting the precarious status quo which insured that these weapons would not be used in the absence of some vital challenge. Our own strategic missiles have never been transferred to the territory of any other nation under a cloak of secrecy and deception; and our history, unlike that of the Soviets since the end of World War II, demonstrates that we have no desire to dominate or conquer any other nation or impose our system upon its people. Nevertheless, American citizens have become adjusted to living daily on the bull's eye of Soviet missiles located inside the U.S.S.R. or in submarines.

In that sense missiles in Cuba add to an already clear and present danger—although it should be noted the nations of Latin America have never previously been subjected to a potential nuclear threat.

But this secret, swift, and extraordinary build-up of Communist missiles—in an area well known to have a special and historical relationship to the United States and the nations of the Western Hemisphere, in violation of Soviet assurances, and in defiance of American and hemispheric policy—this sudden, clandestine decision to station strategic weapons for the first time outside of Soviet soil—is a deliberately provocative and unjustified change in the status quo which cannot be accepted by this country if our courage and our commitments are ever to be trusted again by either friend or foe.

The 1930's taught us a clear lesson: Aggressive conduct, if allowed to grow unchecked and unchallenged, ultimately leads to war. This nation is opposed to war. We are also true to our word. Our unswerving objective, therefore, must be to prevent the use of these missiles against this or any other country and to secure their withdrawal or elimination from the Western Hemisphere.

Our policy has been one of patience and restraint, as befits a peaceful and powerful nation, which leads a worldwide alliance. We have been determined not to be diverted from our central concerns by mere irritants and fanatics. But now further action is required—and it is underway; and these actions may only be the beginning. We will not prematurely or unnecessarily risk the costs of worldwide nuclear war in which even the fruits of victory would be ashes in our mouth—but neither will we shrink from that risk at any time it must be faced.

Acting, therefore, in the defense of our own security and of the entire Western Hemisphere, and under the authority entrusted to me by the Constitution as endorsed by the resolution of the Congress, I have directed that the following initial steps be taken immediately:

First: To halt this offensive build-up, a strict quarantine on all offensive military equipment under shipment to Cuba is being initiated. All ships of any kind bound for Cuba from whatever nation or port will, if found to contain cargoes of offensive weapons, be turned back. This quarantine will be extended, if needed, to other types of cargo and carriers. We are not at this time, however, denying the necessities of life as the Soviets attempted to do in their Berlin blockade of 1948.

Second: I have directed the continued and increased close surveillance of Cuba and its military build-up. The Foreign Ministers of the Organization of American States in their communiqué of October 3 rejected secrecy on such matters in this Hemisphere. Should these offensive military preparations continue, thus increasing the threat to the Hemisphere, further action will be justified. I have directed the Armed Forces to prepare for any eventualities; and I trust that in the interests of both the Cuban people and the Soviet technicians at the sites, the hazards to all concerned of continuing this threat will be recognized.

Third: It shall be the policy of this nation to regard any nuclear missile launched from Cuba against any nation in the Western Hemisphere as an attack by the Soviet Union on the United States, requiring a full retaliatory response upon the Soviet Union.

Fourth: As a necessary military precaution I have reinforced our base at Guantanamo, evacuated today the dependents of our personnel there, and ordered additional military units to be on a standby alert basis.

Fifth: We are calling tonight for an immediate meeting of the Organ of Consultation, under the Organization of American States, to consider this threat to hemispheric security and to invoke articles six and eight of the Rio Treaty in support of all necessary action. The United Nations Charter allows for regional security arrangements—and the nations of this Hemisphere decided long ago against the military presence of outside powers. Our other allies around the world have also been alerted.

Sixth: Under the Charter of the United Nations, we are asking tonight that an emergency meeting of the Security Council be convoked without delay to take action against this latest Soviet threat to world peace. Our resolution will call for the prompt dismantling and withdrawal of all offensive weapons in Cuba, under the supervision of United Nations observers, before the quarantine can be lifted.

Seventh and finally: I call upon Chairman Khrushchev to halt and eliminate this clandestine, reckless, and provocative threat to world peace and to stable relations between our two nations. I call upon him further to abandon this course of world domination and to join in an historic effort to end the perilous arms race and transform the history of man. He has an opportunity now to move the world back from the abyss of destruction—by returning to his Government's own words that it had no need to station missiles outside its own territory, and withdrawing these weapons from Cuba—by refraining from any action which will widen or deepen the present crisis—and then by participating in a search for peaceful and permanent solutions.

This nation is prepared to present its case against the Soviet threat to peace, and our own proposals for a peaceful world, at any time and in any forum in the Organization of American States, in the United Nations, or in any other meeting that could be useful—without limiting our freedom of action.

We have in the past made strenuous efforts to limit the spread of nuclear weapons. We have proposed the elimination of all arms and military bases in a fair and effective disarmament treaty. We are prepared to discuss new proposals for the removal of tensions on both sides—including the possibilities of a genuinely independent Cuba, free to determine its own destiny. We have no wish to war with the

Soviet Union, for we are a peaceful people who desire to live in peace with all other peoples.

But it is difficult to settle or even discuss these problems in an atmosphere of intimidation. That is why this latest Soviet threat—or any other threat which is made either independently or in response to our actions this week—must and will be met with determination. Any hostile move anywhere in the world against the safety and freedom of peoples to whom we are committed—including in particular the brave people of West Berlin—will be met by whatever action is needed.

Finally, I want to say a few words to the captive people of Cuba, to whom this speech is being directly carried by special radio facilities. I speak to you as a friend, as one who knows of your deep attachment to your fatherland as one who shares your aspirations for liberty and justice for all. And I have watched and the American people have watched with deep sorrow how your nationalist revolution was betrayed and how your fatherland fell under foreign domination. Now your leaders are no longer Cuban leaders inspired by Cuban ideals. They are puppets and agents of an international conspiracy which has turned Cuba against your friends and neighbors in the Americas—and turned it into the first Latin American country to become a target for nuclear war, the first Latin American country to have these weapons on its soil.

These new weapons are not in your interest. They contribute nothing to your peace and well being. They can only undermine it. But this country has no wish to cause you to suffer or to impose any system upon you. We know that your lives and land are being used as pawns by those who deny you freedom.

Many times in the past Cuban people have risen to throw out tyrants who destroyed their liberty. And I have no doubt that most Cubans today look forward to the time when they will be truly free—free from foreign domination, free to choose their own leaders, free to select their own system, free to own their own land, free to speak and write and worship without fear or degradation. And then shall Cuba be welcomed back to the society of free nations and to the associations of this Hemisphere.

My fellow citizens, let no one doubt that this is a difficult and dangerous effort on which we have set out. No one can foresee precisely what course it will take or what costs or casualties will be incurred. Many months of sacrifice and self-discipline lie ahead—months in which both our patience and our will will be tested, months in which many threats and denunciations will keep us aware of our dangers. But the greatest danger of all would be to do nothing.

The path we have chosen for the present is full of hazards, as all paths are; but it is the one most consistent with our character and courage as a nation and our commitments around the world. The cost of freedom is always high —but Americans have always paid it. And one path we shall never choose, and that is the path of surrender or submission.

Our goal is not the victory of might but the vindication of right—not peace at the expense of freedom, but both peace and freedom, here in this Hemisphere and, we hope, around the world. God willing, that goal will be achieved.

U.S. PROCLAMATION
OCTOBER 23, 1962

WHEREAS the peace of the world and the security of the United States and of all American States are endangered by reason of the establishment by the Sino-Soviet powers of an offensive military capability in Cuba, including bases for ballistic missiles with a potential range covering most of North and South America:

WHEREAS by a Joint Resolution passed by the Congress of the United States and approved on October 3, 1962, it was declared that the United States is determined to prevent by whatever means may be necessary, including the use of arms, the Marxist-Leninist regime in Cuba from extending, by force or the threat of force, its aggressive or subversive activities to any part of this hemisphere, and to prevent in Cuba the creation or use of an externally supported military capability endangering the security of the United States; and

WHEREAS the Organ of Consultation of the American Republics meeting in Washington on October 23, 1962, recommended that the Member States, in accordance with Articles six and eight of the Inter-American Treaty of Reciprocal Assistance, take all measures, individually and collectively, including the use of armed force, which they may deem necessary to ensure that the Government of Cuba cannot continue to receive from the Sino-Soviet powers military material and related supplies which may threaten the peace and security of the Continent and to prevent the missiles in Cuba with offensive capability from ever becoming an active threat to the peace and security of the Continent:

NOW, THEREFORE, I, JOHN F. KENNEDY, President of the United States of America, acting under and by virtue of the authority conferred upon me by the Constitution and statutes of the United States, in accordance with the aforementioned resolutions of the United States Congress and of the Organ of Consultation of the American Republics, and to defend the security of the United States, do hereby proclaim that the forces under my command are ordered, beginning at 2:00 P.M. Greenwich time October 24, 1962, to interdict, subject to the instructions herein contained, the delivery of offensive weapons and associated material to Cuba.

For the purposes of this Proclamation the following are declared to be prohibited material:

Surface-to-surface missiles; bomber aircraft; bombs, air-to-surface rockets and guided missiles; warheads for any of the above weapons; mechanical or electronic equipment to support or operate the above items; and any other classes of material hereafter designated by the Secretary of Defense for the purpose of effectuating this Proclamation.

To enforce this order, the Secretary of Defense shall take appropriate measures to prevent the delivery of prohibited materiel to Cuba, employing the land, sea and air forces of the United States in cooperation with any forces that may be made available by other American States.

The Secretary of Defense may make such regulations and issue such directives as he deems necessary to ensure the effectiveness of this order, including the designation, within a reasonable distance of Cuba, of prohibited or restricted zones and of prescribed routes.

Any vessel or craft which may be proceeding toward Cuba may be intercepted and may be directed to identify itself, its cargo, equipment and stores and its ports of call, to stop, to lie to, to submit to visit and search, or to proceed as directed. Any vessel or craft which fails or refuses to respond to or comply with directions shall be subject to being taken into custody. Any vessel or craft which it is believed is en route to Cuba and may be carrying prohibited materiel or may itself constitute such materiel shall, wherever possible, be directed to proceed to another destination of its own choice and shall be taken into custody if it fails or refuses to obey such directions. All vessels or craft taken into custody shall be sent into a port of the United States for appropriate disposition.

In carrying out this order, force shall not be used except in case of failure or refusal to comply with directions, or with regulations or directives of the Secretary of Defense issued hereunder, after reasonable efforts have been made to communicate them to the vessel or craft, or in case of self-defense. In any case, force shall be used only to the extent necessary.

IN WITNESS WHEREOF, I have hereunto set my hand and caused the seal of the United States of America to be affixed.

DONE in the City of Washington this twenty-third day of October in the year of our Lord, nineteen hundred (SEAL) and sixty-two, and of the Independence of the United States of America the one hundred and eighty-seventh.

(s) JOHN FITZGERALD KENNEDY
7:06 P.M.
October 23, 1962

By the President:
DEAN RUSK,
Secretary of State

A RESOLUTION OF THE ORGANIZATION
OF AMERICAN STATES
OCTOBER 23, 1962

WHEREAS,

The Inter-American Treaty of Reciprocal Assistance of 1947 (Rio Treaty) recognizes the obligation of the American Republics to "provide for effective reciprocal assistance to meet armed attacks against any American State and in order to deal with threats of aggression against any of them."

Article 6 of the said Treaty states:

"If the inviolability or the integrity of the territory or the sovereignty or political independence of any American State should be affected by an aggression which is not an armed attack or by an extra-continental or intra-continental conflict, or by any other fact or situation that might endanger the peace of America, the Organ of Consultation shall meet immediately in order to agree on the measures which must be taken in case of aggression to assist the victim of the aggression or, in any case, the measures which should be taken for the common defense and for the maintenance of the peace and security of the Continent."

The Eighth Meeting of Consultation of the Ministers of Foreign Affairs of the American Republics in Punta del Este in January, 1962, agreed in Resolution II "To urge the member states to take those steps that they may consider appropriate for their individual and collective self-defense, and to cooperate, as may be necessary or desirable to strength their capacity to counteract threats or acts of aggression, subversion, or other dangers to peace and security resulting from the continued intervention in this hemisphere of Sino-Soviet powers, in accordance with the obligations established in treaties and agreements such as the Charter of the Organization of American States and the Inter-American Treaty of Reciprocal Assistance";

The Ministers of Foreign Affairs of the American Republics meeting informally in Washington, October 2 and 3, 1962, reasserted "the firm intention of the Governments represented and of the peoples of the American Republics to conduct themselves in accordance with the principles of the regional system, staunchly sustaining and consolidating the principles of the Charter of the Organization of American States, and affirmed the will to strengthen the security of the Hemisphere against all aggression from within or outside the Hemisphere and against all developments or situations capable of threatening the peace and security of the Hemisphere through the application of the Inter-American Treaty of Reciprocal Assistance of Rio de Janeiro. It was the view of the Ministers that the existing organizations and bodies of the inter-American system should intensify the carrying out of their respective duties with special and urgent attention to the situation created by the communist regime in Cuba and that they should stand in readiness to consider the matter promptly if the situation requires measures beyond those already authorized."

The same meeting "recalled that the Soviet Union's intervention in Cuba threatens the unity of the Americas and its democratic institutions, and that this intervention has special characteristics which, pursuant to paragraph 3 of Resolution II of the Eighth Meeting of Consultation of Ministers of Foreign Affairs, call for the adoption of special measures, both individual and collective";

Incontrovertible evidence has appeared that the Government of Cuba, despite repeated warnings, has secretly endangered the peace of the Continent by permitting the Sino-Soviet powers to have intermediate and middle-range missiles on its territory capable of carrying nuclear warheads;

THE COUNCIL OF THE ORGANIZATION OF AMERICAN STATES, MEETING AS THE PROVISIONAL ORGAN OF CONSULTATION, RESOLVES:

1. To call for the immediate dismantling and withdrawal from Cuba of all missiles and other weapons with any offensive capability;

2. To recommend that the member states, in accordance with Articles 6 and 8 of the Inter-American Treaty of Reciprocal Assistance, take all measures, individually and collectively, including the use of armed force, which they may deem necessary to ensure that the Government of Cuba cannot continue to receive from the Sino-Soviet powers military material and related supplies which may threaten the peace and security of the Continent and to prevent the missiles in Cuba with offensive capability from ever becoming an active threat to the peace and security of the Continent;

3. To inform the Security Council of the United Nations of this resolution in accordance with Article 54 of the

Charter of the United Nations and to express the hope that the Security Council will, in accordance with the draft resolution introduced by the United States, dispatch United Nations observers to Cuba at the earliest moment;

    4. To continue to serve provisionally as Organ of Consultation and to request the Member States to keep the Organ of Consultation duly informed of measures taken by them in accordance with paragraph two of this resolution.

A STATEMENT BY MR. U THANT TO U.N. SECURITY COUNCIL, INCLUDING TEXT OF LETTER TO PRESIDENT KENNEDY AND CHAIRMAN KHRUSHCHEV

OCTOBER 24, 1962

Mr. President:

Today the United Nations faces a moment of grave responsibility. What is at stake is not just the interests of the parties directly involved, nor just the interests of all Member States, but the very fate of mankind. If today the United Nations should prove itself ineffective, it may have proved itself so for all time.

In the circumstances, not only as Acting Secretary General of the United Nations but as a human being, I would be failing in my duty if I did not express my profound hope and conviction that moderation, self-restraint and good sense will prevail over all other considerations. In this situation, where the very existence of mankind is in the balance, I derive some consolation from the fact that there is some common ground in the resolutions introduced in the Council. Irrespective of the fate of those resolutions, that common ground remains. It calls for urgent negotiations between the parties directly involved, though, as I said earlier, the rest of the world is also an interested party. In this context I cannot help expressing the view that some of the measures proposed or taken, which the Council is called upon to approve, are very unusual, and I might say even extraordinary, except in wartime.

At the request of the Permanent Representatives of a large number of Member Governments, who have discussed the matter amongst themselves and with me, I have sent, through the Permanent Representatives of the two Governments, the following identically worded message to the President of the United States of America and the Chairman of the Council of Ministers of the U.S.S.R.:

"I have been asked by the Permanent Representatives of a large number of Member Governments of the United Nations to address an urgent appeal to you in the present critical situation. These Representatives feel that in the interest of international peace and security all concerned should refrain from any action which may aggravate the situation and bring with it the risk of war. In their view it is important that time should be given to enable the parties concerned to get together with a view to resolving the present crisis peacefully and normalizing the situation in the Caribbean. This involves on the one hand the voluntary suspension of all arms shipments to Cuba, and also the voluntary suspension of the quarantine measures involving the searching of ships bound for Cuba. I believe that such voluntary suspension for a period of two to three weeks will greatly ease the situation and give time to the parties concerned to meet and discuss with a view to finding a peaceful solution of the problem. In this context I shall gladly make myself available to all parties for whatever services I may be able to perform. I urgently appeal to Your Excellency to give immediate consideration to this message."

I have sent an identical message to the President of the United States of America and the Chairman of the Council of Ministers of the U.S.S.R.

I should also like to take this occasion to address an urgent appeal to the President and the Prime Minister of the Revolutionary Government of Cuba. Yesterday Ambassador García-Inchaustegui of Cuba recalled the words of his President, words which were uttered from the rostrum of the General Assembly just over two weeks ago, and I quote:

"Were the United States able to give us proof, by word and deed, that it would not carry out aggression against our country, then, we declare solemnly before you here and now, our weapons would be unnecessary and our army redundant."

Here again I feel that on the basis of discussion, some common ground may be found through which a way may be traced out of the present impasse. I believe it would also contribute greatly to the same end if the construction and development of major military facilities and installations in Cuba could be suspended during the period of negotiations.

Mr. President, I now make a most solemn appeal to the parties concerned to enter into negotiations immediately, even this night, if possible, irrespective of any other procedures which may be available or which could be invoked.

I realize that if my appeal is heeded, the first subject to be discussed will be the modalities, and that all parties concerned will have to agree to comply with those responsibilities which fall on them before any agreement as a whole could become effective. I hope, however, that the need for such discussion will not deter the parties concerned from undertaking these discussions. In my view it would be shortsighted for the parties concerned to seek assurances on the end result before the negotiations have even begun.

I have stated in my message to both the President of the United States of America and the Chairman of the Council of Ministers of the U.S.S.R. that I shall gladly make myself available to all parties for whatever services I may be able to perform. I repeat that pledge now.

During the seventeen years that have passed since the end of World War II, there has never been a more dangerous or closer confrontation of the major powers. At a time when the danger to world peace was less immediate, or so it appears by comparison, my distinguished predecessor said:

"The principles of the Charter are, by far, greater than the Organization in which they are embodied, and the aims which they are to safeguard are holier than the policies of any single nation or people." He went on to say: "The discretion and impartiality . . . imposed on the Secretary General by the character of his immediate task may not degenerate into a policy of expediency. . . . A Secretary General cannot serve on any other assumption than that . . . within the necessary limits of human frailty and honest differences of opinion—all Member Nations honour their pledge to observe all articles of the Charter. . . ."

It is after considerable deliberation that I have decided to send the two messages to which I have referred earlier, and likewise I have decided to make this brief intervention tonight before the Security Council including the appeal to the President and Prime Minister of Cuba.

I hope that at this moment, not only in the Council Chamber but in the world outside, good sense and understanding will be placed above the anger of the moment or the pride of nations. The path of negotiation and compromise is the only course by which the peace of the world can be secured at this critical moment.

Mr. President, I thank you.

PRESIDENT KENNEDY TO MR. U THANT
OCTOBER 25, 1962

Excellency:

I deeply appreciate the spirit which prompted your message of yesterday.

As we made clear in the Security Council, the existing threat was created by the secret introduction of offensive weapons into Cuba, and the answer lies in the removal of such weapons.

In your message and your statement to the Security Council last night, you have made certain suggestions and have invited preliminary talks to determine whether satisfactory arrangements can be assured.

Ambassador Stevenson is ready to discuss these arrangements with you.

I can assure you of our desire to reach a satisfactory and peaceful solution of the matter.

(s) JOHN F. KENNEDY

I have received your appeal, and carefully studied the proposals it contains. I welcome your initiative. I understand your concern about the situation obtained in the Caribbean since the Soviet Government also considers this situation as highly dangerous and requiring an immediate interference by the United Nations.

I am informing you that I agree with your proposal, which meets the interest of peace.

I have today sent a further message to Chairman Khrushchev expressing my grave concern that Soviet ships already on their way to Cuba might challenge the quarantine imposed by your government and produce a confrontation at sea between Soviet ships and United States vessels, which could lead to an aggravation of the situation. I have also stated that what concerns me most is the fact that such a confrontation and consequent aggravation of the situation would destroy any possibility of the discussions that I have suggested as a prelude to negotiations on a peaceful settlement. I have accordingly expressed to him my earnest hope that Soviet ships already on their way to Cuba might be instructed to stay away from the interception area for a limited time only, in order to permit discussions of the modalities of a possible agreement which could settle the problem peacefully in line with the Charter of the United Nations.

In continuation of my message of yesterday and my speech before the Security Council, I would now like to appeal to Your Excellency that instructions may be issued to United States vessels in the Caribbean to do everything possible to avoid direct confrontation with Soviet ships in the next few days in order to minimize the risk of any untoward incident. If I could be informed of the action taken by your government on the basis of this appeal, I could inform

Chairman Khrushchev that I have assurances from your side of your cooperation in avoiding all risk of an untoward incident. I would express the further hope that such cooperation could be the prelude to a quick agreement in principle on the basis of which the quarantine measures themselves could be called off as soon as possible.

(s) U THANT
Acting Secretary General

PRESIDENT KENNEDY TO
MR. U THANT
     OCTOBER 25, 1962

Excellency:
     I have your further message of today and I continue
to understand and welcome your efforts for a satisfactory solution. I appreciate and share your concern that great caution be exercised pending the inauguration of discussions.
     If the Soviet Government accepts and abides by
your request "that Soviet ships already on their way to
Cuba . . . stay away from the interception area" for the
limited time required for preliminary discussion, you may be
assured that this government will accept and abide by your
request that our vessels in the Caribbean "do everything
possible to avoid direct confrontation with Soviet ships in
the next few days in order to minimize the risk of any untoward incident." I must inform you, however, that this is a
matter of great urgency in view of the fact that certain Soviet
ships are still proceeding toward Cuba and the interception
area.
     I share your hope that Chairman Khrushchev will
also heed your appeal and that we can then proceed urgently to meet the requirements that these offensive military
systems in Cuba be withdrawn, in order to end their threat
to peace. I must point out to you that present work on these
systems is still continuing.

In continuation of my message of yesterday and my statement before the Security Council, I would like to bring to Your Excellency's attention my grave concern that Soviet ships already on their way to Cuba might challenge the quarantine imposed by the United States and produce a confrontation at sea between Soviet ships and United States vessels, which could lead to an aggravation of the situation. What concerns me most is that such a confrontation and consequent aggravation of the situation would destroy any possibility of the discussions I have suggested as a prelude to negotiations on a peaceful settlement. In the circumstances I earnestly hope that Your Excellency may find it possible to instruct the Soviet ships already on their way to Cuba to stay away from the interception area for a limited time only, in order to permit discussions of the modalities of a possible agreement which could settle the problem peacefully in line with the Charter of the United Nations.

I am confident that, if such instructions could be issued by Your Excellency, the United States authorities will take action to ensure that a direct confrontation between their ships and Soviet ships is avoided during the same period in order to minimise the risk of any untoward incident taking place.

If I could be informed of the action taken by Your

Government on the basis of this appeal, I could inform President Kennedy that I have assurances from your side of your cooperation in avoiding all risk of an untoward incident.

I am at the same time addressing the enclosed appeal to President Kennedy.

(s) U THANT
Acting Secretary General

CHAIRMAN KHRUSHCHEV TO MR. U THANT

OCTOBER 26, 1962

Dear U Thant,

I have received and studied your telegram of 25 October. I understand your anxiety for the preservation of peace, and I appreciate highly your efforts to avert military conflict.

Indeed, if any conflict should arise on the approaches to Cuba—and this may become unavoidable as a result of the piratical measures taken by the United States—this would beyond question seriously complicate the endeavours to initiate contacts in order to put an end, on a basis of negotiation, to the critical situation that has now been thrust on the world by the aggressive actions of the United States.

We therefore accept your proposal, and have ordered the masters of Soviet vessels bound for Cuba but not yet within the area of the American warships' piratical activities to stay out of the interception area, as you recommend.

But we have given this order in the hope that the other side will understand that such a situation, in which we keep vessels immobilized on the high seas, must be a purely temporary one; the period cannot under any circumstances be of long duration.

I thank you for your efforts and wish you success in your noble task. Your efforts to ensure world peace will always meet with understanding and support on our part.

The Soviet Government has consistently striven, and is striving, to strengthen the United Nations—that international Organization which constitutes a forum for all countries of the world, regardless of their socio-political structure, in order that disputes arising may be settled not through war but through negotiations.

Accept, Sir, the assurances of my highest consideration.

(s) N. KHRUSHCHEV

WHITE HOUSE STATEMENT
ON CONTINUATION OF MISSILE BUILD-UP
IN CUBA
OCTOBER 26,1962

The development of ballistic missile sites in Cuba continues at a rapid pace. Through the process of continued surveillance directly by the President, additional evidence has been acquired which clearly reflects that as of Thursday, October 25, definite build-ups in these offensive missile sites continued to be made. The activity at these sites apparently is directed at achieving a full operational capability as soon as possible.

There is evidence that as of yesterday, October 25, considerable construction activity was being engaged in at the intermediate-range ballistic missile sites. Bulldozers and cranes were observed as late as Thursday actively clearing new areas within the sites and improving the approach roads to the launch pads.

Since Tuesday, October 23, missile-related activities have continued at the medium-range ballistic missiles sites resulting in progressive refinements at these facilities. For example, missiles were observed parked in the open on October 23. Surveillance on October 25 revealed that some of these same missiles have now been moved from their original parked positions. Cabling can be seen running from the missile-ready tents to power generators nearby.

162

In summary, there is no evidence to date indicating that there is any intention to dismantle or discontinue work on these missile sites. On the contrary the Soviets are rapidly continuing their construction of missile support and launch facilities, and serious attempts are under way to camouflage their efforts.

SECOND * LETTER FROM CHAIRMAN
KHRUSHCHEV TO PRESIDENT KENNEDY
OCTOBER 26, 1962

Dear Mr. President:

It is with great satisfaction that I studied your reply to Mr. U Thant on the adoption of measures in order to avoid contact by our ships and thus avoid irreparable fatal consequences. This reasonable step on your part persuades me that you are showing solicitude for the preservation of peace, and I note this with satisfaction.

I have already said that the only concern of our people and government and myself personally as chairman of the Council of Ministers is to develop our country and have it hold a worthy place among all people of the world in economic competition, advance of culture and arts, and the rise in people's living standards. This is the loftiest and most necessary field for competition which will only benefit both the winner and loser, because this benefit is peace and an increase in the facilities by means of which man lives and obtains pleasure.

* On Friday, Oct. 26, Khrushchev sent two letters to President Kennedy. The first, not made public, apparently took the "soft" line that Russia would remove its missiles from Cuba in return for ending of the U.S. quarantine and assurances that the U.S. would not invade Cuba. The second took a harder line seeking the removal of U.S. missiles in Turkey in return for taking Russian missiles out of Cuba [A notation from *Congressional Quarterly*]

In your statement, you said that the main aim lies not only in reaching agreement and adopting measures to avert contact of our ships, and, consequently, a deepening of the crisis, which because of this contact can spark off the fire of military conflict after which any talks would be superfluous because other forces and other laws would begin to operate—the laws of war. I agree with you that this is only a first step. The main thing is to normalize and stabilize the situation in the world between states and between people.

I understand your concern for the security of the United States, Mr. President, because this is the first duty of the president. However, these questions are also uppermost in our minds. The same duties rest with me as chairman of the U.S.S.R. Council of Ministers. You have been worried over our assisting Cuba with arms designed to strengthen its defensive potential—precisely defensive potential—because Cuba, no matter what weapons it had, could not compare with you since these are different dimensions, the more so given up-to-date means of extermination.

Our purpose has been and is to help Cuba, and no one can challenge the humanity of our motives aimed at allowing Cuba to live peacefully and develop as its people desire. You want to relieve your country from danger and this is understandable. However, Cuba also wants this. All countries want to relieve themselves from danger. But how can we, the Soviet Union and our government, assess your actions which, in effect, mean that you have surrounded the Soviet Union with military bases, surrounded our allies with military bases, set up military bases literally around our country, and stationed your rocket weapons at them? This is no secret. High-placed American officials demonstratively declare this. Your rockets are stationed in Britain and in Italy and pointed at us. Your rockets are stationed in Turkey.

You are worried over Cuba. You say that it worries you because it lies at a distance of ninety miles across the sea from the shores of the United States. However, Turkey lies next to us. Our sentinels are pacing up and down and watching each other. Do you believe that you have the right to demand security for your country and the removal of such weapons that you qualify as offensive, while not recognizing this right for us?

You have stationed devastating rocket weapons, which you call offensive, in Turkey literally right next to us. How then does recognition of our equal military possibilities tally with such unequal relations between our great states? This does not tally at all.

It is good, Mr. President, that you agreed for our representatives to meet and begin talks, apparently with the participation of U.N. Acting Secretary General U Thant. Consequently, to some extent, he assumes the role of intermediary, and we believe that he can cope with the responsible mission if, of course, every side that is drawn into this conflict shows good will.

I think that one could rapidly eliminate the conflict and normalize the situation. Then people would heave a sigh of relief, considering that the statesmen who bear the responsibility have sober minds, an awareness of their responsibility, and an ability to solve complicated problems and not allow matters to slide to the disaster of war.

This is why I make this proposal: We agree to re-move those weapons from Cuba which you regard as offen-sive weapons. We agree to do this and to state this commit-ment in the United Nations. Your representatives will make a statement to the effect that the United States, on its part, bearing in mind the anxiety and concern of the Soviet state, will evacuate its analogous weapons from Turkey. Let us reach an understanding on what time you and we need to put this into effect.

After this, representatives of the U.N. Security Council could control on-the-spot the fulfillment of these commitments. Of course, it is necessary that the Govern-ments of Cuba and Turkey would allow these representa-tives to come to their countries and check fulfillment of this commitment, which each side undertakes. Apparently, it would be better if these representatives enjoyed the trust of the Security Council and ours—the United States and the Soviet Union—as well as of Turkey and Cuba. I think that it will not be difficult to find such people who enjoy the trust and respect of all interested sides.

We, having assumed this commitment in order to give satisfaction and hope to the peoples of Cuba and Tur-key and to increase their confidence in their security, will make a statement in the Security Council to the effect that the Soviet Government gives a solemn pledge to respect the integrity of the frontiers and the sovereignty of Turkey, not to intervene in its domestic affairs, not to invade Turkey, not to make available its territory as a *place d'armes* for such in-vasion, and also will restrain those who would think of launching an aggression against Turkey either from Soviet territory or from the territory of other states bordering on Turkey.

The U.S. Government will make the same statement in the Security Council with regard to Cuba. It will declare that the United States will respect the integrity of the frontiers of Cuba, its sovereignty, undertakes not to intervene in its domestic affairs, not to invade and not to make its territory available as [a] *place d'armes* for the invasion of Cuba, and also will restrain those who would think of launching an aggression against Cuba either from U.S. territory or from the territory of other states bordering on Cuba.

Of course, for this we would have to reach agreement with you and to arrange for some deadline. Let us agree to give some time, but not to delay, two or three weeks, not more than a month.

The weapons on Cuba, that you have mentioned and which, as you say, alarm you, are in the hands of Soviet officers. Therefore any accidental use of them whatsoever to the detriment of the United States of America is excluded. These means are stationed in Cuba at the request of the Cuban Government and only in defensive aims. Therefore, if there is no invasion of Cuba, or an attack on the Soviet Union, or other of our allies then, of course, these means do not threaten anyone and will not threaten. For they do not pursue offensive aims.

If you accept my proposal, Mr. President, we would send our representatives to New York, to the United Nations, and would give them exhaustive instructions to order to come to terms sooner. If you would also appoint your men and give them appropriate instructions, this problem could be solved soon.

Why would I like to achieve this? Because the entire world is now agitated and expects reasonable actions from us. The greatest pleasure for all the peoples would be an announcement on our agreement, on nipping in the bud the conflict that has arisen. I attach a great importance to such understanding because it might be a good beginning and, specifically, facilitate a nuclear test ban agreement. The problem of tests could be solved simultaneously, not linking one with the other, because they are different problems. However, it is important to reach an understanding to both these problems in order to make a good gift to the people, to let them rejoice in the news that a nuclear test ban agreement has also been reached and thus there will be no further contamination of the atmosphere. Your and our positions on this issue are very close.

All this, possibly, would serve as a good impetus to searching for mutually acceptable agreements on other disputed issues, too, on which there is an exchange of opinion between us. These problems have not yet been solved, but they wait for an urgent solution which would clear the international atmosphere. We are ready for this.

These are my proposals, Mr. President.

Respectfully yours,
(s) NIKITA KHRUSHCHEV

PRESIDENT KENNEDY TO CHAIRMAN KHRUSHCHEV

OCTOBER 27, 1962

[Reply to Chairman Khrushchev's first letter of October 26]

I have read your letter of October 26th with great care and welcomed the statement of your desire to seek a prompt solution to the problem. The first thing that needs to be done, however, is for work to cease on offensive missile bases in Cuba and for all weapons systems in Cuba capable of offensive use to be rendered inoperable, under effective United Nations arrangements.

Assuming this is done promptly, I have given my representatives in New York instructions that will permit them to work out this weekend—in cooperation with the Acting Secretary General and your representative—an arrangement for a permanent solution to the Cuban problem along the lines suggested in your letter of October 26th. As I read your letter, the key elements of your proposals—which seem generally acceptable as I understand them—are as follows:

1) You would agree to remove these weapons systems from Cuba under appropriate United Nations observation and supervision; and undertake, with suitable safeguards, to halt the further introduction of such weapons systems into Cuba.

2) We, on our part, would agree—upon the estab-

lishment of adequate arrangements through the United Nations to ensure the carrying out and continuation of these commitments—(a) to remove promptly the quarantine measures now in effect and (b) to give assurances against an invasion of Cuba. I am confident that other nations of the Western Hemisphere would be prepared to do likewise.

If you will give your representative similar instructions, there is no reason why we should not be able to complete these arrangements and announce them to the world within a couple of days. The effect of such a settlement on easing world tensions would enable us to work toward a more general arrangement regarding "other armaments," as proposed in your second letter which you made public. I would like to say again that the United States is very much interested in reducing tensions and halting the arms race; and if your letter signifies that you are prepared to discuss a detente affecting NATO and the Warsaw Pact, we are quite prepared to consider with our allies any useful proposals.

But the first ingredient, let me emphasize, is the cessation of work on missile sites in Cuba and measures to render such weapons inoperable, under effective international guarantees. The continuation of this threat, or a prolonging of this discussion concerning Cuba by linking these problems to the broader questions of European and world security, would surely lead to an intensified situation on the Cuban crisis and a grave risk to the peace of the world. For this reason I hope we can quickly agree along the lines outlined in this letter and in your letter of October 26th.

(s) JOHN F. KENNEDY

Several inconsistent and conflicting proposals have been made by the U.S.S.R. within the last twenty-four hours, including the one just made public in Moscow. The proposal broadcast this morning involves the security of nations outside the Western Hemisphere. But it is the Western Hemisphere countries and they alone that are subject to the threat that has produced the current crisis—the action of the Soviet Government in secretly introducing offensive weapons into Cuba. Work on these offensive weapons is still proceeding at a rapid pace. The first imperative must be to deal with this immediate threat, under which no sensible negotiations can proceed.

It is therefore the position of the United States that as an urgent preliminary to consideration of any proposals work on the Cuban bases must stop; offensive weapons must be rendered inoperable; and further shipment of offensive weapons to Cuba must cease—all under effective international verification.

As to proposals concerning the security of nations outside this hemisphere, the United States and its allies have long taken the lead in seeking properly inspected arms limitation, on both sides. These efforts can continue as soon as the present Soviet-created threat is ended.

CHAIRMAN KHRUSHCHEV TO
PRESIDENT KENNEDY
OCTOBER 28, 1962

Dear Mr. President:

I have received your message of 27 October. I express my satisfaction and thank you for the sense of proportion you have displayed and for realization of the responsibility which now devolves on you for the preservation of the peace of the world.

I regard with great understanding your concern and the concern of the United States people in connection with the fact that the weapons you describe as offensive are formidable weapons indeed. Both you and we understand what kind of weapons these are.

In order to eliminate as rapidly as possible the conflict which endangers the cause of peace, to give an assurance to all people who crave peace, and to reassure the American people, all of whom, I am certain, also want peace, as do the people of the Soviet Union, the Soviet Government, in addition to earlier instructions on the discontinuation of further work on weapons constructions sites, has given a new order to dismantle the arms which you described as offensive, and to crate and return them to the Soviet Union.

Mr. President, I should like to repeat what I had already written to you in my earlier messages—that the Soviet Government has given economic assistance to the Republic of Cuba, as well as arms, because Cuba and the Cuban people were constantly under the continuous threat of an invasion of Cuba.

A piratic vessel had shelled Havana. They say that this shelling was done by irresponsible Cuban *émigrés*. Perhaps so. However, the question is from where did they shoot. It is a fact that these Cubans have no territory, they are fugitives from their country, and they have no means to conduct military operations.

This means that someone put into their hands these weapons for shelling Havana and for piracy in the Caribbean in Cuban territorial waters. It is impossible in our time not to notice a piratic ship, considering the concentration in the Caribbean of American ships from which everything can be seen and observed.

In these conditions, pirate ships freely roam around and shell Cuba and make piratic attacks on peaceful cargo ships. It is known that they even shelled a British cargo ship. In a word, Cuba was under the continuous threat of aggressive forces, which did not conceal their intention to invade its territory.

The Cuban people want to build their life in their own interests without external interference. This is their right, and they cannot be blamed for wanting to be masters of their own country and disposing of the fruits of their own labor. The threat of invasion of Cuba and all other schemes for creating tension over China are designed to strike the Cuban people with a sense of insecurity, intimidate them, and prevent them from peacefully building their new life.

Mr. President, I should like to say clearly once more

that we could not remain indifferent to this. The Soviet Government decided to render assistance to Cuba with means of defense against aggression—only with means for defense purposes. We have supplied the defense means which you describe as offensive means. We have supplied them to prevent an attack on Cuba—to prevent rash acts.

I regard with respect and trust the statement you made in your message of 27 October 1962 that there would be no attack, no invasion of Cuba, and not only on the part of the United States, but also on the part of other nations of the Western Hemisphere, as you said in your same message. Then the motives which induced us to render assistance of such a kind to Cuba disappear.

It is for this reason that we instructed our officers—these means as I had already informed you earlier are in the hands of the Soviet officers—to take appropriate measures to discontinue construction of the aforementioned facilities, to dismantle them, and to return them to the Soviet Union. As I had informed you in the letter of 27 October, we are prepared to reach agreement to enable U.N. representatives to verify the dismantling of these means. Thus in view of the assurances you have given and our instructions on dismantling, there is every condition for eliminating the present conflict.

I note with satisfaction that you have responded to the desire I expressed with regard to elimination of the aforementioned dangerous situation as well as with regard to providing conditions for a more thoughtful appraisal of the international situation, fraught as it is with great dangers in our age of thermonuclear weapons, rocketry, spaceships, global rockets, and other deadly weapons. All people are interested in insuring peace.

Therefore, vested with trust and great responsibility, we must not allow the situation to become aggravated and must stamp out the centers where a dangerous situation fraught with grave consequences to the cause of peace has arisen. If we, together with you, and with the assistance of other people of good will, succeed in eliminating this tense atmosphere, we should also make certain that no other dangerous conflicts, which could lead to a world nuclear catastrophe, would arise.

In conclusion, I should like to say something about a detente between NATO and the Warsaw Treaty countries that you have mentioned. We have spoken about this long since and are prepared to continue to exchange views on this question with you and to find a reasonable solution.

We should like to continue the exchange of views on the prohibition of atomic and thermonuclear weapons, general disarmament, and other problems relating to the relaxation of international tension.

Although I trust your statement, Mr. President, there are irresponsible people who would like to invade Cuba now and thus touch off a war. If we do take practical steps and proclaim the dismantling and evacuation of the means in question from Cuba, in so doing we, at the same time, want the Cuban people to be certain that we are with them and are not absolving ourselves of responsibility for rendering assistance to the Cuban people.

We are confident that the people of all countries, like you, Mr. President, will understand me correctly. We are not threatening. We want nothing but peace. Our country is now on the upsurge. Our people are enjoying the fruits of their peaceful labor. They have achieved tremendous successes since the October Revolution, and created the greatest material, spiritual, and cultural values. Our people are enjoying these values; they want to continue developing their achievements and insure their further development on the way of peace and social progress by their persistent labor.

I should like to remind you, Mr. President, that military reconnaissance planes have violated the borders of the Soviet Union. In connection with this there have been conflicts between us and notes exchanged. In 1960 we shot down your U-2 plane, whose reconnaissance flight over the U.S.S.R. wrecked the summit meeting in Paris. At that time, you took a correct position and denounced that criminal act of the former U[nited] S]tates] administration.

But during your term of office as president another violation of our border has occurred, by an American U-2 plane in the Sakhalin area. We wrote you about that violation on 30 August. At that time you replied that that violation had occurred as a result of poor weather, and gave assurances that this would not be repeated. We trusted your assurance, because the weather was indeed poor in that area at that time.

But had not your plane been ordered to fly about our territory, even poor weather could not have brought an American plane into our airspace, hence, the conclusion that this is being done with the knowledge of the Pentagon, which tramples on international norms and violates the borders of other states.

A still more dangerous case occurred on 28 October, when one of your reconnaissance planes intruded over Soviet borders in the Chukotka Peninsula area in the north and flew over our territory. The question is, Mr. President: How should we regard this? What is this, a provocation? One of your planes violates our frontier during this anxious time we are both experiencing, when everything has been put into combat readiness. Is it not a fact than an intruding American plane could be easily taken for a nuclear bomber, which might push us to a fateful step; and all the more so since the U[nited] S[tates] Government and Pentagon long ago declared that you are maintaining a continuous nuclear bomber patrol?

Therefore, you can imagine the responsibility you are assuming; especially now, when we are living through such anxious times.

I should like also to express the following wish; it concerns the Cuban people. You do not have diplomatic relations. But through my officers in Cuba, I have reports that American planes are making flights over Cuba.

We are interested that there should be no war in the world, and that the Cuban people should live in peace. And besides, Mr. President, it is no secret that we have our people on Cuba. Under a treaty with the Cuban Government we have sent there officers, instructors, mostly plain people: specialists, agronomists, zootechnicians, irrigators, land reclamation specialists, plain workers, tractor drivers, and others. We are concerned about them.

I should like you to consider, Mr. President, that violation of Cuban airspace by American planes could also lead to dangerous consequences. And if you do not want this to happen, it would be better if no cause is given for a dangerous situation to arise. We must be careful now and refrain from any steps which would not be useful to the defense of the states involved in the conflict, which could only cause irritation and even serve as a provocation for a fateful step. Therefore, we must display sanity, reason, and refrain from such steps.

We value peace perhaps even more than other peoples because we went through a terrible war with Hitler. But our people will not falter in the face of any test. Our people trust their government, and we assure our people and world public opinion that the Soviet Government will not allow itself to be provoked. But if the provocateurs unleash a war, they will not evade responsibility and the grave consequences a war would bring upon them. But we are confident that reason will triumph, that war will not be unleashed, and peace and the security of the peoples will be insured.

In connection with the current negotiations between Acting Secretary General U Thant and representatives of the Soviet Union, the United States, and the Republic of Cuba, the Soviet Government has sent First Deputy Foreign Minister V. V. Kuznetsov to New York to help U Thant in his noble efforts aimed at eliminating the present dangerous situation.

Respectfully yours,
(s) N. KHRUSHCHEV

STATEMENT BY PRESIDENT KENNEDY
ON RECEIPT OF
CHAIRMAN KHRUSHCHEV'S LETTER
OCTOBER 28, 1962

I welcome Chairman Khrushchev's statesmanlike decision to stop building bases in Cuba, dismantling offensive weapons and returning them to the Soviet Union under United Nations verification. This is an important and constructive contribution to peace.

We shall be in touch with the Secretary General of the United Nations with respect to reciprocal measures to assure peace in the Caribbean area.

It is my earnest hope that the governments of the world can, with a solution of the Cuban crisis, turn their urgent attention to the compelling necessity for ending the arms race and reducing world tensions. This applies to the military confrontation between the Warsaw Pact and NATO countries as well as to other situations in other parts of the world where tensions lead to the wasteful diversion of resources to weapons of war.

Dear Mr. Chairman:

I am replying at once to your broadcast message of October twenty-eight, even though the official text has not yet reached me, because of the great importance I attach to moving forward promptly to the settlement of the Cuban crisis. I think that you and I, with our heavy responsibilities for the maintenance of peace, were aware that developments were approaching a point where events could have become unmanageable. So I welcome this message and consider it an important contribution to peace.

The distinguished efforts of Acting Secretary General U Thant have greatly facilitated both our tasks. I consider my letter to you of October twenty-seventh and your reply of today as firm undertakings on the part of both governments which should be promptly carried out. I hope that the necessary measures can at once be taken through the United Nations, as your message says, so that the United States in turn will be able to remove the quarantine measures now in effect. I have already made arrangements to report all these matters to the Organization of American States, whose members share a deep interest in a genuine peace in the Caribbean area.

You referred in your letter to a violation of your frontier by an American aircraft in the area of the Chukotsk

Peninsula. I have learned that this plane, without arms or photographic equipment, was engaged in an air-sampling mission in connection with your nuclear tests. Its course was direct from Eielson Air Force Base in Alaska to the North Pole and return. In turning south, the pilot made a serious navigational error which carried him over Soviet territory He immediately made an emergency call on open radio for navigational assistance and was guided back to his home base by the most direct route. I regret this incident and will see to it that every precaution is taken to prevent recurrence.

Mr. Chairman, both of our countries have great unfinished tasks and I know that your people as well as those of the United States can ask for nothing better than to pursue them free from the fear of war. Modern science and technology have given us the possibility of making labor fruitful beyond anything that could have been dreamed of a few decades ago.

I agree with you that we must devote urgent attention to the problem of disarmament, as it relates to the whole world and also to critical areas. Perhaps now, as we step back from danger, we can together make real progress in this vital field. I think we should give priority to questions relating to the proliferation of nuclear weapons, on earth and in outer space, and to the great effort for a nuclear test ban. But we should also work hard to see if wider measures of disarmament can be agreed and put into operation at an early date. The United States government will be prepared to discuss these questions urgently, and in a constructive spirit, at Geneva or elsewhere.

(s) JOHN F. KENNEDY

ADDRESS BY PRESIDENT KENNEDY ON CUBA
NOVEMBER 2, 1962

My fellow citizens: I want to take this opportunity to report on the conclusions which this Government has reached on the basis of yesterday's aerial photographs which will be made available tomorrow, as well as other indications, namely, that the Soviet missile bases in Cuba are being dismantled, their missiles and related equipment are being crated, and the fixed installations at these sites are being destroyed.

The United States intends to follow closely the completion of this work through a variety of means, including aerial surveillance, until such time as an equally satisfactory international means of verification is effected.

While the quarantine remains in effect, we are hopeful that adequate procedures can be developed for international inspection of Cuba-bound cargoes. The International Committee of the Red Cross, in our view, would be an appropriate agent in this matter.

The continuation of these measures in air and sea, until the threat to peace posed by these offensive weapons is gone, is in keeping with our pledge to secure their withdrawal or elimination from this hemisphere. It is in keeping with the resolution of the Organization of American States, and it is in keeping with the exchange of letters with Chairman Khrushchev of October 27th and 28th.

Progress is now being made toward the restoration of peace in the Caribbean, and it is our firm hope and purpose that this progress shall go forward. We will continue to keep the American people informed on this vital matter.

PRESIDENT KENNEDY'S STATEMENT ON CUBA
NOVEMBER 20, 1962

I have today been informed by Chairman Khrushchev that all of the IL-28 bombers now in Cuba will be withdrawn in thirty days. He also agrees that these planes can be observed and counted as they leave. Inasmuch as this goes a long way toward reducing the danger which faced this Hemisphere four weeks ago, I have this afternoon instructed the Secretary of Defense to lift our naval quarantine.

In view of this action I want to take this opportunity to bring the American people up to date on the Cuban crisis and to review the progress made thus far in fulfilling the understandings between Soviet Chairman Khrushchev and myself as set forth in our letters of October 27 and 28. Chairman Khrushchev, it will be recalled, agreed to remove from Cuba all weapons systems capable of offensive use, to halt the further introduction of such weapons into Cuba, and to permit appropriate United Nations observation and supervision to insure the carrying out and continuation of these commitments. We on our part agreed that, once these adequate arrangements for verification had been established, we would remove our naval quarantine and give assurances against invasion of Cuba.

The evidence to date indicates that all known offensive missile sites in Cuba have been dismantled. The missiles and their associated equipment have been loaded on Soviet ships. And our inspection at sea of these departing ships has confirmed that the number of missiles reported by the Soviet Union as having been brought into Cuba, which closely corresponded to our own information, has now been removed. In addition the Soviet Government has stated that all nuclear weapons have been withdrawn from Cuba and no offensive weapons will be reintroduced.

Nevertheless, important parts of the understanding of October 27th and 28th remain to be carried out. The Cuban Government has not yet permitted the United Nations to verify whether all offensive weapons have been removed, and no lasting safeguards have yet been established against the future introduction of offensive weapons back into Cuba.

Consequently, if the Western Hemisphere is to continue to be protected against offensive weapons, this Government has no choice but to pursue its own means of checking on military activities in Cuba. The importance of our continued vigilance is underlined by our identification in recent days of a number of Soviet ground combat units in Cuba, although we are informed that these and other Soviet units were associated with the protection of offensive weapons systems and will also be withdrawn in due course.

I repeat, we would like nothing better than adequate international arrangements for the task of inspection and verification in Cuba, and we are prepared to continue our efforts to achieve such arrangements. Until that is done, difficult problems remain. As for our part, if all offensive weapons are removed from Cuba and kept out of the Hemisphere in the future, under adequate verification and safeguards, and if Cuba is not used for the export of aggressive Communist purposes, there will be peace in the Caribbean. And as I said in September, we shall neither initiate nor permit aggression in this Hemisphere.

We will not, of course, abandon the political, economic, and other efforts of this Hemisphere to halt subversion from Cuba nor our purpose and hope that the Cuban people shall some day be truly free. But these policies are very different from any intent to launch a military invasion of the island.

In short, the record of recent weeks shows real progress, and we are hopeful that further progress can be made. The completion of the commitment on both sides and the achievement of a peaceful solution to the Cuban crisis might well open the door to the solution of other outstanding problems.

May I add this final thought. In this week of Thanksgiving there is much for which we can be grateful as we look back to where we stood only four weeks ago—the unity of this Hemisphere, the support of our allies, and the calm determination of the American people. These qualities may be tested many more times in this decade, but we have increased reason to be confident that those qualities will continue to serve the cause of freedom with distinction in the years to come.

Slage

Cologne — topes   6.99

100162

VOUCHER	INVOICE		GROSS	DISCOU
112156	CON 112156		30.00	
CHECK NO.	VENDOR	CHECK DATE	TOTAL GROSS	TOTA
100162	99103	11-25-81	30.00	

Index

Index

DATE DUE

PRINTED IN U.S.A.

THE WHITE HOUSE STAFF AND THE NATIONAL SECURITY ASSISTANT

The White House Staff and the National Security Assistant

FRIENDSHIP AND FRICTION AT THE WATER'S EDGE

Joseph G. Bock

CONTRIBUTIONS IN POLITICAL SCIENCE, NUMBER 170

Greenwood Press
NEW YORK · WESTPORT, CONNECTICUT · LONDON

Library of Congress Cataloging-in-Publication Data

Bock, Joseph G.
  The White House staff and the national security
assistant.

  (Contributions in political science, ISSN 0147-1066 ;
no. 170)
  Bibliography: p.
  Includes index.
  1. Presidents—United States—Staff. 2. United
States. Special Assistant to the President for National
Security Affairs. I. Title. II. Series.
JK518.B63   1987   353.03'4   86-29619
ISBN 0-313-25698-5 (lib. bdg. : alk. paper)

Library of Congress Catalog Card Number: 86-29619
ISBN: 0-313-25698-5
ISSN: 0147–1066

First published in 1987

Greenwood Press, Inc.
88 Post Road West, Westport, Connecticut 06881

Printed in the United States of America

The paper used in this book complies with the
Permanent Paper Standard issued by the National
Information Standards Organization (Z39.48-1984).

10 9 8 7 6 5 4 3 2 1

Copyright Acknowledgments

The author gratefully acknowledges permission to quote copy-
righted material from the following:

Zbigniew Brzezinski for material from *Power and Principle: Memoirs
of the National Security Adviser 1977–1981* (New York: Farrar, Straus
& Giroux, 1981).

New Republic Books for material from John Osborne's *White
House Watch: The Ford Years* (Washington: New Republic Books,
1977).

For Sue,
and for Mom and Dad
Bock, Lyke, Harmon, Rogers, and Zumbrunn

Contents

Preface

The relationships between the national security assistant and the president's political advisers have been crucial to the integration of foreign policy with domestic politics. It is often alleged that intrigue and power struggle characterize the president's "inner circle," sometimes to the detriment of policy coherence.

This volume compares these relationships and their apparent policy consequences from 1947 to 1984. In addition to memoirs and periodicals; staff memoranda; oral histories; and meeting minutes at the Truman, Eisenhower, Kennedy, and Johnson presidential libraries; the National Archives were consulted. Clarification of written material was possible and further information was collected by conducting interviews with forty-three former senior White House staff members, some on numerous occasions.

This book also identifies the extent to which political aides controlled the national security assistant's access to and affected his influence on the president, compares the rigidity with which presidents delineated domestic political and foreign policy responsibilities among the staff, and describes the evolution of staff relations.

Contrary to conventional belief, these relationships have generally been cordial and cooperative although there has been periodic, issue-oriented friction. When there was incongruency between perceived diplomatic imperatives and domestic sentiment, friction sometimes resulted, especially when staff responsibilities were delineated rigidly. This friction, on occasion, caused the na-

tional security assistant to retain a tight hold on sensitive information, thereby preventing other aides from injecting domestic political considerations during the decision-making process.

Friction also tended to develop when the national security assistant was an extensive diplomatic operative and foreign policy spokesman. These two responsibilities made the assistant a potential lightning rod for criticism about domestically unpopular foreign policies. Furthermore, when the assistant became popular through these activities, political aides sought to ensure that his popularity did not detract from the president's popularity.

Therefore, although intra–White House relationships are normally cordial and cooperative, friction among the staff can develop and have a detrimental impact on foreign policy coherence. The conditions under which they tend to become contentious are relatively easy to identify.

The original idea for the research that underpins this work was Duncan L. Clarke's, professor of International Relations at the School of International Service, American University. It had occurred to Dr. Clarke that no systematic study existed about the influence of the White House staff on foreign policy. In the summer of 1983, he asked me if I was interested in writing a chapter on the subject for a book he was putting together on defense and foreign policy.

I was guided into this research that summer by Dr. Clarke, General Andrew J. Goodpaster, I. M. Destler, and Robert L. Beckman. I am indebted to them for identifying important questions and helping me with the art of interviewing.

I quickly learned through the initial interviews that general questions were of little utility. I decided, therefore, to exhaust written material, including archival information, before talking to former members of the White House staff and to tailor questions to the individual. During the interviews, I was often struck by inaccuracies in some journalistic accounts and by the extent to which archival evidence can be misleading. For their part, the interviewees often found the inaccuracies amusing and were forthright when they did not remember a given memorandum that I had dug up in one of the presidential libraries. Without their assistance, this study would be much less accurate than it is. Those who granted interviews truly had a sense of what it means to be a "civil ser-

vant" by giving their time for the sake of history. For service "above and beyond the call of duty," I cannot thank adequately these former officials (along with six who remain anonymous), some of whom granted numerous interviews: Zbigniew Brzezinski; McGeorge Bundy; S. Douglass Cater, Jr.; George E. Christian, Jr.; Clark M. Clifford; Lloyd N. Cutler; Ralph A. Dungan; John Ehrlichman; John S. D. Eisenhower; Stuart E. Eisenstat; George M. Elsey; Frank Gannon; Leonard Garment; Andrew J. Goodpaster; Bryce N. Harlow; Karl G. Harr; Stephen H. Hess; Carl Kaysen; Winston Lord; Henry R. McPhee; Harry C. McPherson, Jr.; L. Arthur Minnich; Charles W. Murphy, son of deceased Charles S. Murphy; Robert Pastor; Bradley Patterson; William B. Quandt; George E. Reedy; Walt W. Rostow; Donald Rumsfeld; Pierre E. G. Salinger; Jerrold Schector; Brent Scowcroft; Theodore C. Sorensen; Elmer B. Staats; David H. Stowe; Paul A. Theis; Jack Watson; and Lee C. White.

What is contained herein is my attempt to represent what these former White House officials told me about the written record. I did not ask them to comment on my drafts. The synthesis is mine, as are the mistakes.

While this book is a personal initiative and was completed on my own time, I would like to recognize my employer, BDM International, Inc., a professional and technical services company headquartered in McLean, Virginia. I found that BDM's emphasis on excellence and individual initiative has instilled an inquisitive spirit in its employees that also assisted me in this project.

Archivists Dennis Bilger, Herb Pankratz, Michael Desmond, and Dr. Gary Gallagher at the Truman, Eisenhower, Kennedy, and Johnson libraries, respectively, were most helpful in showing me how to use finding aids and in identifying relevant files. Dr. Gallagher deserves special mention for helping me while I was stranded in Austin, Texas, without enough cash for a hotel while using the Johnson Library. I also must thank the Lyndon Baines Johnson Foundation for the generous research grant that not only paid for the flight to Austin, but also provided the funds that allowed Dr. Gallagher to help me out of my "liquidity crisis." My parents, Dorothy and Jim Bock, my "adopted parents," Dan and Noreen Zumbrunn, and close friends Bob and Kathy Fanning deserve special thanks for providing me—and sometimes my wife Sue—a place

to stay while doing research in Independence, Missouri; Abilene, Kansas; and Boston, Massachusetts.

Drs. Llewellyn Howell and Jeffrey Richelson of American University made helpful recommendations about research design and offered constructive comments about my conclusions. My father-in-law, Doug Lyke, and my grandfather-in-law, Hiram Lyke, read the draft and offered their ideas about targeting the book specifically to foreign policy specialists. Hiram deserves special mention since he read and commented on the draft while cancer was slowly pulling him from this life. He exemplified the human capacity to maintain vitality and generosity despite the knowledge of imminent death.

Very special thanks go to my wife, Susan Lyke, for her active interest, her skillful editing of the drafts, her patience with a habitual researcher who often slacked in giving her the personal attention she deserved and sometimes needed, her agreement to let our home become my "office," her continued encouragement, and, most important, her help in keeping my work in perspective by reminding me that the work of God is more important.

1

Introduction

It is not uncommon to pick up a book, memoir, newspaper, or periodical and read about power struggles and intrigue within the president's "inner circle." His close assistants, the stories often go, vie for power and clash with one another as they seek to influence important decisions.[1] Frequently, such stories have emphasized the assistants' personalities, their propensity to seek supremacy, or the traits of one that triggered the petty jealousies of another. The accounts speculate how an emotional quibble might have caused the president to lean a certain way on a given issue.

These stories have not, generally, focused on the different responsibilities that the president delegated to his assistants, with some operating primarily in foreign policy and others in domestic politics. They have not identified what happens when a given foreign policy course is inconsistent with domestic sentiment, and how that is played out among the president's staff in light of their different areas of responsibility. Nor have they described these relationships during different presidencies, comparing alternative staff arrangements, identifying common tendencies, and, where possible, distilling prescriptive statements about how to prevent, or at least not encourage, staff problems that have a negative influence on U.S. foreign policy process or substance.

This book addresses such matters. More specifically, it focuses on the interaction between the presidents' political advisers[2] and his national security assistant,[3] starting with Harry S Truman's

staff and ending with Ronald W. Reagan's. During the Truman administration, the National Security Act became law. Among other things, it authorized the creation of a National Security Council (NSC) "to advise the President with respect to the integration of *domestic*, foreign, and military policies relating to the national security so as to enable the military services and the other departments and agencies of the Government to cooperate more effectively in matters involving the national security."[4] The NSC was also authorized to have a staff "headed by a civilian executive secretary who shall be appointed by the President."[5] While other presidents before Truman had key staffers to assist them in the conduct of foreign affairs, he was the first to be authorized to appoint a separate staff whose exclusive focus was the integration of national security policy.

President Truman, unlike his successors, regarded the executive secretary and the NSC staff as nonpartisan assistants. This changed with the Eisenhower administration, when the national security assistant was made a political appointee in order to vest him with greater authority in his dealings with departmental and agency officials.[6] By the time of the Kennedy administration—and in every subsequent administration—the national security assistant was a *de facto* member of the president's personal staff. The assistants' primary responsibility has been national security policy. Their involvement with domestic political issues has generally been minimal.[7]

Despite the legislative mandate to integrate domestic *policy* with foreign and military policies, the coordination between domestic *politics* and national security policy has been, in large part, a catch-as-catch-can process. This is a central problem addressed in this study. The real or imagined domestic political pressures confronting an administration have sometimes conflicted with the perceived imperatives of national security policy. The president's staff, with varying degrees of domestic *political* and national security *policy* responsibilities, represents a critical focal point for understanding how these conflicts are handled. The interpersonal relationships among White House staff members have affected presidential decision making. Although all presidents have found it necessary to coordinate national security policy with domestic

politics, the staffing arrangements within the White House to serve that function have been very different.

Problems in the interrelationship between foreign policy and domestic politics in the United States were noted by Alexis de Tocqueville:

it is especially in the conduct of their foreign relations that democracies appear to me decidedly inferior to other governments. Foreign politics demand scarcely any of those qualities which are peculiar to a democracy; they require, on the contrary, the perfect use of almost all those in which it is deficient. . . . [A] democracy can only with great difficulty regulate the details of an important undertaking, persevere in a fixed design, and work out its execution in spite of serious obstacles. It cannot combine its measures with secrecy or await their consequences with patience.[8]

Sections of this book focus on the extent to which the national security assistants shared their "secrets," or, conversely, guarded sensitive information lest it be leaked at times when it was beneficial for the president's domestic political standing but harmful for U.S. foreign relations. Moreover, it describes reactions of the political assistants when citizens protested, congressmen became intransigent, or public opinion approval ratings plummeted subsequent to a foreign policy change of which the national security assistant was a major architect.

Certainly, personality differences and disagreements over foreign policy substance or the procedures by which it is formulated can and have contributed to friction within the White House "inner circle." However, the presence of an assistant and his staff whose major focus is *policy*, not *politics*, creates an environment especially conducive to friction. As John Osborne, a respected White House correspondent, noted:

It must be understood that tensions have existed between presidential staffs and NSC staffs since the NSC was created in 1947. They [have] existed . . . *partly for reasons that have to do only incidently with personalities.* One reason is and always has been that NSC staff members consider themselves creatures apart from the ordinary run of White House hacks.[9]

When the national security assistant appears to be insensitive to the president's political stakes, other presidential assistants—whose

primary responsibilities include working with the press, dealing with Congress, speech writing, or focusing on domestic policy—take measures to protect the chief executive. Sometimes these measures have harmful consequences on U.S. foreign relations. However, cordial personal relations between the national security assistant and other White House staffers combined with a *common* sense of domestic political considerations increase the influence of the assistant on presidential decision making relative to agency and departmental heads.

Each chapter of this study opens with an explanation of each president's decision making style, including the rigidity or flexibility with which he delegated domestic political and foreign policy responsibilities among his staff. The extent to which the president relied on the national security assistant to perform diplomatic or public relations functions is also identified since such functions invariably have domestic political consequences.

Two primary issues are addressed in this book: One is *access*, the other *influence*. In most administrations, national security assistants have had direct access to the president; their access was not subject to the approval of other White House staffers. But this has not always been the case. Even when other White House aides impeded the assistant's access to the Oval Office at the explicit behest of the president, this generally had significant foreign policy ramifications.

A related consideration regarding access concerns non–White House actors. Executive departments and agencies rely often on the national security assistant for channeling their position papers and reports to the president. But when this information is not brought to the president's attention by the national security assistant, it has been alleged that other White House staff memers provided a "back door" for departmental and agency officials.

The second major issue addressed in this study concerns the extent to which White House assistants form alliances, thereby adding greater credence to their advice relative to the counsel of senior departmental and agency officials. The national security assistant's influence can be affected also by other members of the White House staff who take measures to ensure that policy deliberations are not dominated by him. The staff may, for instance,

assure that the secretary of state has an adequate high-level hearing.

The overriding purpose of this study is to marshal available evidence to describe the personal interrelationships and interactions within this critically important decision-making circle and, ultimately, to assess their impact on foreign policy process and substance. The concluding chapter offers observations about the White House "inner circle," given the environment each president created and the different responsibilities assigned to the national security assistant relative to other senior assistants. Finally, prescriptions are offered for mitigating the problems identified.

Both written and oral sources were consulted for this research. Fortunately, many memoirs have been written by former senior White House staff members and departmental and agency officials. Yet each of these accounts represents one person's *post hoc* description about a historical period during which they were intimately involved. Rarely are they scrupulously objective, despite attempts by the authors to provide what they no doubt consider a fair rendition of events. Only when diary recordings are published verbatim—and one never knows what has been deleted—do the words reflect what that individual saw or thought he saw at that time without the benefit of hindsight.[10] And while what is contained in many memoirs might be accurate, the material that is omitted may be very significant indeed. To the extent possible, memoirs have been "balanced" by presenting the recollections of two or more authors who "tilt" in different directions.

Other sources were utilized, including the meeting minutes contained in the National Archives; records and staff memoranda in the Truman, Eisenhower, Kennedy, and Johnson presidential libraries; and various other secondary sources. In addition, the generosity of former NSC and other White House staff members who granted interviews made it possible to clarify issues about which the written record raised questions but provided few, if any, answers.

NOTES

1. According to Patrick Anderson, former White House reporter for the *New York Times*, the president's assistants "almost certainly develop

an enemy or two among . . . [their] fellow staff members. . . . [Presidents] deliberately balance liberals against conservatives, intellectuals against non-intellectuals, on their staffs, and the certain result is friction, rivalry, and hostility." Patrick Anderson, *The Presidents' Men: White House Assistants of Franklin D. Roosevelt, Harry S Truman, Dwight D. Eisenhower, John F. Kennedy, and Lyndon B. Johnson* (Garden City, N.Y.: Doubleday, 1968), p. 5. Similar statements were made by, among others, Louis W. Keonig, in "The Invisible Presidency," in *The Presidential Office*, eds. Sidney Wise and Richard Schier (New York: Thomas Y. Crowell, 1968), pp. 203–207; and Charles Peters, "What Happened to the American Public," in *Politics and the Oval Office: Towards Presidential Governance*, ed. Arnold T. Meltsner (San Francisco: Institute for Contemporary Studies, 1981), pp. 13–30, see especially p. 23.

2. These assistants will usually be referred to as "political assistants," "political advisers," or "political aides" since their main responsibilities pertained to domestic politics and policy, although some were heavily involved in foreign policy decisions.

3. The title given the person charged with administering and operating the National Security Council, which was authorized by Congress in July 1947, has changed numerous times. The original career post of "executive secretary" was superseded during the Eisenhower administration by the "special assistant to the president for national security affairs," who shared responsibility with the staff secretary. The staff secretary's responsibilities, almost in their entirety, were absorbed by the special assistant during the Kennedy administration. After Lyndon B. Johnson appointed his second national security assistant, Walt W. Rostow, the end of the title, "for national security affairs," was dropped. President Nixon dropped the word "special" and again added "for national security affairs." That title—"assistant to the president for national security affairs"—has remained to this day. Henceforth, the title "national security assistant" will be used generically, except for the Eisenhower years.

4. U.S., *Statutes at Large*, 80th Cong., 1st sess., Vol. 61, pt. 1, "National Security Act of 1947" (Washington, D.C.: U.S. Government Printing Office, 1948), p. 496. Emphasis added.

5. Ibid., p. 497.

6. David K. Hall, "The 'Custodian-Manager' of the Policymaking Process," *Report of the Commission on the Organization of the Government for the Conduct of Foreign Policy* [commonly referred to as the *Murphy Commission*], Appendix E, Vol. 2, Ch. XII (Washington, D.C.: Government Printing Office, 1975), pp. 107–109. This was done at the suggestion of Sidney W. Souers, Truman's first executive secretary, and accepted by Eisenhower's transition advisers. Thus, the *de jure* change to

appointing a "Special Assistant to the President for National Security Affairs" was enacted mainly for bureaucratic, not partisan, reasons. David K. Hall's interview with Sidney W. Souers, June 3, 1971, reported in David K. Hall, "Implementing Multiple Advocacy in the National Security Council, 1947–1980" (Ph.D. diss., Stanford University, 1982), pp. 311–312.

7. Hall, "Implementing Multiple Advocacy," pp. 464–465.

8. Alexis de Tocqueville, *Democracy in America*, vol. I (reprint; New York: Vintage Books, 1945), p. 243.

9. John Osborne, *White House Watch: The Ford Years* (Washington, D.C.: New Republic Books, 1977), p. 109. Emphasis added.

10. Most memoirs contain partial diary entries, but few diaries have been published in their entirety. There are exceptions. For instance, see Walt Millis, ed., *The Forrestal Diaries* (New York: Viking, 1951); and John J. Casserly, *The Ford White House: The Diary of a Speechwriter* (Boulder, Colo.: Colorado Associated Press, 1977).

2

The Truman Administration

Harry S Truman wanted his foreign affairs advisers to give him advice on foreign affairs, not domestic politics. He considered it his responsibility to handle the domestic political implications of foreign policy. According to George M. Elsey, one of his close assistants, Truman "used to say over and over again that politics should stop at the water's edge. . . . [He approached] foreign and domestic affairs very differently."[1] And this sometimes cost Truman popularity in the polls.[2]

This separation between domestic politics and foreign policy was evident in how Truman regarded his different staff members. Truman considered it both appropriate and desirable for his *personal* staff to be concerned with the political repercussions of both foreign and domestic developments. In contrast, the executive secretary of the National Security Council, a member of the *career* staff, was to be concerned mainly with the foreign policy process, not domestic politics. However, he had to be *sensitive* to public sentiment and inform Truman's personal staff about international events or foreign policy initiatives with likely domestic political consequences.

TRUMAN'S STAFF

Foremost among Truman's personal staff was Clark M. Clifford. Clifford entered the White House in 1945 as a naval aide.

Not restricted solely to military assignments, he assisted Samuel I. Rosenman, Truman's leading speech writer, and exhibited shrewd political understanding. In January 1946, Clifford succeeded Rosenman, was given the title "Special Counsel to the President," and, by virtue of his control over the speech writing process, acquired substantial responsibility for domestic policy formulation. Moreover, in line with his earlier experience in the military and his general interest in foreign affairs, Clifford became an important liaison with the Atomic Energy Commission, the Pentagon, and the State Department. Among other things, he had a major role in shaping the U.S. policy of containment toward the Soviet Union and was a major draftsman of Truman's message to Congress in the spring of 1947, which rallied domestic sentiment behind aid to Greece and Turkey by stressing that their fall to communism would be a threat to the West.[3]

When Clifford returned to private law practice in early 1950, he was replaced by Charles S. Murphy. Murphy had been an assistant in the Senate Office of Legislative Counsel before being recruited to the White House in 1947. Under Truman, his task was to improve relations with Congress, and his excellent speech writing abilities made him one of Truman's leading political aides. He continued his speech writing and congressional liaison work when he replaced Clifford, but Murphy did not assume the extensive national security policy responsibilities of his predecessor.[4]

Working under the special counsel were the administrative assistants, who served mainly as a support staff. Murphy himself had worked in this capacity before replacing Clifford. Other administrative assistants included (by seniority) Donald S. Dawson, David H. Stowe, George M. Elsey, David E. Bell, David D. Lloyd, Philleo Nash, and Joseph G. Feeney.[5]

The first executive secretary of the National Security Council was Sidney W. Souers. Souers, who served from August 1947 to January 1950, had previously been the president's "cloak-and-dagger man," having been a chief naval intelligence officer during World War II, drafter of recommendations for the Navy's Eberstadt Committee in the summer of 1945, and then the director of the new Central Intelligence Group in 1946.[6] His experience on the Eberstadt Committee had convinced him that the NSC staff should be headed by a nonpartisan, neutral, careerist official,

modeled after the secretariat of the British Committee on Imperial Defense.[7]

His successor and previous assistant, James S. Lay, who served as executive secretary from January 1950 to January 1953,[8] had worked as secretary of the Joint Intelligence Committee of the Joint Chiefs of Staff during World War II and was later transferred to the Central Intelligence Group. Working under Souers, he, too, saw the wisdom in remaining as a nonpartisan, neutral, and careerist assistant.[9] Symbolic of their career status, the executive secretaries were provided an office in the Executive Office Building rather than in the White House with other senior staff members.[10]

AREAS OF RESPONSIBILITY AND STAFF RELATIONS

The one area in which the executive secretaries had a near-exclusive domain was the operation of the National Security Council. Truman's political advisers almost never attended NSC meetings. The only exceptions were Stowe's attendance on May 18, 1950 (regarding defense expenditures), Elsey's on November 28, 1950, and December 4, 1951 (regarding congressional leaks of national security information), and Press Secretary Joseph H. Short's on January 12 and July 11, 1951 (regarding press announcements about the Korean War).[11]

The executive secretary's main responsibility was to oversee the national security policy process and coordinate the activities of agency and departmental officials. Truman expected his White House staff, both personal and careerist, to assist him in handling the executive departments, not to be an embodiment of those departments in miniature. And while friction between departmental heads was not considered desirable, Truman was much more tolerant of it than he was of conflict among his own staff.[12] According to Richard Neustadt, who worked under Murphy as a special assistant, the president "had an abhorrence of caterwauling, knife-throwing, in-fighting, among his subordinates. And his staff . . . learned, perforce, that for their own survival it was essential to keep their quarrels beneath the surface, maintaining at least the appearance of reasonably good relations with one another."[13]

At least as between Souers and Lay and Truman's personal as-

sistants, the inner–White House relationships were apparently cooperative and friendly. When asked about Souers, Clifford mentioned that they had known each other prior to working together in the White House, that both were from St. Louis, and that he "thought very highly of Souers."[14] All former Truman administration officials who were interviewed invariably spoke about their deep admiration for and friendship with both Souers and Lay. None could remember any friction between either of the two executive secretaries and anyone on the White House staff.[15]

STAFF BEHAVIOR REGARDING THE AUTHORITY OF THE NSC AND ITS EXECUTIVE SECRETARY

While drafting the National Security Act, Clifford, Murphy, and Elsey worked with Budget Bureau Director James E. Webb and Secretary of State George C. Marshall to limit the authority of the NSC (contrary to the position of Secretary of Defense James V. Forrestal) by making it an *advisory* rather than policy-*enforcing* body.[16] Webb apparently felt that the initial drafts of the 1947 legislation would, if adopted, diminish his bureau's defense budgetary authority. Marshall warned Truman that, if enacted in its original form, the Act would "dissipate the constitutional responsibility of the President for the conduct of foreign affairs . . . and at the same time markedly . . . diminish the responsibility of the Secretary of State."[17]

As a matter of procedure the National Security Act was scrupulously written. It carefully specified the authority of the new body so as to prevent misinterpretation among the executive departments.[18] The only statutory authority provided by the Act for the executive secretary was to "appoint and fix the compensation of such personnel as may be necessary to perform such duties as may be prescribed by the Council in connection with the performance of its functions."[19] By establishing the Council, the intent of Congress was "to provide for the establishment of integrated policies and procedures for the departments, agencies, and functions of the Government relating to the national security."[20] Clearly, the executive secretary and his staff were to facilitate the advisory

process and not infringe upon the prerogatives of the statutory Council members.

Clifford and Elsey, two of the primary White House drafters of the National Security Act, also prepared a "guidance statement" for Truman and the future executive secretary in collaboration with Budget Director Webb. This statement, among other things, specified that in the president's absence "the Secretary of State shall preside at meetings of the [National Security] Council"; that recommendations or reports submitted to the president by the NSC "shall include a statement of the minority or divergent views of any member of the Council"; and that "information concerning the affairs of the Council will be made available to the public only upon my explicit authorization."[21] But this, too, was considered normal procedure in the creation of any post of such importance.

When asked whether they felt the "guidance statement" had been written in order to specify Souers's responsibilities and, hence, prevent him from usurping presidential authority or departmental secretaries' prerogatives, neither Clifford nor Elsey could remember the document, but, in any case, considered the thought that Souers would do any such thing absolutely ludicrous.[22] According to Elsey, "Truman didn't want a Harry Hopkins."[23] Moreover, he stressed that neither of the executive secretaries were the type to seek personal power or publicity, but, regardless, it was not really a question of *personalities*. As he put it, "If Souers, Lay, or an X [person] were of a Kissinger/Brzezinski personality type, [they] . . . would have been inconsistent with everything else in the White House."[24] Under Truman, neither Souers nor Lay, nor any member of the White House staff were to assume foreign policy spokesmanship or diplomatic responsibilities.

Indeed, reporters who sought interviews with Souers found him to be "tight-lipped" and "blandly uncommunicative."[25] When interviewed about the NSC, Souers invariably insisted that his neutral, nonpartisan status be reported.[26] Both Souers and Lay tended to cooperate with reporters and members of Congress only on *procedural* questions.[27] Furthermore, Souers's contact with foreign dignitaries was confined to information gathering, not diplomacy.[28] There is no evidence that Lay made any foreign contacts.

It is important to recognize, however, that various members of the White House staff, at certain times, thought the executive sec-

retary's responsibilities should be expanded. In one case, Clifford clearly did take measures to extend Souers's procedural responsibility. Because the original "guidance" for the executive secretary specified that "the Council . . . has no policy-making or supervisory functions, except in its direction of the Central Intelligence Agency," [29] Souers felt it was not his responsibility to follow up on presidentially approved NSC decisions throughout the executive bureaucracy. Nor did he consider it his role to present NSC papers to the president. Instead, this was left to the secretary of state, who was frequently out of town, and who therefore delegated the responsibility to Under Secretary of State Robert A. Lovett. After witnessing the awkwardness of this process and realizing the strong potential for delay and miscommunication, Clifford apparently discussed the matter with Souers, suggesting that he assume complete responsibility for seeking presidential approval of NSC papers and communicating the decision to the NSC members. As a result, in October 1948, Souers was authorized to, among other things, "advise members of the Council of the President's approval of each paper and . . . transmit to the members the President's designation of the coordinating agency" that would "notify all departments and agencies of the actions for which each is responsible in implementation of the paper, and ensure that such actions are taken in a coordinate manner." [30] But Clifford's motive was not to increase Souers's authority vis-à-vis the secretary of state. Instead, he apparently wanted to improve the policy process. There was no concern that Souers would exploit the new arrangement for his own ends. [31]

While Lay was executive secretary, the question of policy enforcement authority reemerged. After policy coordination problems grew substantially during the operational expansion associated with the Korean War, and an article in *Harper's*, published in the summer of 1951, argued that the National Security Council "lacks the tools for enforcing its decisions," Elsey wrote Lay that he had an "uneasy suspicion that there may be some truth to this." [32] Indeed, when interviewed, Elsey recalled feeling this way at the time but stressed that it was mainly because of the growing animosity between Secretary of Defense Louis Johnson and Secretary of State Dean Acheson, which made policy coordination between the two departments rather difficult. Moreover, the attempted so-

lution to the problem was not to increase Lay's authority. Instead, Truman had already sought the help of W. Averell Harriman, who had served as U.S. ambassador to both Great Britain and the Soviet Union, and who was then senior Marshall Plan administrator. In early June 1950, Truman appointed Harriman special assistant to the president for foreign affairs, with the expectation that he would increase the administration's policy enforcement capability.[33]

There were others on the White House staff, however, who thought the executive secretary should be given more enforcement authority and additional responsibilities. Elsey remembered David E. Bell, in particular, as having this opinion.[34]

COMMUNICATION AMONG THE STAFF

Clearly, the coordination between foreign policy and domestic politics depended—in *ad hoc* fashion—on Souers and Lay informing the president's other assistants about impending NSC decisions and international developments. According to Richard Neustadt, the gap between foreign policy and domestic politics was "never bridged in Truman's time on any systematic basis. On a relatively few occasions, Murphy, Bell and others of this group got a rope across, but never intensively or for long."[35]

However, the available evidence suggests that both Souers and Lay were sensitive to domestic politics and would notify other political assistants when they considered it warranted. For instance, mindful of the Jewish constituency, Souers sent Clifford an NSC report in March 1948 on Palestine.[36] Another, more revealing, example of the executive secretary's sharing of information on sensitive matters was the exchange between Souers and Clifford and his aide Stephen J. Springarn about the announcement of new NSC arrangements in the area of internal security.[37] In June 1939, President Franklin D. Roosevelt had established a committee responsible for "coordinating the investigation of all domestic espionage, counter espionage, sabotage, and subversion" called the Interdepartmental Intelligence Conference (ICC). By April 1949, in the thick of the cold war, it was decided that the ICC would come under the supervision of the National Security Council, as would a new committee established for "everything other

than straight counter-intelligence activity," called the Interdepartmental Committee on Internal Security (ICIS). Souers was aware that these new arrangements could quickly create political difficulties.[38]

Souers was apparently more than happy to let Springarn handle the publicity on the NSC action, informing him that "the Executive Secretary does not make news announcements to the press, [so] it appears that the release of this information would have to be made by the White House."[39] Accordingly, Press Secretary Charles G. Ross broke the news, as standard operating procedure by announcing the new governmental body, along with the names of the appointed members, in early May 1949.[40]

ACCESS TO THE PRESIDENT

Given this kind of cooperation and sharing of information, it is not surprising that political aides felt no compulsion to obstruct the executive secretaries' access to the president. The executive secretaries did not attend the daily meetings of the White House staff. Instead, they had a private morning meeting with the president. There is no evidence that this access was ever obstructed by the president's assistants. Truman was accessible to his staff and his door was always, at any hour, open if there was an emergency.[41]

However, sometimes the political advisers, rather than Souers or Lay, received subcabinet State and Defense Department officials' proposals that suggested new policies or programs that might be introduced in a presidential speech. For example, the "Point Four" program, announced by Truman in his inaugural address on January 20, 1949, was the idea of Benjamin Hardy of the Public Affairs Division of the State Department. Hardy had met with Elsey some six months previously, saying he was having difficulty getting his idea accepted at State.[42] When Truman requested an inaugural address containing something "unique and outstanding," Elsey and Clifford put Hardy's idea into the address as the final crescendo—the fourth point. When asked whether Souers knew about the proposal prior to the address, Elsey was virtually certain that he did not, since speeches were routinely cleared through the

State Department, not the NSC. Elsey was certain that State had cleared the draft.[43]

But this type of "backdoor" access channel was, according to Elsey, "highly unusual."[44] Nor were such ideas or any information hoarded by the political advisers as a means of enhancing their power vis-à-vis the executive secretaries. For instance, in early spring of 1950, after receiving a confidential report on U.S. defense, Murphy, astonished at what he had read, recommended to Truman that the document "be referred to the National Security Council and put in the National Security Council staff machinery." The decision on that report came to be known as NSC 68, which substantially changed U.S. defense posture.[45]

THE EXECUTIVE SECRETARIES' POLITICAL ADVICE

Since Truman drew distinctions between career and personal staff, the executive secretaries tended not to offer their advice about domestic political problems. When they did offer such advice, the political assistants were not reluctant to express their opinion on the feasibility of proposals. For instance, during the National Security Council meeting that Elsey attended in December 1951, Lay presented a synopsis of a paper he had written about how to handle the problem of the leaks of national security information from Congress. Lay suggested that Truman pursue an "informal approach" and discuss the matter with congressional leaders behind closed doors, particularly with the "Big Four."[46] Recording the events of the meeting afterward, Elsey wrote:

> My participation was limited to a fairly blunt statement to the effect that I thought . . . the "informal approach" . . . would be completely ineffectual. I said that it would do no good for the President to just mention the matter to Congressional leaders; he would have to designate an official or an agency to follow through with the Big Four if anybody expected anything to come of his conversation.[47]

Consequently, Lay agreed to draft another paper.[48]

But Lay rarely offered political advice. Instead, he tended to

forward the opinions of others, without any interpretive remarks, to whomever was handling a domestically sensitive matter.[49]

Even Souers, whose stature within the White House far surpassed Lay's, usually did not offer political advice. He apparently did so only after the normal procedure for political counsel was exhausted. If he disagreed with a political aide's advice, he would suggest to Truman that he get the opinion of another political aide, but, if the president declined, he would then offer his personal view. This was evident in the background deliberations about when and how to announce the Soviet Union's first successful atomic explosion in late August 1949.

By September 14 a panel of U.S. and British experts who had analyzed the atmospheric data concluded that it was virtually certain that a man-made explosion had occurred. Since more than three hundred people in the United States and Great Britain were aware of it, a leak was probable and would have been politically disastrous in light of the requirement that the Joint Atomic Energy Committee of Congress be kept "fully and currently informed" (which it was not). Both Secretary of State Acheson and Under Secretary Webb opposed the announcement, apparently for two reasons. First, the British pound had just been devalued and British Foreign Minister Ernest Bevin thought an announcement of the blast would prompt financial panic. Second, Acheson had recently witnessed conciliatory signs by the Soviet Union at the United Nations and thought an announcement would refreeze the potential thaw in relations. Press Secretary Ross agreed with Acheson and Webb on domestic political grounds.[50]

On September 19, Truman—who was disturbed about news of the blast—informed Atomic Energy Commission Chairman David E. Lilienthal that he was not convinced that there had indeed been a man-made explosion despite Lilienthal's adamant testimony to the contrary. Accordingly, Truman said that he planned to defer action by at least a week, until the British devaluation crisis had subsided. It was then that Souers, who had arranged Lilienthal's meeting with the president, advised Truman that Clifford be informed, given the possible political implications of a leak.[51] But the president did not take Souers's suggestion. By the afternoon of September 20, having failed to get the president to hear Clifford challenge Ross's views, Souers did it himself. When the NSC

executive secretary and the press secretary approached Truman, Souers argued for an immediate announcement, which Ross opposed, saying that Truman "couldn't let Acheson down."[52] But Souers's efforts were in vain. Truman waited until September 23, when he had Ross announce the explosion during a press conference.[53]

It was not unusual for Souers to suggest that Truman consult Clifford, and later Murphy, on a national security matter with possible domestic political implications.[54] And if one of Truman's assistants consulted Souers about a national security matter that had the potential for creating a political problem, the executive secretary would sometimes escort the assistant to the Oval Office.

During a meeting with congressional leaders after the announcement of the Soviet Union's atomic explosion had been made, Truman indicated that he was not fully convinced that it had happened. Stowe, who was attending the meeting in place of Murphy, noticed that Senator Brien McMahon, chairman of the Joint Committee on Atomic Energy, became visibly shaken by the president's comments. After the meeting Stowe spoke with the senator and, the next day, he informed Souers of McMahon's concern. Souers then escorted Stowe into Truman's office to discuss the matter in order, in Stowe's words, "to make sure the president was not wishfully thinking."[55]

CONCLUSION

Cooperation between the NSC executive secretaries and the president's personal assistants served as the integrative mechanism for foreign policy and domestic politics during the Truman administration. There were no written guidelines about exchanging information between the two staffs, nor did there need to be since they shared it freely. Therefore, the Truman administration provides evidence that friction between the national security assistant and the president's political advisers is not *necessarily* and *invariably* endemic to the functional division of staff responsibilities. *So long as information is exchanged freely*, rigidly delineated areas of responsibility need not result in friction between staff members.

But it should be emphasized that information flowed freely and tension was averted during the Truman administration mainly for

four reasons. First, the president mandated that this be the case, and he took sufficient interest in his own policy process to see that his wishes were followed. Second, the executive secretary adopted a low *public* profile and concentrated on managing and coordinating the foreign policy process. He did not interfere with the turf of political aides, nor did he unduly threaten the traditional roles of the secretaries of state or defense. Third, the executive secretaries and political aides interacted well on a *personal* level. Finally, the NSC staff was small and did not raise the spector of a "mini–State Department" or "mini–Defense Department" lodged near the president.

NOTES

1. Oral history interview with George M. Elsey, 9 March 1965, Truman Library, Independence, Mo., pp. 97–98. Indicative of this separation is the response to a senator who asked about "the domestic political implications" during the Greek and Turkey military aid controversy, to which Truman fired, "Political implications? To hell with that. So long as I am President and so long as we are discussing a matter of this kind I don't ever want to hear those . . . words mentioned again." Quoted in William S. White, *The Responsibles* (New York: Harper and Row, 1971), pp. 55–56. Another example of this separation was the response to Under Secretary of State James E. Webb when he asked Truman about the political aspects of the Korean War. The president snapped, "We're not going to talk about politics. I'll handle the political affairs." Quoted in Glenn D. Paige, *The Korean Decision* (New York: The Free Press, 1968), p. 141.

2. Some observers assert that Truman's separation of foreign policy from domestic politics might partly explain why, after eighteen months in office, a Gallup poll indicated that Truman's public approval rating had plummeted from 87 to 32 percent, and the Republicans gained control of both chambers of Congress in the 1946 election. See James D. Barber, *The Presidential Character* (Englewood Cliffs, N.J.: Prentice-Hall, 1972), p. 278; and Margaret Truman, *Harry S. Truman* (New York: Morrow, 1973), p. 322.

On Truman's decision making style, see, among others, Richard Tanner Johnson, *Managing the White House: An Intimate Study of the Presidency* (New York: Harper and Row, 1974), pp. 39–73; Alexander L. George, *Presidential Decisionmaking in Foreign Policy: The Effective Use of Information and Advice* (Boulder, Colo.: Westview, 1981), pp. 150–152; Barber, *The*

Presidential Character, pp. 261–262; Richard Neustadt, *Presidential Power* (New York: Wiley, 1960), pp. 163, 166; and the special commemorative edition on Truman by the *Kansas City Star*, 6 May 1984, especially Section C.

3. Stephen Hess, *Organizing the Presidency* (Washington, D.C.: The Brookings Institution, 1976), p. 47; Patrick Anderson, *The Presidents' Men: White House Assistants of Franklin D. Roosevelt, Harry S Truman, Dwight D. Eisenhower, John F. Kennedy, and Lyndon B. Johnson* (Garden City, N.Y.: Doubleday, 1968), pp. 114–132; Michael Medved, *The Shadow Presidents* (New York: Times Books, 1979), pp. 223–224; and Eleanora W. Schoenebaum, ed., *Political Profiles: The Truman Years* (New York: Facts on File, 1978), p. 101.

4. Hess, *Organizing the Presidency*, p. 47; Schoenebaum, ed., *Political Profiles: The Truman Years*, p. 400; Richard E. Neustadt, "Notes on the White House Staff Under President Truman," essay written for the Public Administration Clearinghouse, Truman Library, June 1953, Independence, Mo., p. 14. On the influence of Clifford and Murphy among the White House staff, see the statement by Elmer B. Staats, assistant and later deputy director of the Budget Bureau under Truman, in Francis H. Heller, ed., *The Truman White House* (Lawrence, Kans.: Regents Press of Kansas, 1980), p. 170.

5. These assistants also supported John Steelman, a senior adviser who handled primarily labor relations and disputes among executive departments. Interview with David H. Stowe, Washington, D.C., 15 August 1984.

6. Neustadt, "Notes on the White House Staff," pp. 40–41; and Schoenebaum, ed., *Political Profiles: The Truman Years*, pp. 509–510. For Souers's intelligence background, see John Prados, *The Soviet Estimate: U.S. Intelligence Analysis and Russian Military Strength* (New York: Dial Press, 1982), pp. 5–6.

7. David K. Hall, "Implementing Multiple Advocacy in the National Security Council, 1947–1980" (Ph.D. diss., Stanford University, 1982), pp. 158–159.

8. For a short period, in October 1952, S. Everett Gleason was Acting Executive Secretary. Minutes of the 124th and 125th Meetings of the National Security Council, 14 October and 19 November 1952, National Archives of the United States, Washington, D.C.

9. Hall, "Implementing Multiple Advocacy," p. 161; Neustadt, "Notes on the White House Staff," pp. 40–41.

10. This location was retained during the Eisenhower administration. McGeorge Bundy, John F. Kennedy's national security assistant, was the first to have a White House Office. Kenneth P. O'Donnell and David F.

Powers with Joe McCarthy, *"Johnny, We Hardly Knew Ye"* (Boston: Little, Brown, 1970), pp. 277–278.

11. W. Averell Harriman attended NSC meetings frequently after he was appointed a special assistant in June 1950, but he was more of a roving ambassador than a political adviser. Minutes of the National Security Council, 26 September 1947 to 9 January 1953, National Archives, Washington, D.C.

12. As Elsey saw it, there was a feeling that there was a choice between having friction inside the White House among a staff of specialists, or having a staff of generalists who worked to settle disputes among cabinet secretaries. Truman, he said, decided to have the friction outside rather than within the White House. Interview with George M. Elsey, Washington, D.C., 24 August 1984.

13. Neustadt, "Notes on the White House Staff," p. 43. According to David H. Stowe, if anyone on the staff was "struggling about turf, . . . [Truman would] kick your ass right out of the White House. The president wouldn't tolerate that business." Interview with David H. Stowe, Washington, D.C., 15 August 1984.

14. Telephone interview with Clark M. Clifford, Washington, D.C., 15 August 1984.

15. As evidence of the closeness of the entire staff to the first executive secretary, Stowe mentioned that only the president's senior staff went with Truman to Key West for vacation, but Souers, even though he was on the career staff, went along also. Although Lay did not join in the Key West vacations, his family had a summer cottage right next to the Murphy and Stowe family cottages, and, according to Stowe, the three men were close friends. During the summer, the three rode to work together. Interview with David H. Stowe, Washington, D.C., 15 August 1984; and telephone interview with Charles W. Murphy [Charles S. Murphy's son], Washington, D.C., 14 August 1984.

16. Forrestal, who was secretary of the Navy during World War II, had been frustrated by President Roosevelt's failure to consult him and other senior officials prior to major military decisions, or even inform them of those decisions after they were made. (For instance, Roosevelt did not consult the military before espousing his "unconditional surrender" doctrine near the close of the war.) Forrestal authorized a study, headed by Ferdinand Eberstadt, whose 1945 report suggested, among other things, that a council be established that could be used by future presidents as a forum for consultation, a National Security Council.

During the legislative negotiations to authorize the formation of the Council, the sensitive matter of military unification surfaced. Since 1798, the U.S. military had been divided between two separate organizations—

the War Department and the Navy Department—with the president as the only common superior. During World War II, it was evident that the Army, Navy, and evolving Air Force (that had previously operated semiautonomously within the War Department) needed some kind of unified command.

Forrestal, being an ardent advocate of military unification, felt that the National Security Council could serve that purpose. After the momentous debate between the Army and Navy on unification under a single Defense Department, Forrestal proposed, in his first National Security Act draft, that the Secretary of Defense (he would be the first) be chairman of the NSC, that the NSC staff be drawn largely from the soon-to-be-formed Joint Staff of the Army and Navy, and, "subject to the authority of the President," the NSC have the power to "integrate our foreign and military policies" and "establish the approved policy of the departments and agencies represented in the Council." (Quoted in Hall, "Implementing Multiple Advocacy," p. 150.)

On the background pertinent to Forrestal's early proposals, see Walter Millis, ed., *The Forrestal Diaries* (New York: Viking, 1951), p. 11; Robert J. Donovan, *Tumultuous Years: The Presidency of Harry S Truman* (New York: W. W. Norton, 1982), pp. 53–65; and Harry Truman, *Memoirs, Volume Two: Years of Trial and Hope* (Garden City, N.Y.: Doubleday, 1956), pp. 46–54.

17. Quoted in Demetrios Caraley, *The Politics of Military Unification: A Study of Conflict and the Policy Process* (New York: Columbia University Press, 1966), p. 314, n. 11.

18. As Clifford put it, "we just didn't want to create a new organization and have it go freewheeling off everywhere." Telephone interview with Clark M. Clifford, Washington, D.C., 22 August 1984. Apparently, one of the biggest concerns during the drafting of the National Security Act was that the president's freedom to consult outside, non-NSC officials not be restricted. Interview with Elmer B. Staats, Washington, D.C., 27 August 1984. Staats was working under Webb at the Budget Bureau during the drafting of the Act.

19. U.S., *Statutes at Large*, 80th Cong., 1st sess., Vol. 61, pt. 1, "National Security Act of 1947" (Washington, D.C.: U.S. Government Printing Office, 1948), p. 497.

20. Ibid., p. 496.

21. Quotes taken from a draft copy of the statement contained in Clifford's file. Memorandum for the Executive Secretary, National Security Council, Papers of Clark M. Clifford, Subject File, Box 11, Folder: National Military Establishment–Security Council, Truman Library, Independence, Mo. Hall has pointed out that much of the impetus for this

guidance statement came from Budget Director Webb, who was in collaboration with Clifford and Elsey. Hall, "Implementing Multiple Advocacy," p. 256, n. 110.

22. Telephone interview with Clark M. Clifford, Washington, D.C., 22 August 1984. Interview with George M. Elsey, Washington, D.C., 24 August 1984.

23. Harry L. Hopkins was Roosevelt's assistant, to whom he delegated substantial responsibility in the area of foreign and defense policy. See Anderson, *The Presidents' Men*, pp. 45–49, 66–84

24. Interview with George M. Elsey, Washington, D.C., 24 August 1984.

25. Joseph Alsop and Stewart Alsop, "How Foreign Policy Is Made," *The Saturday Evening Post* 221 (30 April 1949): 30–31, 114. According to John Fischer, Souers and Lay "are regarded as mysterious . . . because they behave in a fashion almost without precedent in the capital. . . . [N]either has used [the position] to enhance his personal power, or to harvest publicity . . . or even to press his own views about government policy." John Fischer, "Mr. Truman's Politburo," *Harper's* 202 (June 1951): 32.

26. See, for example, *The Reporter*, (10 May 1949): 9; and *New York Post*, 17 December 1948. In his own publication about the National Security Council, Souers wrote that his responsibilities demanded that he be a "non-political confidant of the President." Sidney W. Souers, "Policy Formulation and National Security," *American Political Science Review*, 43 (June 1949): 537.

27. While testifying before a House Committee, Lay once said, "I am not an authorized spokesman for the policies recommended [by the National Security Council]." U.S., Congress, House, Committee on Appropriations, *Hearings on Department of Defense Appropriations for 1953*, pt. 1, hearings (Washington: U.S. Government Printing Office, 1952), p. 18.

28. That foreign dignitaries wanted Souers to assume a diplomatic role although he refused is reflected in H. H. Kung [New York City Head of the Bank of China], Letter to Sidney W. Souers, 12 March 1948, Papers of Sidney W. Souers, Box 1, Truman Library, Independence, Mo., which pleads for U.S. assistance for the Chinese Nationalists; and Sidney W. Souers, Letter to H. H. Kung, 16 March 1948, Papers of Sidney W. Souers, Box 1, Truman Library, Independence, Mo., which thanks Kung for the information he acquired at a meeting with him, but does not indicate that Souers planned to talk with Truman about it. This contact, and one with a Peruvian ambassador for technical assistance to organize a secret police force, which Souers referred to the CIA and State Department, are Souers's only apparent potentially diplomatic activities. Sidney W. Souers, Mem-

orandum for Edward G. Miller, Jr., [assistant secretary of state] 20 December 1949, Papers of Sidney W. Souers, Truman Library, Independence, Mo.

29. Memorandum for the Executive Secretary, National Security Council, p. 1.

30. NSC Action 123, "Record of Actions Taken by the National Security Council, 1947–1948," 6 October 1948, Papers of Harry S Truman, President's Secretary's Files, Subject File, National Security Council, Box 191, Truman Library, Independence, Mo. On the awkwardness of the earlier process see Hall, "Implementing Multiple Advocacy," pp. 225–226.

31. Elsey could not remember this change in procedure, but surmised that it was probably along the lines of a "meeting of the minds." He was certain that there was no consideration that Souers would use it for his own ends. Interview with George M. Elsey, Washington, D.C., 24 August 1984.

Clifford said that he "didn't think there was any intention of infringing on the authority of a cabinet member. Things were just working out well with Mr. Souers and the president, and we decided to make it as useful as we could." Telephone interview with Clark M. Clifford, Washington, D.C., 22 August 1984.

32. Fischer, "Mr. Truman's Politburo," p. 35; George M. Elsey, Memorandum to James S. Lay, 17 April 1951, Papers of George M. Elsey, Truman Library, Independence, Mo. Fischer had provided the White House with an advanced copy.

33. Interview with George M. Elsey, Washington, D.C., 24 August 1984; and *New York Times*, 17 June 1950, p. 4. Hall referred to the Harriman appointment as "A Flawed Attempt to Fill the Gap" in the NSC's inability to integrate the policies of various departments. Hall, "Implementing Multiple Advocacy," pp. 243–249. On the animosity between Acheson and Johnson, see Dean Acheson, *Present at the Creation: My Years at the State Department* (New York: W. W. Norton, 1969), pp. 405–407, 430–431, 441.

34. Apparently, after witnessing this happening in later administrations, Bell changed his mind. Interview with George M. Elsey, Washington, D.C., 24 August 1984.

35. Neustadt, "Notes on the White House Staff," p. 40. An example of when there was no "rope across" was the decision to airlift supplies to Berlin in the summer of 1948. According to Elsey, the White House staff, except those assigned to the NSC, was not involved in the decision. Oral history interview with George M. Elsey, 7 July 1970, Truman Library, Independence, Mo., p. 391.

36. See the note on the receipt of "1 TOP SECRET document" for Mr. Clark M. Clifford from Sidney Souers, 11 March 1948, Papers of Clark M. Clifford, Subject File, Box 11, Truman Library, Independence, Mo. A newspaper article contained within this file mentioned that Truman had to consider the "domestic political factor" along with "military and economic factors" in making his decision about Palestine "in this Presidential year." "Latest U.S. Policy on Palestine Based on Study by National Security Council," *St. Louis Post-Dispatch*, 29 February 1948, p. C1.

37. Souers's initial contact with Clifford about this matter was apparently in the fall of 1948. See Stephen J. Springarn, Memorandum for Clark M. Clifford, 21 September 1948, Papers of Harry S Truman, Official File 10-B, Truman Library, Independence, Mo., reprinted in Arthur G. Theoharis, *The Truman Presidency: The Origins of the Imperial Presidency and the National Security State* (New York: Earl M. Coleman Enterprises, 1979), p. 280. Springarn worked under Clifford as a special assistant from 1949 to 1950.

38. Apparently, Secretary of Defense Forrestal had been accused of "wanting to set up a Gestapo" when his internal security proposal was leaked in the early fall of 1948. Stephen J. Springarn, Memorandum for Mr. Clifford, 11 April 1949, Papers of Clark M. Clifford, Box 11, Truman Library, Independence, Mo., pp. 1–3.

39. Ibid. Reference to the White House was made because Souers's office was in the Executive Office Building.

40. Souers's full cooperation is apparent in Sidney W. Souers, Memorandum for Mr. Clark M. Clifford, 22 April 1949, Papers of Clark M. Clifford, Subject File, Box 11, Truman Library, Independence, Mo.; and Stephen J. Springarn, Memorandum for Mr. Clifford, 22 April 1949, Papers of Clark M. Clifford, Subject File, Box 11, Truman Library, Independence, Mo.

41. Those published works that mention Souers's and Lay's access to the president make no reference to obstruction. See, for instance, Raymond P. Brandt, "Sidney Souers May Become Truman's Military Adviser," *St. Louis Post-Dispatch*, 3 December 1948; Neustadt, "Notes on the White House Staff," pp. 26–28, 40, 47; Richard E. Neustadt, "The Constraining of the President: The Presidency after Watergate," *British Journal of Political Science* 4 (October 1974): 389–390; Fischer, "Mr. Truman's Politburo," p. 33; Alsop and Alsop, "How Foreign Policy Is Made": 114; Anderson, *The Presidents' Men*, p. 204; Alfred Steinberg, *The Man from Missouri: The Life and Times of Harry S Truman* (New York: G. P. Putnam's Sons, 1962), p. 349; and U.S., Congress, Senate, Subcommittee on National Policy Machinery of the Committee on Government Op-

erations, *Organizing for National Security*, pt. 1, 87th Cong., 1st sess., hearings (Washington: D.C.: U.S. Government Printing Office, 1961), p. 574. Robert Allen and William Shannon describe as one of Appointment Secretary Matthew J. Connelly's "certain fixed constants" the scheduling of Souers's and then Lay's daily briefing. Robert S. Allen and William V. Shannon, *The Truman Merry-Go-Round* (New York: Vanguard, 1950), p. 51.

42. Oral history interview with George M. Elsey, 7 July 1970, Truman Library, Independence, Mo., p. 426; and Anderson, *The Presidents' Men*, p. 127.

43. Interview with George M. Elsey, Washington, D.C., 24 September 1984.

44. Interview with George M. Elsey, Washington, D.C., 24 August 1984. This is consistent with Murphy's recollection, that the Point Four idea "did not come through the regular channels." Oral history interview with Charles S. Murphy, 15 July 1969, Truman Library, Independence, Mo., p. 285. This is at variance, however, with Clifford's statement: "*this was not a rare instance*. Persons working in the different departments would get ideas, and I knew a great many of those individuals who would send ideas over." Emphasis added. Oral history interview with Clark M. Clifford, 16 March 1972, Truman Library, Independence, Mo., p. 354.

45. Oral history interview with Charles S. Murphy, 19 May 1970, Truman Library, Independence, Mo., pp. 521–522. The National Security Council was, of course, already aware of the report since it had been produced under the direction of the secretaries of state and defense. Other evidence that political aides did not hoard information includes a memorandum that indicates Elsey shared a Budget Bureau report with Lay that he thought would be of "interest and value" to the NSC staff. George M. Elsey, Memorandum for Mr. Lay, 21 February 1951, Papers of George M. Elsey, Subject File, Box 89, Folder: National Defense–Defense Mobilization, Truman Library, Independence, Mo.

46. House Speaker Sam Rayburn, Senate Majority Leader Scott Lucus, House Majority Leader John W. McCormick, and Vice President Alben W. Barkley were commonly referred to as the "Big Four," with whom Truman had weekly meetings. Steinberg, *The Man from Missouri*, p. 348.

47. George M. Elsey, Memorandum for General Roberts, 4 December 1951, Papers of George M. Elsey, Subject File, Box 89, Folder: National Defense–National Security Council, Truman Library, Independence, Mo.

48. Ibid. However, Elsey felt it was entirely appropriate for Lay to offer his advice on matters like congressional leaks. Interview with George M. Elsey, Washington, D.C., 24 August 1984.

49. For example, in the winter of 1950, Elsey was contacted by Wayne

Grover of the Joint Committee on Atomic Energy about the release of documents from the Roosevelt Library. The documents held sensitive records about the exchange of atomic energy information with the British government during World War II. Disclosure of the information could have been embarrassing to the British if it was leaked, but lack of disclosure might have caused a congressional confrontation. Elsey asked Lay to solicit the opinions of Secretary of State Acheson, Acting Chairman of the Atomic Energy Commission Sumner T. Pike, and Secretary of Defense Johnson. After receiving memoranda from all three, Lay merely forwarded them with a cover letter containing no opinion of his own. George M. Elsey, Memorandum [and Note attached] for Dr. Wayne Grover, 11 January 1950; Louis Johnson, Memorandum for James S. Lay, 1 February 1950; Sumner T. Pike, Memorandum for James S. Lay, 7 February 1950; Dean Acheson, Memorandum for James S. Lay, 7 February 1950; James S. Lay, Memorandum for George M. Elsey, 7 February 1950; George M. Elsey, Memorandum for the President, 8 February 1950, Papers of George M. Elsey, Subject File, Box 88, Folder: National Defense–Atomic Energy, 1950, Truman Library, Independence, Mo.

50. Richard G. Hewlett and Francis Duncan, *Atomic Shield, 1947–1952* (University Park: The Pennsylvania State University Press, 1969), pp. 364–366; and Hall, "Implementing Multiple Advocacy," p. 202. Ross felt that "the American people had about all the bad news they could stand" with frequent stories about labor unrest. Ross, quoted in U.S., Department of State, "Memorandum of the Executive Secretary of the Policy Planning Staff (Savage)," *Foreign Relations of the United States, 1949: Volume I* (Washington, D.C.: U.S. Government Printing Office, 1976), p. 536.

51. David E. Lilienthal, *The Atomic Energy Years, 1945–1950* (New York: Harper and Row, 1964), pp. 623–632; and David K. Hall's interview with Sidney W. Souers, 3 June 1971, as reported in Hall, "Implementing Multiple Advocacy," p. 203.

52. See Elsey's longhand notes of the chronology of events in the White House prior to the announcement. Notes Regarding White House Press Release, 23 September 1949, Papers of George M. Elsey, Box 88, Folder: National Defense–Atomic Energy–Announcement of Russian Atomic Bomb, Truman Library, Independence, Mo. See also the article by Raymond Brandt, who apparently had an interview with Elsey. Raymond Brandt, "Inside Story of Announcement of Red's Atomic Blast Revealed," *Washington Star*, 28 September 1949, p. 1, which is contained within Elsey's file.

53. Truman, *Memoirs, Volume Two*, pp. 306–308; and Brandt, "Inside Story of Announcement," p. 1.

54. Sidney W. Souers, "The National Security Council Under President Truman," in Henry M. Jackson, ed., *The National Security Council: Subcommittee Papers on Policy-making at the Presidential Level* (New York: Praeger, 1965), p. 104; and David K. Hall's interview with Sidney W. Souers, 3 June 1971, as reported in Hall, "Implementing Multiple Advocacy," p. 174.

55. Truman's comments may have been a slip of the tongue since, according to Stowe, "there was no question in his mind" about the explosion that day. Neither Stowe nor Souers called the senator afterward. Interview with David H. Stowe, Washington, D.C., 15 August 1984.

3

The Eisenhower Administration

Dwight D. Eisenhower's method of decision making was developed and refined while he was a commanding general during World War II. During the war he relied on the advice and analysis of professional subordinates in deciding upon and adjusting overall military strategy. He maintained this approach during his presidency. After leaving office Eisenhower remarked that "the one way in which you can be sure to make a wise decision . . . is to get all of the people who have a partial and definable responsibility in this particular field . . . in front of you, and listen to them debate."[1]

As president, Eisenhower sought an NSC system that would sharpen the views of his advisers and delineate their differences before hearing them advocate their positions at Council meetings. Such an advisory system necessitated a drastic revamping of the national security policy process. Eisenhower had criticized Truman's NSC system, saying he would move from "shadow to substance."[2]

Eisenhower chose Robert Cutler to be his national security assistant. Cutler had been a primary draftsman of Eisenhower's campaign speeches that criticized Truman's NSC system and later became a member of Eisenhower's transition team, which recommended ways to reorganize the national security policy machinery. In line with Eisenhower's preference that his advisers' positions be clearly delineated, the NSC Planning Board was es-

tablished. Cutler chaired the Board, which was composed of senior departmental and agency officials. It produced policy papers with "splits" (delineations of disagreements), which were to be used to force debate at NSC sessions.[3] Cutler filled the position during two different periods (January 1953 to April 1955, and January 1957 to July 1958). He was replaced by Dillon Anderson (May 1955 to August 1956), who had worked under Cutler at the Department of Defense during World War II and then as an NSC consultant beginning in 1953. Anderson was succeeded by Gordan Gray (July 1958 to January 1961), who had worked with Cutler at the Pentagon in 1948, became director of President Truman's Psychological Strategy Board, and then served under Eisenhower as assistant secretary of defense for international security affairs and director of the Office of Defense Mobilization before becoming national security assistant.[4]

Although Cutler and his successors bore the new title Special Assistant to the President for National Security Affairs (hereafter called national security assistant), they were not considered to be partisan members of the president's personal staff. The new position was created not for the purpose of moving away from a careerist head of the NSC, but—on the advice of Souers, who assisted in the transition—to enhance the national security assistant's credibility and clout when dealing with executive departmental and agency officials.[5]

The national security assistant was to coordinate the foreign and defense policy process and facilitate long-range planning. Responsibility for overseeing policy implementation was given to the Operations Coordinating Board (OCB), the meetings of which Cutler attended but did not chair.[6] Diplomatic and policy spokesmanship functions were left to departmental heads, especially Secretary of State John Foster Dulles.[7]

Domestic politics and overall supervision of the White House staff were the concern, not of a "special" assistant, but of *the* assistant to the president, Sherman Adams, and his staff. Adams was one of Eisenhower's key political advisers during the 1952 campaign. While governor of New Hampshire he had endorsed Eisenhower for the Republican nomination and later joined the campaign team aboard the candidate's train, serving as a political adviser and chief of staff.[8]

Two other key political advisers were Wilton B. ("Jerry") Persons and Bryce N. Harlow. Persons, who replaced Adams in September 1958 as assistant to the president, had worked as director of legislative liaison for the Army and then for the entire Department of Defense after World War II. In early 1951 he became a special adviser to Eisenhower, who was then commanding the NATO forces in Europe. During the 1952 presidential campaign, he served as a liaison between congressional Republicans and Eisenhower and then directed executive-legislative liaison in the new administration. Harlow, a House Armed Services Committee staff member after World War II, was one of Eisenhower's chief speech writers and also assisted Persons. He became chief of congressional liaison when Persons replaced Adams.[9]

To handle day-to-day operations of both domestic and international matters, the office of staff secretary was created. It was established early in the administration because the president had complained about some paperwork getting "crossed up" and said he did not intend to be his own "sergeant major." He then appointed Paul T. Carroll, who had earlier handled military liaison, to the new post of staff secretary. Carroll had the responsibility of coordinating all documents headed to the Oval Office. After serving for a year and a half, Carroll suddenly died of a heart attack. In September 1954, Andrew J. Goodpaster was recruited to fill the staff secretary post. Like Persons, Goodpaster had worked under Eisenhower in Europe, organizing NATO forces.[10]

In addition to coordinating paper flow, the staff secretary had some mundane "house-keeping" tasks. Goodpaster also helped Sherman Adams coordinate the work of other assistants. Some of this work pertained directly to domestic politics.[11] Furthermore, by 1955, he was put in charge of handling some press and congressional matters, particularly those relating both to "the content of the message and the timing of its submission to the Congress." And in October, the State and Defense Departments' memoranda that had hitherto been channeled through Adams's office were to be routed to Goodpaster, who would, among other things, "advise as to press release."[12]

However, Goodpaster's duties pertained to foreign, defense, and intelligence matters much more than to domestic politics. The correspondence he handled for the president was mostly foreign

or defense policy related. It was Goodpaster, not the special assistant for national security affairs, who almost daily briefed Eisenhower on the latest intelligence. It seems appropriate to consider him, as most observers have, as himself being a national security assistant. Goodpaster's responsibilities paralleled, complemented, and supplemented those of the national security assistants, whose time was filled by their Planning Board and NSC activities.[13]

COMMUNICATION AMONG THE STAFF

According to L. Arthur Minnich, who served under both Carroll and Goodpaster, the office of the staff secretary was composed of "the most generalist of all the generalists." It was their job, said Minnich, "to look at everything that went through to the president and make sure it was coordinated with everyone we thought should be involved or who others thought should be involved."[14] Hence, Goodpaster and his staff had to work closely with both the national security staff and the president's political advisers, handling day-to-day operations of both and coordinating matters of common concern. For example, during *ad hoc* national security meetings that he would periodically call, Goodpaster invited the political advisers to attend if the discussion was "directly related to domestic affairs."[15]

But there were other means of communication between the national security assistant and the political assistants. In contrast to the Truman administration, where information· exchange hinged critically on the executive secretary's personal sensitivity to an issue with domestic political ramifications, information flow was built into the staff system.[16] In addition to the link Goodpaster and his staff provided, there were three ways the political assistants kept informed about impending NSC actions and international developments. First, Adams, Persons, and Harlow were invited to attend NSC meetings. When they were able to attend they did so, although, according to Fred I. Greenstein, they were "observers" rather than "participants."[17] Second, Cutler and his successors attended and "participated regularly" in general White House staff meetings that averaged three per week.[18] Finally, it was regular practice for the national security assistants to send weekly reports about NSC activities to Adam's office.[19]

ACCESS TO THE PRESIDENT AND STAFF RELATIONS

These institutionalized channels of communication were probably one reason for the evident lack of friction between the national security assistant and the political assistants. Nor was the national security assistant's access to the president ever obstructed by the political aides.[20] Despite assertions by some observers that Adams's mark of approval—"O.K, S.A."—had to appear on everything the president read, in fact, the national security assistants' and staff secretarys' memoranda did *not* require that inscription.[21]

The only control over national security information that Adams apparently had was to decide which State and Defense Department memoranda would be forwarded to the president. This apparently was changed, however, during the fall of 1955, when Adams gave Goodpaster's office this responsibility.[22]

THE STAFF'S INFLUENCE ON THE NATIONAL SECURITY ASSISTANTS' RESPONSIBILITIES

It does not appear that Eisenhower's political assistants sought to expand the responsibilities of the national security assistant, except in two ways. It was generally not considered appropriate for members of the White House staff to appear in public as officially representing the administration.[23] However, in the midst of public and congressional outcry about the defense budget in the late 1950s, Adams and Persons apparently persuaded the president to allow Cutler, and then Gray, to *preside* over the annual meetings of the Advertising Council, an influencial group of businessmen, where top administration officials explained and answered questions about national security policy.[24] The national security assistants were not asked to defend a particular policy but, instead, to coordinate presentations and introduce top officials. They did so for four consecutive years (1956 to 1960). When asked about this, Karl G. Harr, who was vice chairman of the Operations Coordinating Board, pointed out how Cutler and Gray were obvious choices to *monitor* the presentations at the meetings and make sure the executive officials "wouldn't go too far" in revealing sensitive information.[25]

Another understanding among the White House staff was that they would not offer advice during formal policy deliberations. It was their job to manage the policy process and to facilitate the work of the cabinet secretaries and agency directors. On at least one occasion, however, Harlow suggested that Gray make a recommendation at an NSC meeting, with the understanding that it would be appropriate to do so in light of the extremely slight chance that someone else would make it. In September 1958, Harlow received a letter from a private citizen that contained a newspaper article reporting the recommendation of the president of R.C.A., John L. Burns, to establish a "National Council for Long Range [Defense] Planning" at a Harvard Business School conference.[26] In response, Harlow sent the article to Gray, with a note attached:

Certainly if it is needed, it will not be recommended by the dominant powers in our government, such as State and Defense, who would see in such a venture an intrusion of their daily activities and perhaps some loss of jurisdiction and freedom of action. This means—probably—that the impetus for such a venture, if it makes any sense, would have to come from someone such as yourself.[27]

Gray considered the recommendation, but indicated to Harlow that the NSC Planning Board already had thought of responsibilities similar to those proposed for the suggested body.[28]

In general, members of the White House staff probably helped each other resist the temptation to be champions of their own views or to emerge as public figures. For example, Adams referred to Cutler as being "quite out of order" when the national security assistant argued against tariffs at a cabinet meeting.[29] Moreover, although the political advisers often asked the national security assistants to brief reporters on an off-the-record basis, even this had to be cleared with Press Secretary James C. Hagerty.[30]

CONCLUSION

The exchange of national security information during the Eisenhower administration was built into the staff system and was not, at least primarily, contingent on the political sensitivity of the na-

tional security assistant, as it was during the Truman administration. Hence, there was little danger that an oversight about the potential for political repercussions of national security developments would cause friction among the staff; everyone was generally kept informed of all relevant matters. This is probably one reason for the evident lack of friction within the Eisenhower White House. Furthermore, as in the Truman administration, when the political assistants were recipients of information provided by departmental officials, they did not hoard it, and eventually gave full control of that information to the office of the staff secretary.

Apparently, political advisers were instrumental in furthering the national security assistants' public exposure, but only to *monitor* departmental and agency officials, not to *present and defend* the administration's policy. Moreover, it appears that the political advisers helped prevent the national security assistants from being advocates of their own views at official meetings and would only encourage them to present proposals that would not likely be presented by the officials themselves.

NOTES

1. Oral history interview with Dwight D. Eisenhower, 20 June 1967, Eisenhower Library, Abilene, Kans., p. 103. On Eisenhower's decision making style, see, among others, Chester Wilmot, *The Struggle for Europe* (New York: Harper, 1952), pp. 467–468; Fred I. Greenstein, *The Hidden-Hand Presidency: Eisenhower as Leader* (New York: Basic Books, 1982), pp. 132–136; Richard Tanner Johnson, *Managing the White House: An Intimate Study of the Presidency* (New York: Harper and Row, 1974), pp. 74–119; and Alexander L. George, *Presidential Decisionmaking in Foreign Policy: The Effective Use of Information and Advice* (Boulder, Colo.: Westview, 1981), pp. 152–154.

2. Greenstein, *The Hidden-Hand Presidency*, p. 125; and Patrick Anderson, *The Presidents' Men* (Garden City, N.Y.: Doubleday, 1968), pp. 172–174.

3. Anderson, *The Presidents' Men*, pp. 172–173; David K. Hall, "Implementing Multiple Advocacy in the National Security Council, 1947–1980" (Ph.D. diss., Stanford University, 1982), p. 307; Robert Cutler, *No Time for Rest* (Boston: Little, Brown, 1966), p. 292; and Greenstein, *The Hidden-Hand Presidency*, pp. 125–127.

4. For a brief time, William H. Jackson was Acting Special Assistant

(September to December 1956). National Archives and Records Service, General Services Administration, *Historical Materials in the Dwight D. Eisenhower Library*, Abilene, Kans., 1981, p. 17; Anderson, *The Presidents' Men*, pp. 172–173; and Hall, "Implementing Multiple Advocacy," p. 353.

5. David K. Hall's interview with Sidney W. Souers, 3 June 1971, as reported in Hall, "Implementing Multiple Advocacy," pp. 311–312.

6. The predecessor of the OCB was the Psychological Strategy Board, which was formed under Truman. Under Eisenhower, it was felt that psychological strategy could not be "grafted" onto the NSC, but, instead, had to be integrated with overall policy implementation. Hence, the OCB was created. Interview with Karl G. Harr, former vice chairman of the OCB, Washington, D.C., 20 August 1984. See also Greenstein, *The Hidden-Hand Presidency*, pp. 132–134.

7. On Dulles's role as primary spokesman of the administration's foreign policy, see Greenstein, *The Hidden-Hand Presidency*, pp. 87–92.

Although Cutler traveled in an official capacity while national security assistant, his foreign contacts were, like Souers's, *informational*. On one occasion, he did perform diplomatic functions, but that was to negotiate the *procedures* that would govern the 1957 NATO Council meeting in Paris, and he acted in that capacity as an assistant to Dulles. Hall, "Implementing Multiple Advocacy," p. 723.

8. Greenstein, *The Hidden-Hand Presidency*, pp. 138–139; and Eleanora W. Schoenebaum, ed., *Political Profiles: The Eisenhower Years* (New York: Facts on File, 1977), p. 5.

9. Greenstein, *The Hidden-Hand Presidency*, p. 107; and Schoenebaum, ed., *Political Profiles: The Eisenhower Years*, pp. 250–251, 482–483.

10. Greenstein, *The Hidden-Hand Presidency*, p. 142; Dwight D. Eisenhower, *The White House Years: Mandate for Change, 1953–1956* (Garden City, N.Y.: Doubleday, 1963), p. 117; and Schoenebaum, ed., *Political Profiles: The Eisenhower Years*, p. 233.

11. For instance, he once reminded Persons to mention at a cabinet meeting "the need for great care to head off the press from creating divisions and dissensions between principal officials in the government." Andrew J. Goodpaster, Note to General Persons, 7 October 1955, White House Office, Office of the Staff Secretary, Subject Series, White House Subseries, A67-49, 67-50, Box 7, Folder: Staff Secretary File (4), Eisenhower Library, Abilene, Kans. Similarly, he once told Press Secretary James C. Hagerty about Adams's suggestion to present a report on the Commission on Veterans' Pensions "in such a way as to get [the] best possible impact from it" among the public. Andrew J. Goodpaster, Memorandum for Mr. Hagerty, 12 November 1955, White House Of-

fice, Office of the Staff Secretary, Subject Series, White House Subseries, Folder: Staff Secretary File, 1955 (5), Eisenhower Library, Abilene, Kans.

12. Andrew J. Goodpaster, Memorandum for the Record, 23 April 1955, White House Office, Office of the Staff Secretary, Subject Series, White House Subseries, A67-49, 67-50, Box 1, Folder: Administrative Arrangements (1), Eisenhower Library, Abilene, Kans.; and Andrew J. Goodpaster, Memorandum for the Record, 1 October 1955, White House Office, Office of the Staff Secretary, Subject Series, White House Subseries, A67-49, 67-50, Box 1, Folder: Administration Arrangements (2), Eisenhower Library, Abilene, Kans.

13. Those who consider the two posts as parallel and complementary to each other include I. M. Destler, "National Security Management: What Presidents Have Wrought," *Political Science Quarterly* 95 (Winter 1980–1981): 573–588; Greenstein, *The Hidden-Hand Presidency*, p. 134; Dwight D. Eisenhower, *The White House Years: Waging Peace, 1956-1961* (Garden City, N.Y.: Doubleday, 1965), p. 319n; and Richard M. Moose, "The White House National Security Staffs Since 1947," in *The President and the Management of National Security*, eds. Keith Clark and Laurence Legere (New York: Praeger, 1969), pp. 61–62. These positions were collapsed into one during the Kennedy administration. However, before the Bay of Pigs incident, Kennedy, despite Goodpaster's warning that it would be hazardous, did not give the responsibility for daily intelligence briefings to his national security assistant, McGeorge Bundy, but instead gave it to military aide Chester Clifton. After the Bay of Pigs incident, Bundy was given that responsibility. Interview with Andrew J. Goodpaster, Washington, D.C., 11 July 1983.

14. Telephone interview with L. Arthur Minnich, McLean, Va., 27 August 1984. As Harlow put it, Goodpaster's job was to make sure "everything was staffed properly." Telephone interview with Bryce N. Harlow, Washington, D.C., 7 September 1984.

15. Interview with Andrew J. Goodpaster, Washington, D.C., 11 July 1983.

16. It was fortunate that the exchange of information was not contingent on the national security assistant's personal sensitivity about domestic politics during the Eisenhower administration since Adams apparently considered Cutler deficient in this regard. For instance, during a staff meeting Cutler argued that senior staff members on leave did not need to pay transportation taxes since high government officials should be considered "on duty all the time." In response, Adams, aware of how such handling of taxes could be misconstrued, closed the meeting "by reminding the staff that Mr. Cutler's philosophy is exactly what this Administration is trying to avoid." L. Arthur Minnich, Note, 27 March 1953,

White House Office, Office of the Staff Secretary, L. Arthur Minnich Series, A67-49, Box 1, Eisenhower Library, Abilene, Kans.

Reflecting back years later, Adams referred to Cutler as a "political neuter" and still remembered the time he wanted to hire a speech writer who, Adams found out later, was an Adlai Stevenson supporter. David K. Hall's interview with Sherman Adams, 18 July 1977, as reported in Hall, "Implementing Multiple Advocacy," p. 386.

17. Oral history interview with Sherman Adams, 12 April 1967, Eisenhower Library, Abilene, Kans., p. 152; Greenstein, *The Hidden-Hand Presidency*, p. 143. Apparently, Harlow attended NSC meetings more frequently than Adams or Persons. When he took the position of speech writer, Harlow said he did so under the condition that he "could be in on everything the president was doing." Telephone interview with Bryce N. Harlow, Washington, D.C., 7 September 1984.

During NSC meetings, Goodpaster, Persons, Adams, and Harlow sat on the fringes, not directly at the table as Cutler did. Cutler's NSC-meeting seating chart is contained in Robert Cutler, Letter to Hon. Bryce Harlow, 26 June 1958, Bryce N. Harlow File, Moscow Exhibition, Box 6, Folder: National Security Council, Eisenhower Library, Abilene, Kans.

18. Regular participants were listed in L. Arthur Minnich, Note, 1 July 1953, White House Office, Office of the Staff Secretary, L. Arthur Minnich Series, A67-49, Box 1, Folder: Staff Meetings (3), Eisenhower Library, Abilene, Kans. When interviewed, Minnich indicated that Cutler's successors also regularly attended White House staff meetings. Telephone interview with L. Arthur Minnich, McLean, Va., 27 August 1984. The frequency of these meetings was noted in Stephen Hess, *Organizing the Presidency* (Washington, D.C.: The Brookings Institution, 1976), p. 70. This channel of sharing national security information should not be exaggerated since, according to Harlow, foreign policy matters were usually only discussed when they appeared on Adams's meeting agenda. However, Minnich stressed that Press Secretary James C. Hagerty often prompted discussion about foreign policy, particularly before presidential press conferences. Telephone interview with Bryce N. Harlow, Washington, D.C., 7 September 1984; and with L. Arthur Minnich, McLean, Va., 27 August 1984.

19. See, for instance, William H. Jackson, Memorandum for Sherman Adams, 11 September 1956, White House Office, Office of the Staff Secretary, Subject Series, White House Subseries, Folder: William H. Jackson (4), Eisenhower Library, Abilene, Kans. The information contained in this memorandum indicated that this was a common practice.

20. Those interviewed who indicated good relations and no obstruc-

tion of access include: Andrew J. Goodpaster, Washington, D.C., 11 July 1983; Bradley Patterson, deputy cabinet secretary, Washington, D.C., 29 June 1983; Karl G. Harr, vice chairman of the Operations Coordinating Board, Washigton, D.C., 30 June 1983 and 20 August 1984; John S. D. Eisenhower, the president's son, who was Goodpaster's assistant, Kimberton, Pa., 25 July 1983; Stephen H. Hess, special assistant to the White House office, Washington, D.C., 14 August 1984; Henry R. McPhee, assistant, then associate, special counsel to the president, Washington, D.C., 14 August 1984; L. Arthur Minnich, McLean, Va., 27 August 1984; and Bryce N. Harlow, Washington, D.C., 7 September 1984.

Gray indicated that he had to work through Adams to get to the president while he was director of the Office of Defense Mobilization, but not after he became the special assistant to the president for national security affairs. Oral history interview with Gordan Gray, 10 October 1967, Eisenhower Library, Abilene, Kans., pp. 288–290.

21. The original speculation on this matter appeared in "O.K., S.A.," *Time* (9 January 1956: 18–22. It appears that such speculation may have been encouraged. For instance, Persons apparently told one of Kennedy's political aides, Theodore C. Sorensen, that both he and Adams had total control over access to the president. See Theodore C. Sorensen, *Kennedy* (New York: Harper and Row, 1965), p. 232; and Sorensen's remarks in John Hughes, "The Presidency after Watergate," in *Has the President Too Much Power?* ed. Charles Roberts (New York: Harper's Magazine Press, 1973), p. 21. Evidence to the contrary comes from interview with Andrew J. Goodpaster, Washington, D.C., 11 July 1983; and Greenstein, *The Hidden-Hand Presidency*, pp. 144–145. One explanation for Persons's statements to Sorensen is that the myth of Adams's total control of access to Eisenhower was a useful way of directing anger at Adams rather than the president when the latter did not want to see someone. This would fit into Adams's role as "lightning rod." On the lightning-rod effect, see Greenstein, *The Hidden-Hand Presidency*, pp. 238–239, 260fn. 79; and Robert J. Donovan, *Eisenhower: The Inside Story* (New York: Harper and Brothers, 1956), p. 71.

22. Eisenhower's memoir indicates that this arrangement was changed in September 1958 after Adams resigned. Eisenhower wrote that Persons was not given the burden to sift the memoranda, but, instead, they went directly to him, Gordan Gray (who was then national security assistant), Goodpaster, or Goodpaster's assistant, and the president's son, John. Eisenhower, *Waging Peace*, p. 318. However, this is inconsistent with a memorandum that indicated Adams had given the responsibility to Goodpaster in October 1955. Andrew Goodpaster, Memorandum for the

Record, 1 October 1955, White House Office, Office of the Staff Secretary, Subject Series, White House Subseries, A67-49, 67-50, Box 1, Folder: Administrative Arrangements (2), Eisenhower Library, Abilene, Kans.

23. Cutler, *No Time for Rest*, pp. 314–315; Oral history interview with Sherman Adams, 12 April 1967, Eisenhower Library, Abilene, Kans., p. 152; and Greenstein, *The Hidden-Hand Presidency*, p. 107n.

24. Cutler, *No Time for Rest*, p. 355; and Wilton B. Persons, Memorandum for Gordan Gray, 14 January 1960, Files of Special Assistant Relating to the Office of Coordinator of Government Public Service Advertising (James M. Lambie, Jr.), Box 55, Folder: Gordan Gray, Eisenhower Library, Abilene, Kans.

25. Interview with Karl G. Harr, Washington, D.C., 20 August 1984.

26. "R.C.A. President Urges 4th Federal Branch for Defense Planning," *Boston Daily Globe* 6 September 1958; and Frederick C. McKee, Letter to Bryce N. Harlow, 19 September 1958, Records of Bryce N. Harlow, 1953–61, A67-56, Box 6, Folder: National Security Council, 1958, Eisenhower Library, Abilene, Kans.

27. Bryce Harlow, Memorandum for Gordan Gray, 12 November 1958, Records of Bryce N. Harlow, 1953–61, A67-56, Box 6, Folder: National Security Council, 1958, Eisenhower Library, Abilene, Kans.

28. Gordan Gray, Memorandum for Bryce N. Harlow, 16 December 1958, Records of Bryce N. Harlow, 1953–61, A67-56, Box 6, Folder: National Security Council, 1958, Eisenhower Library, Abilene, Kans.

29. Sherman Adams, *Firsthand Report: The Story of the Eisenhower Administration* (New York: Harper and Brothers, 1961), p. 388.

30. David K. Hall, "The National Security Assistant as Public Spokesman, 1947–1981," paper prepared for the American Political Science Association Convention, New York, 3 September 1981, p. 14; and telephone interview with L. Arthur Minnich, McLean, Va., 27 August 1984. See also Andrew J. Goodpaster, Note to Mr. Hagerty, 15 May 1955, White House Office, Office of the Staff Secretary, Subject Series, White House Subseries, A67-50, Folder: Staff Secretary File, 1957–60, Eisenhower Library, Abilene, Kans., which indicated that all press contact was cleared with the press secretary.

4

The Kennedy Administration

John F. Kennedy's only administrative experience prior to entering the White House was overseeing his staff while serving in the U.S. Congress. This lack of administrative experience, as contrasted with Dwight D. Eisenhower's, may have been a factor in Kennedy's skepticism about his predecessor's elaborate national security policy system. This skepticism was strengthened by the hearings of the Subcommittee on National Policy Making of the Committee on Government Operations, chaired by Senator Henry M. Jackson, Jr., which criticized the Eisenhower NSC's Planning Board as being a "paper mill."[1] Kennedy abolished the office of the staff secretary as well as the Planning Board and Operations Coordinating Board, which he, according to his close aide Theodore C. Sorensen, felt imposed "needless paperwork and machinery between the President and his responsible officers."[2]

Not a believer in hierarchical organization, Kennedy organized his staff as "spokes of a wheel," with himself at the hub.[3] He expected his staff to be of diverse backgrounds and to feel free to express opinions independent of those given by cabinet and agency officials. Said Kennedy: "I can't afford to confine myself to one set of advisers. If I did that, *I* would be on *their* leading strings."[4]

Each "spoke" did not represent an exclusive area of responsibility. Kennedy often assigned staffers overlapping responsibilities in order to encourage diverse points of view on an issue. Indeed, he did not hold general White House staff meetings partly because

he feared that redundant assignments would be discovered. However, on their own the aides—who often discovered such overlapping assignments—divided up tasks to reduce their work load.[5]

KENNEDY'S STAFF AND ACCESS TO THE OVAL OFFICE

Open access to the president was an integral part of Kennedy's spokes-of-a-wheel method of staff organization. But entry into the Oval Office was regulated by Appointments Secretary Kenneth P. O'Donnell and Personal Secretary Evelyn Lincoln. O'Donnell had worked for Kennedy during his 1952 Senate campaign and then for his brother Robert on the Senate Rackets Committee staff, beginning in 1957. He later served as a senior political adviser during the 1960 presidential race. During the administration O'Donnell, mindful of the president's time, sternly regulated access to the Oval Office.[6] However, Evelyn Lincoln had a list of White House staff members who were granted easy access to the Oval Office. This provided a "back door" to the president for senior aides, offsetting the restrictive O'Donnell "front door." These staff members were aware that at various times of the day Kennedy would be able to see them. When the door between Evelyn Lincoln's office and the Oval Office was ajar, it meant that the president was "open for business."[7]

White House assistants with open access to Kennedy included Theodore C. Sorensen, Lawrence F. O'Brien, Pierre E. G. Salinger, Arthur M. Schlesinger, Jr., and McGeorge Bundy. They often saw the president several times a day. Science adviser Jerome B. Wiesner, political adviser Ralph A. Dungan, and NSC staffers Walt W. Rostow, Carl Kaysen, Robert Komer, Michael V. Forrestal, and Bromley Smith also had open access to the president, though their Oval Office visits were not as frequent as the others.[8]

Sorensen joined Kennedy's Senate staff in 1953, emerging as chief speech writer and senior political adviser. After the 1960 election, Kennedy appointed him special counsel with responsibility to formulate the budget, the legislative program, and the administration's domestic policy. Moreover, he remained Kennedy's chief speech writer and senior political adviser and served as a primary administration spokesman on domestic affairs.

O'Brien had organized Kennedy's successful senatorial campaigns in 1952 and 1958. He was also a principal strategist during the 1960 presidential race. During the administration, O'Brien's main duty was congressional liaison.

Salinger had served as press officer for Adlai Stevenson's California campaign in 1952. In 1957 Robert Kennedy recruited him to be an investigator on the Senate Rackets Committee, where he worked alongside O'Donnell. In 1961 he became President Kennedy's press secretary.[9]

Schlesinger, a professor of history at Harvard University, had helped organize a group of scholars to advise Kennedy on foreign policy matters during the 1960 presidential campaign. In 1961, he was appointed special assistant to the president. He functioned as a point of access for intellectuals seeking the president's attention, became extensively involved in U.S. policy toward Latin America, and assisted in writing speeches.[10]

Bundy had become a foreign affairs specialist following his service in the Army during World War II. After helping his former superior, Secretary of War Henry L. Stimson, write his autobiography, he became a speech writer and foreign policy adviser for Republican presidential candidate Thomas Dewey during the 1948 campaign. Thereafter, he became an analyst at the Council on Foreign Relations. In 1953, he was appointed dean of arts and sciences at Harvard College, where he met Senator Kennedy, who was then serving as a university overseer. During the 1960 campaign Bundy, Schlesinger, and others helped organize a group of foreign policy advisers for Kennedy. After the election Bundy became Kennedy's national security assistant.[11]

Bundy's access to the president was never obstructed by other White House staff members.[12] Moreover, Bundy and the State Department, not O'Donnell, regulated the access of foreign officials who sought the president's ear.[13]

Apparently, Kennedy's spokes-of-a-wheel method of access, on occasion, created misunderstandings in parts of the executive bureaucracy. Departmental officials, particularly at State, found it difficult to recognize when a White House staff member spoke with presidential authority. Kennedy's accessibility made it possible for numerous staff members to appear to be speaking at the president's behest. Their actual authority was sometimes unclear.

Eventually, the State Department centralized its communications with the White House, thereby mitigating the problem. Benjamin H. Read, State's executive secretary, was authorized to clear White House instructions through Bundy. According to Read, Bundy was often obliged to indicate that the directives of his colleagues had not been cleared with the president.[14]

THE NATIONAL SECURITY ASSISTANT AS PUBLIC SPOKESMAN AND AN ANALYSIS OF STAFF RELATIONS

In contrast to President Truman, Kennedy felt no compulsion to separate foreign policy from domestic political considerations. In the words of Kennedy NSC staffer Carl Kaysen: "We all knew that there was no such thing as something not being political."[15] Thus, Kennedy fully intended that Bundy and his subordinates would be part of his *personal* staff, modifying the concept of a nonpartisan, careerist NSC head.[16] As one way of generating public support, Kennedy asked Bundy to be an official spokesman to "educate" the public and the press about the administration's foreign policy.[17]

Influential columnists were Bundy's regular press contacts. His interviews with foreign journalists were often arranged by Jay Gildner, a member of the White House press office who handled foreign coverage. On occasion, Bundy appeared as an administration official before congressmen. He periodically delivered a speech to groups like the Association of National Advertisers, the American Society of Newspaper Editors, and the Economic Club of Chicago, and he appeared on "Issues and Answers" and "Meet the Press."[18]

Bundy also spoke occasionally with foreign officials in a diplomatic capacity. But most of the NSC's diplomatic functions were delegated to Bundy's subordinates.[19]

There are three reasons why Bundy's public spokesmanship and limited diplomatic activities did not produce friction with other White House staff members or cabinet officials.[20] First, Bundy did not become popular through his spokesmanship. Journalists found him somewhat abrasive, and he did not have wide appeal among

the general public. Nor did Bundy seek to upstage the president. He therefore did not detract from Kennedy's popularity.[21]

Second, Bundy respected the prerogatives of both Secretary of State Dean Rusk and Secretary of Defense Robert McNamara. Hence, a national security assistant–cabinet secretary rift did not develop and become a political issue. In fact, early in the administration, Kennedy specifically asked Bundy to keep his public statements consistent with those of cabinet officials. The president informed other senior staff members of this request. Throughout the administration they felt Bundy complied with this request and handled his public statements with great care.[22]

Third, Kennedy's treatment of his staff served to minimize friction. He did not play favorites. He instilled a sense of collegiality and rewarded team effort more than an individual tour de force. He treated his key staff members equally—both in their salaries and their access to him. Finally, his leadership provided a common focus and inspiration for the staff; only after his assassination did sharp internal antagonisms surface.[23]

INFORMATION EXCHANGE AND LACK OF TURF-MINDEDNESS

These cordial relations within the White House contributed to spontaneous sharing of information. Schlesinger frequently communicated with Bundy about the foreign policy ideas of U.S. officials, academics, and foreign dignitaries, as well as how foreign policy initiatives were being portrayed by the media. O'Brien informed Bundy about congressional sentiments pertinent to foreign and defense policy.[24]

The Kennedy staff also developed several institutionalized arrangements for exchanging information on national security and domestic matters. Early in the administration, David E. Bell, a former member of President Truman's staff and Kennedy's first director of the Budget Bureau, initiated exclusive, weekly private meetings with Sorensen and Bundy in which information was exchanged on fiscal, domestic, and national security policy.[25] Also, after the Bay of Pigs incident, Bundy created the Situation Room in the White House basement—an information center tapping State, Defense, and CIA cable traffic. Since Bundy allowed other senior

staff members to read the cables (with only a few exceptions),[26] the Situation Room greatly enhanced the dissemination of national security information. This helped eliminate one potential cause for tension within the White House staff. Another information exchange technique, also initiated by Bundy after the Bay of Pigs incident, was the morning briefing about international developments by the NSC staff. Other White House aides were invited to attend. Presidential assistant Richard N. Goodwin, Schlesinger, and Dungan attended regularly. Salinger, or another member of the press office, attended when a major foreign policy story was imminent.[27] Dungan's presence at these briefings was particularly significant since it resulted not from a presidential request but, instead, from a meeting he had with O'Donnell and O'Brien after the Bay of Pigs episode temporarily jeopardized Kennedy's political standing. According to Dungan, at that time the three of them felt that: "there was not enough [input] from us, the old loyalists"; that the department and agency "professionals," who were strangers to the president, were dominating foreign policy deliberations, leaving Kennedy "by himself" before the Bay of Pigs incident; and that "Bundy had a tendency to go with the professionals." Dungan, O'Donnell, and O'Brien had no personal quarrel with Bundy, nor did they necessarily object to the military rationale of the Bay of Pigs invasion plan. But they *did* want representation in future national security policy meetings to protect the president's domestic political interests.[28]

Kennedy himself felt that he needed to include his political advisers in foreign policy deliberations after the Bay of Pigs incident. He requested that thereafter his brother Robert (who was attorney general) and Sorensen attend even the most sensitive national security meetings. O'Donnell also sometimes got a personal invitation to attend.[29] Furthermore, Bundy and his staff began offering their views about domestic political risks inherent in certain foreign policy options and sought the active participation of the domestic advisers in sensitive decisions, such as those relating to Middle East policy and foreign economic relations.[30]

Fluid boundaries of responsibility among the presidential assistants helped prevent turf-mindedness. Bundy did not resist the involvement of the political advisers in national security matters. In fact, he often delegated responsibilities to other assistants.[31]

The political aides were not turf-minded either. For instance, Sorensen requested input from Bundy and other members of the NSC staff while drafting presidential speeches. More than merely asking for their ideas, he sent entire drafts and requested, as he once did of Bundy, to "feel free to *delete* or *add* words, sentences, paragraphs or entire sections."[32]

THE IMPORTANCE OF DIRECTING PRESIDENTIAL REQUESTS ABOUT THE POLICY PROCESS TO THE ENTIRE WHITE HOUSE STAFF

At the very outset of the administration, Kennedy asked Bundy to ensure that all options were presented during national security policy meetings and to see that each department and agency pertinent to a given issue had an opportunity to present its view. In this capacity, as Assistant Secretary of State Roger Hilsman later wrote, Bundy served as a "midwife of policy."[33] In addition, when he felt a point of view was not being presented adequately, Bundy was charged with expressing that view, regardless of whether he felt it was the appropriate policy to pursue. Although this was largely Bundy's responsibility in the national security field, shortly after being elected Kennedy had asked the entire staff to try to ensure that all options were presented during policy meetings and that they seek to prevent premature foreclosure of policy deliberations.[34]

The Bay of Pigs incident highlighted the importance of and gave substance to Kennedy's original request. Schlesinger, among others, has argued that without the lesson learned from the Bay of Pigs fiasco, the Cuban missile crisis would have been handled differently: "that failure in Cuba in 1961 contributed to success in Cuba in 1962."[35] Henceforth, the entire White House staff understood the importance of presenting various options.[36] Had this not been so, Bundy's numerous policy shifts during the Cuban missile crisis would have confused the political assistants and could have caused friction.

On the morning of October 13, after Bundy informed the president about the photographic evidence of the construction of Soviet missile bases in Cuba, Kennedy ordered the national security

assistant to assemble a group of top advisers, later known as the Executive Committee (Ex Comm). Both Robert Kennedy and Sorensen were members of this group. At first, Bundy agreed with the president that if the initial evidence was confirmed, the United States would probably have to bomb the missile sites. But at the first Ex Comm meeting on October 13, Bundy advocated a strictly diplomatic approach. During the next three days he reverted back to an air strike, eventually becoming chair of a team supporting it (the other team, headed by Under Secretary of State George W. Ball, supported a naval blockade).[37]

By the evening of October 18, members of Ex Comm came to a near–unanimous decision—the Joint Chiefs of Staff and their chairman, Maxwell Taylor, dissenting—to establish a naval blockade to prevent further delivery of Soviet missiles, along with a public demand that the missiles already on Cuban soil be removed. However, in the early stages of the meeting, in Sorensen's words, "somewhat to everyone's surprise, Mac Bundy urged that we not overlook the justification of no action at all."[38]

The next morning, after speaking with the Joint Chiefs about their preference for a military assault (including a ground invasion), the president, before departing on a campaign trip (an appointment he kept to project a sense of normalcy), spoke with Robert Kennedy and Sorensen, indicating that, in Sorensen's words, "he was rather concerned and hoped we would be able to get more of a consensus."[39] But during the Ex Comm meeting that morning, according to notes taken by Leonard C. Meeker, the State Department's deputy legal adviser, Bundy indicated that he favored "decisive action with its advantages of surprise and confronting the world with a *fait accompli*." At that point, according to Meeker's notes, "Sorensen intervened, saying it was not fair to the President to reconsider a matter on which they had all [except the JCS] reached a decision the day before." Thereafter, Dean Acheson (who also attended the meetings), CIA Director John McCone, Treasury Secretary Douglas Dillon, and Taylor spoke out in favor of an air strike.[40]

Bundy was following instructions to ensure that all options received due consideration while Robert Kennedy and Sorensen were complying with the president's request to try to bring the meetings to closure. These instructions conflicted with each other. But

Sorensen understood Bundy's behavior because of the president's previous requests about preserving policy options. His "intervention" during the Friday meeting in all likelihood merely reflected his desire to bring the group closer to a consensus. Sorensen stated: "Mac changed his position but that was in part his role. That was what he was supposed to do."[41] If Sorensen had been upset with Bundy it is unlikely that he would have maintained freely flowing communication with him. The next weekend, for instance, when Sorensen sent a memorandum to the president advising how to handle a Soviet tanker headed toward the blockade, he sent a copy to Bundy.[42]

THE INFLUENCE OF MUTUAL ADVICE BY STAFF MEMBERS

Because in the Truman and Eisenhower administrations the national security assistant was not normally expected to offer substantive policy views, he had little incentive to form alliances with other senior officials in support of his position on foreign policy issues. Conversely, cabinet officials and White House aides had little reason to conclude alliances to thwart the national security assistant's influence with the president. On the other hand, since Kennedy expected his entire staff to offer their opinions, the formation of alliances was a strong possibility. More weight could thereby have been added to a particular option, possibly even circumventing the advice of cabinet secretaries or agency heads. However, probably due to Bundy's careful consideration of Kennedy's statutory advisers, this rarely occurred.

In fact, it seems that White House staff collaboration was, if anything, strongly supportive of cabinet secretaries. For instance, Sorensen and Bundy together mustered intelligence estimates and sought legislation pertinent to Agriculture Secretary Orville Freeman's suggestion that U.S. grain be sold to the Soviet Union. Sorensen and Bundy later recommended to Kennedy that the sales be made and worked the agreement through Congress and the executive bureaucracy.[43]

As with policy questions, Kennedy often requested the advice of his staff on matters related to his presidential functions. But when two aides had similar opinions, this advice did not consti-

tute an alliance. Their mutual counsel represented common positions taken by those who agreed on certain issues, not a "ganging up" on the president to enhance their persuasive power vis-à-vis another aide. Their expression of opinion often enhanced coordination. For instance, Sorensen's and Bundy's opposition to Salinger's recommendation for live presidential press conferences probably made the entire staff more meticulous in briefing Kennedy before he appeared on television.[44]

CONCLUSION

In the Kennedy administration the national security assistant was, for the first time, a primary foreign policy adviser. Bundy did not merely coordinate, manage, and monitor the policy-making process. Kennedy *required* Bundy to present unrepresented options during policy deliberations and requested that he be a *public* spokesman for U.S. foreign policy, a role traditionally reserved for the secretary of state.

Among the factors that help explain this relative absence of friction, two are especially critical. First was Kennedy's collegial style and his active interest in—indeed promotion of—hearing divergent views on foreign policy matters. Kennedy himself was a listener, a reader, someone open to different and clashing views, and virtually all significant foreign policy actors had easy access to him. An analogy to a graduate-level university seminar conducted by a flexible, tolerant professor is an imperfect one, yet it is suggestive of the ambiance at the highest policy levels. The participants in the "seminar" not only shared the president's values concerning national security policy, but they were also comfortable with his style. Moreover, the president himself made the rules of the policy-making process known early in the administration. It was explained at the outset that Bundy was to be *both* a policy advocate—often taking different sides on the same issue—and, on occasion, a policy spokesman. This greatly mitigated the possibility of friction between Bundy and Secretary of State Rusk. Furthermore, Bundy did not abuse his authority vis-à-vis cabinet secretaries. Bundy was conscious of the secretary of state's prominent policy advisory role; if anything, he *facilitated* Rusk's access to the president. And Bundy's public role was handled so tactfully that

there was never any doubt that the president ran the show; there was no danger that Bundy's appearances would detract from Kennedy's popularity. Therefore, other White House staff members had no reason to clash with Bundy over his spokesmanship or policy advocate roles.

A second factor in explaining the relative lack of friction was Bundy's style, personality, and mode of operation. He worked harmoniously with White House political aides. Following the Bay of Pigs incident, he was not only receptive to suggestions from O'Donnell, O'Brien, and Dungan that domestic political considerations be better integrated into national security policy discussions, but he enthusiastically supported such suggestions. Some political aides, thereafter, participated in key foreign policy meetings and attended daily NSC staff briefings. Furthermore, Bundy created the Situation Room, thereby facilitating dissemination of national security information among the White House staff, reducing the possibility that they would be, or would feel, left out of an important foreign policy matter.

NOTES

1. Fred I. Greenstein, *The Hidden-Hand Presidency: Eisenhower as Leader* (New York: Basic Books, 1982), p. 263, fn. 39. The Subcommittee hearings appear in Henry M. Jackson, Jr., ed., *The National Security Council: Subcommittee Papers on Policy-Making at the Presidential Level* (New York: Praeger, 1965).

2. Theodore C. Sorensen, *Kennedy* (New York: Harper and Row, 1965), p. 281.

3. Ibid., p. 262; Richard Tanner Johnson, *Managing the White House: An Intimate Study of the Presidency* (New York: Harper and Row, 1974), p. 125; Stephen Hess, *Organizing the Presidency* (Washington, D.C.: The Brookings Institution, 1976), p. 78; and Michael Medved, *The Shadow Presidents* (New York: Times Books, 1979), p. 271.

4. Quoted in Arthur M. Schlesinger, Jr., *A Thousand Days: John F. Kennedy in the White House* (Boston: Houghton Mifflin, 1965), p. 124. Emphasis in original. On this aspect of Kennedy's style, see also p. 631 and Patrick Anderson, *The Presidents' Men: White House Assistants of Franklin D. Roosevelt, Harry S Truman, Dwight D. Eisenhower, John F. Kennedy, and Lyndon B. Johnson* (Garden City, N.Y.: Doubleday, 1968), p. 201.

5. Johnson, *Managing the White House*, p. 127; Anderson, *The Presidents' Men*, p. 201; Hess *Organizing the Presidency*, p. 80; and Schlesinger, *A Thousand Days*, p. 687. According to one senior White House official, Kennedy "did not want other staff members to know what the others were doing." Interview with anonymous source, Washington, D.C., 19 July 1983. In the words of Ralph A. Dungan, a senior political assistant, Kennedy "did not sort the staff out. The staff sorted themselves out." Telephone interview with Ralph A. Dungan, Washington, D.C., 3 October 1984. At lower levels, the staff did specialize, serving to support the senior aides. Telephone interview with Lee C. White, who served as assistant special counsel, Washington, D.C., 5 October 1984.

6. Pierre Salinger, *With Kennedy* (Garden City, N.Y.: Doubleday, 1966), pp. 64–65; Nelson Lichtenstein, ed., *Political Profiles: The Kennedy Years* (New York: Facts on File, 1976), p. 394; Kenneth P. O'Donnell and David F. Powers with Joe McCarthy, *"Johnny, We Hardly Knew Ye": Memories of John Fitzgerald Kennedy* (Boston: Little, Brown, 1972), pp. vii–viii; Joseph Kraft, "Kennedy's Working Staff," *Harper's* 225 (December 1962): 30; and Anderson, *The Presidents' Men*, pp. 198–199.

7. Sorensen, *Kennedy*, p. 263; Anderson, *The Presidents' Men*, pp. 201, 206; Schlesinger, *A Thousand Days*, p. 687; Kraft, "Kennedy's Working Staff": 33; and Arthur M. Schlesinger, Jr., "What's Wrong with the President's War Powers?" in *Has the President Too Much Power?* ed. Charles Roberts (New York: Harper's Magazine Press, 1973), p. 217.

8. Sorensen, *Kennedy*, p. 374; I. M. Destler, *Presidents, Bureaucrats and Foreign Policy* (Princeton: Princeton University Press, 1974), p. 101; Anderson, *The Presidents' Men*, p. 265; Schlesinger, *A Thousand Days*, p. 422; and Charles W. Roberts, *LBJ's Inner Circle* (New York: Delacorte, 1965), p. 70.

9. Kraft, "Kennedy's Working Staff": 31; Salinger, *With Kennedy*, pp. 66, 68–69; Anderson, *The Presidents' Men*, p. 289; Medved, *The Shadow Presidents*, p. 261; Hess, *Organizing the Presidency*, p. 87; Lichtenstein, ed., *Political Profiles: The Kennedy Years*, pp. 391–394, 457–458; and Sorensen, *Kennedy*, p. 117.

10. Kraft, "Kennedy's Working Staff": 30; Salinger, *With Kennedy*, p. 69; Lichtenstein, ed., *Political Profiles: The Kennedy Years*, pp. 464–465; and Arthur M. Schlesinger, Jr., Papers, Subject Files, 1961–1964, Boxes 1–24, Kennedy Library, Boston, Mass, passim.

11. O'Donnell and Powers, *"Johnny, We Hardly Knew Ye,"* p. 235; Salinger, *With Kennedy*, pp. 67–68; Helen Fuller, *Year of Trial: Kennedy's Crucial Decisions* (New York: Harcourt, Brace & World, 1962), p. 42; and Lichtenstein, ed., *Political Profiles: The Kennedy Years*, pp. 59–60.

12. Telephone interview with McGeorge Bundy, New York, N.Y.,

14 July 1983; with Ralph A. Dungan, Washington, D.C., 3 October 1984, with Carl Kaysen, Cambridge, Mass., 3 October 1984; and with Theodore C. Sorensen, New York, N.Y., 18 October 1984. Referring to Bundy's unchallenged access, former *New York Times* journalist David Halberstam wrote: "Bundy was always there, darting in and out of the President's office (' . . . dammit Mac,' someone heard Kennedy say, 'I've been arguing with you about this all week,' and *that* was power, the access to argue all week long)." David Halberstam, "The Very Expensive Education of McGeorge Bundy," *Harper's* 239 (July 1969): 22.

13. O'Donnell and Powers, *"Johnny, We Hardly Knew Ye,"* p. 266.

14. David K. Hall's interview with Benjamin H. Read, 17 May 1971, as reported in David K. Hall, "Implementing Multiple Advocacy in the National Security Council, 1947–1980" (Ph.D. diss., Stanford University, 1982), pp. 510–511.

15. Telephone interview with Carl Kaysen, Cambridge, Mass., 3 October 1984. See also Hall, "Implementing Multiple Advocacy," pp. 488–489.

16. Symbolically, Bundy's office was eventually moved from the Executive Office Building to the basement of the White House. O'Donnell and Powers, *"Johnny, We Hardly Knew Ye,"* p. 277.

17. David K. Hall, "The National Security Assistant as Policy Spokesman, 1947–1981" (Paper prepared for the American Political Science Association Convention, New York, 3 September 1981), pp. 18–20; Hall, "Implementing Multiple Advocacy," pp. 464, 543; and interview with anonymous source, Washington, D.C., 19 July 1983.

18. Salinger, *With Kennedy*, pp. 131–132; Sorensen, *Kennedy*, pp. 362–363; Elmer E. Cornwell, Jr., *Presidential Leadership of Public Opinion* (Bloomington: Indiana University Press, 1965), p. 199; and Hall, "Implementing Multiple Advocacy," p. 544.

19. Hall, "Implementing Multiple Advocacy," pp. 552–554; and Schlesinger, *A Thousand Days*, pp. 566–567.

20. Good relations are reflected in Salinger, *With Kennedy*, p. 64; Sorensen, *The Kennedy Legacy* (New York: Macmillan, 1969), pp. 80–81; Medved, *The Shadow Presidents*, p. 271; Jim F. Heath, *Decade of Disillusionment: The Kennedy-Johnson Years* (Bloomington: Indiana University Press, 1975), p. 58; Anderson, *The Presidents' Men*, p. 289; Schlesinger, *A Thousand Days*, p. 208; and Theodore C. Sorensen, Confidential letter to McGeorge Bundy, 5 March 1963; and McGeorge Bundy, Memorandum to Mr. Sorensen, 8 March 1963, Papers of President Kennedy, National Security Files, Meetings and Memoranda, Box 327, Folder: Staff Memoranda, Theodore Sorensen, 1961–63, Kennedy Library, Boston, Mass.

21. Oral history interview with Peter Lisagor, White House reporter,

22 April 1966, Kennedy Library, Boston, Mass., p. 53; Sidney Hyman, "When Bundy Says . . . ," *New York Times Magazine* (2 December 1962): 132; and Anderson, *The Presidents' Men*, pp. 196–197.

22. Telephone interview with Theodore C. Sorensen, New York, N.Y., 18 October 1984; Salinger, *With Kennedy*, p. 68; Sorensen, *The Kennedy Legacy*, pp. 82–83; W. W. Rostow, *The Diffusion of Power: An Essay in Recent History* (New York: Macmillan, 1972), p. 169; oral history interview with Peter Lisagor, 22 April 1966, Kennedy Library, Boston, Mass., pp. 52–53; Anderson, *The Presidents' Men*, p. 289; and David Wise, "Scholars of a Nuclear Age," in *The Kennedy Circle*, ed. Lester Tanzer (Washington, D.C.: Luce, 1961), p. 31.

23. Johnson, *Managing the White House*, pp. 144, 152; Sorensen, *Kennedy*, p. 262; Theodore C. Sorensen, *The Kennedy Legacy*, p. 80; and telephone interview with Ralph A. Dungan, Washington, D.C., 3 October 1984. On Kennedy's "collegial style," see Alexander L. George, *Presidential Decisionmaking in Foreign Policy: The Effective Use of Information and Advice* (Boulder, Colo.: Westview, 1981), pp. 157–159.

24. See Schlesinger's memoranda contained throughout Papers of President Kennedy, National Security Files, Meetings and Memoranda, Box 327, Kennedy Library, Boston, Mass.; and Larry O'Brien, Memoranda for McGeorge Bundy, 5 March 1962, Papers of President Kennedy, National Security Files, Box 327, Folder: Staff Memoranda, Maxwell Taylor, 1/62–4/62, Kennedy Library, Boston, Mass.

25. Telephone interview with Theodore C. Sorensen, New York, N.Y., 18 October 1984.

26. According to Kaysen, some satellite information and cables—such as those between Kennedy and Soviet Communist Party Chairman Nikita Krushchev during the Cuban missile crisis—were "closely held." Telephone interview with Carl Kaysen, Cambridge, Mass., 3 October 1984. Dungan indicated that he often reviewed cables about Latin America and gave no indication of being excluded from sensitive information. Telephone interview with Ralph A. Dungan, Washington, D.C., 3 October 1984. When asked about the Situation Room, Sorensen said: "I don't know whether I had free access or not but the few times I went there . . . I was never restricted from entering." Telephone interview with Theodore C. Sorensen, New York, N.Y., 18 October 1984. See also Schlesinger, *A Thousand Days*, pp. 422–423.

27. Salinger, *With Kennedy*, p. 68; Schlesinger, *A Thousand Days*, p. 297; telephone interview with Ralph A. Dungan, Washington, D.C., 3 October 1984; and with Pierre E.G. Salinger, New York, N.Y., 27 October 1984.

28. As Dungan said: "Everybody liked Mac. Everybody respected him." Telephone interview with Ralph A. Dungan, Washington, D.C., 3 October 1984.

29. Salinger, *With Kennedy*, pp. 250, 257; O'Donnell and Powers, *"Johnny, We Hardly Knew Ye,"* pp. 311–312; Fuller, *Year of Trial*, pp. 60, 67; Anderson, *The Presidents' Men*, p. 202; Irving L. Janis, *Victims of Groupthink: A Psychological Study of Foreign-Policy Decisions and Fiascoes* (Boston: Houghton Mifflin, 1972), p. 148; Graham T. Allison, *Essence of Decision: Explaining the Cuban Missile Crisis* (Boston: Little, Brown, 1971), p. 57; and Peter Collier and David Horowitz, *The Kennedy's: An American Drama* (New York: Summit Books, 1984), p. 297.

30. Charles A. Stevenson, *The End of Nowhere* (Boston: Beacon Press, 1972), pp. 147–148; Schlesinger, *A Thousand Days*, pp. 422–423; Roger Hilsman, *To Move a Nation: The Politics of Foreign Policy in the Administration of John F. Kennedy* (Garden City, N.Y.: Doubleday, 1967), p. 56; and Hall, "Implementing Multiple Advocacy," pp. 488–489. Hall's point that Bundy and his staff became more sensitive to domestic political considerations after the Bay of Pigs fiasco is probably correct. But it would be incorrect to say that Bundy was not aware of the potential domestic political repercussions of the invasion before it happened. Three days before the Cuban exiles landed on the beaches of Cuba, Bundy sent a memorandum to Schlesinger (who was involved in the final phases of the planning) to suggest how Kennedy might respond to the "tough question" of "is CIA involved in this operation?" McGeorge Bundy, Memorandum to Mr. Schlesinger, 11 April 1961, Arthur M. Schlesinger, Jr., Papers, Subject Files, 1961–1964, Box 5, Folder: Cuba 4/3/61–4/23/61, Kennedy Library, Boston, Mass.

31. For instance, after the president had asked Bundy to check into the extent to which the British and Canadians wanted to participate in a joint development assistance program for British Guiana, he wrote a memorandum to Schlesinger ending with: "Will you handle this?" McGeorge Bundy, Memorandum for Mr. Arthur Schlesinger, 18 October 1961, Arthur M. Schlesinger, Jr., Papers, Subject Files, 1961–64, Box 3B, Folder: British Guiana 4/28/61–10/30/61, Kennedy Library, Boston, Mass. On Bundy's tendency to delegate, see George, *Presidential Decisionmaking in Foreign Policy*, p. 197.

32. Theodore C. Sorensen, Memorandum for McGeorge Bundy, 6 January 1963, Box 327, Folder: Staff Memoranda, Theodore Sorensen, State of the Union Message, 1963, Kennedy Library, Boston, Mass. Emphasis in original. See also Sorensen, *The Kennedy Legacy*, p. 82; and Cornwell, *Presidential Leadership of Public Opinion*, p. 199.

33. Hilsman, *To Move a Nation*, p. 56.

34. Rostow, *The Diffusion of Power*, p. 168; Schlesinger, *A Thousand Days*, p. 421; Anderson, *The Presidents' Men*, p. 270; Sorensen, *Kennedy*, pp. 259, 260, 282; and telephone interview with Theodore C. Sorensen, New York, N.Y., 18 October 1984.

35. Schlesinger, *A Thousand Days*, p. 297.

36. Ibid.; and Janis, *Victims of Groupthink*, p. 148.

37. Sorensen, *The Kennedy Legacy*, p. 192; Sorensen, *Kennedy*, p. 675; Hugh Sidney, *John F. Kennedy, President* (New York: Atheneum, 1963), pp. 326–329; Allison, *Essence of Decision*, pp. 56–62, 196; and Hall, "Implementing Multiple Advocacy," p. 526.

38. Oral history interview with Theodore C. Sorensen, 6 April 1964, Kennedy Library, Boston, Mass., p. 53. See also Arthur M. Schlesinger, Jr., *Robert Kennedy and His Times* (Boston: Houghton Mifflin, 1978), p. 508.

39. Oral history interview with Theodore C. Sorensen, 6 April 1964, Kennedy Library, Boston, Mass., p. 53. Aside from the need to soon make a decision due to the pace of the construction of missile launch pads in Cuba, the president requested this because he felt that a lack of consensus among his advisers when he made his decision would cause dissension and implementation delays. Ibid.; and Sorensen, *Kennedy*, p. 692. In an interview, Sorensen stated that the president did not particularly want a *complete* consensus, but was "concerned about people changing their position." Telephone interview with Theodore C. Sorensen, New York, N.Y., 18 October 1984.

40. Leonard C. Meeker, Memorandum of October 19, 1962, meeting of the Executive Committee of the National Security Council, Arthur M. Schlesinger, Jr., Papers, Box 5, Kennedy Library, Boston, Mass. as cited in Schlesinger, *Robert Kennedy and His Times*, pp. 508–509.

41. Telephone interview with Theodore C. Sorensen, New York, N.Y., 18 October 1984.

42. Theodore C. Sorensen, Memorandum for the President, 27 October 1962, Papers of President Kennedy, National Security Files, Meetings and Memoranda, Box 327, Folder: Staff Memoranda, Theodore Sorensen, 1961–1963, Kennedy Library, Boston, Mass. At the bottom of this memorandum, "CC to McGeorge Bundy" is followed with a check mark.

43. Oral history interview with Theodore C. Sorensen, 15 April 1964, Kennedy Library, Boston, Mass., p. 87; and Sorensen, *Kennedy*, pp. 740–743.

44. At the beginning of the administration, Sorensen and Bundy opposed this recommendation for fear that a presidential slip of the tongue

would have major foreign policy repercussions. See Salinger, *With Kennedy*, pp. 56, 137; Anderson, *The Presidents' Men*, pp. 233–234; Sorensen, *Kennedy*, p. 324; Schlesinger, *A Thousand Days*, p. 716; and Sidney, *John F. Kennedy, President*, pp. 49–50.

5

The Johnson Administration

Lyndon B. Johnson's decision-making style relied heavily on the cultivation of tension among his advisers to forge agreements, similar to his technique of pressuring his fellow congressmen to pass legislation while he was Senate majority leader. He was demanding of his White House staff. He often used intimidation to challenge their self-respect, thereby encouraging them to seek to redeem themselves in his eyes. This created tension within the White House and triggered numerous staff resignations during the administration. Former White House Fellow Doris Kearns wrote that this "seemed to work as a safety valve for his fears of becoming dependent on those who worked for him."[1]

Much like Kennedy, President Johnson kept his staff members organized loosely and considered them generalists. Johnson's management style was more *ad hoc* than Kennedy's. He tended to assign staffers to areas of responsibility to which they were drawn by their own inclinations. As his former press secretary, George E. Christian, Jr., put it, Johnson had the attitude that "you should do anything you were big enough to do."[2] According to another aide, S. Douglass Cater, Jr., Johnson "administered the White House, certainly, rather loosely. It was not what you'd call an administrator's dream."[3]

JOHNSON'S STAFF AND INTRA-WHITE HOUSE RELATIONS

Johnson's White House staff included ten or so special assistants, with a support staff of nearly thirty. George E. Reedy had first worked with Johnson while serving as staff counsel to the Senate Armed Services Preparedness Subcommittee. He coordinated speech writing and press relations during Johnson's vice presidency and replaced Pierre Salinger as White House press secretary in March 1964. The administration's declining public approval ratings led Johnson to ease Reedy out of the White House in July 1965, replacing him with Bill D. Moyers.

Moyers was probably the most influential assistant in the Johnson White House. He had worked at various times on Johnson's congressional staff while attending college and helped manage his 1960 presidential campaign. He became publicity director of the Peace Corps when Johnson was elected vice president. At the beginning of Johnson's presidency, Moyers became a special assistant on the White House staff. He was a major strategist during the 1964 presidential campaign and emerged as *de facto* chief of staff shortly thereafter. Moyers contributed to foreign policy speeches, attended NSC meetings, and, when he was press secretary, participated in the Tuesday luncheon meetings, during which sensitive national security decisions were made. However, as public criticism of U.S. involvement in the Indochina conflict mounted and Moyer's dovish stance became widely known, his standing with the president diminished. He resigned in December 1966, and was replaced by Christian, who had begun working in the press office eight months previously. Christian also attended NSC and Tuesday luncheon meetings when he was press secretary.[4]

Johnson's coordinator for the 1964 Democratic Convention, Marvin Watson, became the appointments secretary in January 1965. In addition to his secretarial responsibilities, Watson served as liaison with the Democratic National Committee, Democratic governors, and the Federal Bureau of Investigation. He left the White House in April 1968 to become Postmaster General.[5]

The staff member with the most intimate personal relationship with the president was probably Jack J. Valenti. Valenti had han-

dled Johnson's political advertising in Texas during the 1960 presidential campaign. Shortly after becoming president, Johnson commissioned Valenti and Horace W. Busby, Jr., another political aide, to write position papers on urban affairs, civil rights, and foreign policy for the new administration. Subsequently, Valenti worked extensively on foreign policy speeches, participated in informal national security policy discussions, and sat in on NSC meetings. Valenti, and later Watson, not the national security assistant, worked with the president in deciding who would attend the Tuesday luncheons. Valenti resigned from the White House staff in May 1966.[6]

Busby had been a chief speech writer and adviser during Johnson's vice presidential overseas trips. As a special assistant during Johnson's presidency, he continued to be a foreign policy speech writer, attended NSC meetings, worked with members of Congress, and was a chief administration contact for the United States Information Agency and various international organizations. Busby remained on the White House staff only eighteen months, but worked unofficially for the president at various times during the rest of the administration.[7]

Two other senior speech writers were Cater and Harry C. McPherson, Jr. Although his initial involvement was in foreign policy, Cater subsequently became an influential architect of the administration's domestic policy, particularly regarding education. However, he retained some involvement in foreign policy by virtue of his participation in speech writing. McPherson began working in the White House in August 1965 after serving for a year as assistant secretary of defense. In addition to speech writing, he served as a political adviser and legal counselor.[8]

Johnson initially retained McGeorge Bundy as his national security assistant. Bundy resigned, however, on February 28, 1966. He was replaced one month later by Walt W. Rostow, who had served briefly on the NSC staff under Bundy during the Kennedy administration prior to becoming chairman of the State Department's Policy Planning Council. Relations among the political aides and the national security assistants were generally amiable and cooperative.[9]

NEAR-ABSENCE OF STAFF MACHINERY FOR COORDINATION

Though Johnson invited his senior political assistants to NSC and Tuesday luncheon meetings, any other communication among them in efforts to coordinate foreign policy with domestic politics was spontaneous, without any integrative machinery, unless they erected such machinery themselves. As a rule, the White House staff did this on their own. An attempt was made to hold general White House staff meetings, but there was insufficient enthusiasm for them and they were soon discontinued.[10]

This increased the chances that someone might be overlooked; that a staff member who should have been informed was not kept abreast of sensitive developments. This happened at least once to Reedy. In the summer of 1964, Reedy was surprised to learn, while attending an NSC meeting, that the administration planned to request a congressional resolution to authorize military retaliation after the second attack on U.S. naval vessels by North Vietnamese torpedo boats in the Gulf of Tonkin. Immediately thereafter the request was made public, and Reedy was left to explain it to the press without knowing any background.[11]

In contrast to Reedy, when Christian was press secretary he took specific measures to ensure that he was kept informed about such matters. He frequented Rostow's office and read intelligence cables. He requested, and Johnson approved, that NSC staffers Edward K. Hamilton and William J. Jorden be assigned to the press office "part time as needed." He had Rostow's office send him a daily summary of world events as well as State and Defense Department communications about impending press announcements.[12]

ESSENTIAL TRUST

Since the political aides lacked institutionalized mechanisms for information sharing, they had to trust that the national security assistant would take the initiative to keep them informed about sensitive developments. One aide who clearly had this trust was McPherson. When asked about his access to the Situation Room, he remarked that he was not informed about all cables, probably

because of the perennial concern about leaks.[13] According to Rostow, members of the NSC staff shared information with other White House staffers whenever they had a legitimate need to know. He said he took special pains to cultivate a collegial atmosphere among the staff—such as inviting political aides to NSC staff meetings—and that, consequently, the political aides trusted that they would be kept informed about pertinent matters.[14]

Reedy did not seem to enjoy the same degree of trust that McPherson had. Given his Gulf of Tonkin Resolution experience, he was understandably skeptical about the timeliness of the national security assistant's sharing of information. When asked whether he had free access to the Situation Room, he responded affirmatively, but added: "The problem with that is knowing when to enter it."[15]

SPONTANEOUS COORDINATION BY THE STAFF

Johnson did have reason to believe that his staff would coordinate foreign policy with domestic politics on their own, without presidentially created integrative machinery. With some notable exceptions (as with Reedy during the meetings on the Gulf of Tonkin Resolution), aides notified the other appropriate staff members, and usually the president, whenever something sensitive arose. For example, in October 1964, prior to Johnson's campaign debate with presidential candidates Barry M. Goldwater and Richard M. Nixon, Busby requested that Bundy prepare the president for questions regarding the delegation of control of nuclear weapons to commanders in the field. Both Goldwater and Nixon had hinted at such questions in previous statements. Since the president was in Dallas and Bundy was in Washington, Busby had to make a special effort to ensure that briefing papers were sent.[16]

Congressional matters also were coordinated. In December 1965, Moyers was notified by Senator George McGovern that he and another senator, Gaylord Nelson, while in Rome, had been approached by a businessman who said he could arrange a meeting concerning the Indochina conflict with a "North Vietnamese trade man" in Paris. Moyers quickly informed Bundy, indicating that he felt "some appropriate follow-through" was needed.[17] Simi-

larly, one month later, Moyers received a call from Senator Edward Kennedy during which he advocated a continuation of the administration's bombing pause and proposed that negotiations with the National Liberation Front be initiated separately from negotiations (which were then nonexistent) with the North Vietnamese since their political interests, he reasoned, might have been different. Kennedy mentioned also that he planned to make a speech to that effect on the Senate floor two days later. Moyers immediately wrote a memorandum to the president about the call, which ended with: "I suggested that he [Kennedy] may want to talk in detail to McGeorge Bundy before deciding to speak or completing his statement." Johnson did not wait for Kennedy to initiate a call to Bundy. He sent Moyer's memorandum to Bundy, who called Kennedy the next day to discuss the potential speech.[18]

There were also times when the national security assistant felt impelled to warn political aides about possible consequences of impending presidential actions. During the summer of 1964, Bundy explained to Valenti and Reedy why he felt the president should not have a press conference while the issue of reconnaissance flights over Laos was "still hot." He also prepared a statement for them on this matter that he felt would not upset the Laotian prime minister if they thought a press conference had to be given.[19] Similarly, in October 1965, Bundy advised Johnson on how he should handle his meeting with Pope Paul VI in light of the Vatican's statements about U.S. involvement in Vietnam. Bundy provided Moyers and Valenti with a copy of his memorandum to the president on this matter so that, in his own words, "they will know the diplomatic background as I see it."[20]

Normally, the president was included in the information flow between the aides. However, at least once he was left out and was subsequently upset about what happened. In September 1965, the State Department sent the NSC staff a draft presidential message regarding German reunification, to be read by Ambassador W. Averell Harriman during the Steuben Day Parade in New York City. The president was on the plane to Texas, so NSC staffer Hamilton cleared it with Moyers at the White House. A few days later, the president read about Harriman's statement in the newspaper and was, in the words of another NSC staffer, Francis M. Bator, "surprised to see himself in print." In light of Moyers's

pervasive influence in the White House, Hamilton had not felt it necessary to clear the message with Bundy, who heard about it only later, after Watson called from Texas expressing Johnson's annoyance.[21]

ACCESS TO THE PRESIDENT

Johnson was usually accessible to his staff. However, Bundy, as well as other senior staffers, on occasion apparently had difficulty getting through to the president. According to presidential scholar Richard Tanner Johnson, Appointments Secretary Watson

imposed a far more comprehensive grip on Johnson's calendar than O'Donnell had done with Kennedy's. Watson's surly gatekeeping brought him into serious conflict with Bill Moyers and McGeorge Bundy during the course of his service. This was exacerbated by LBJ's tendency to periodically require even his closest aides to go through Watson as a kind of purgative discipline.[22]

Clearly, it was Johnson himself who periodically cut off the access of certain members of the White House staff. According to McPherson, Watson always had to decide whether the president had the desire and time to see somebody. In no instance, said McPherson, did Watson cut off another staff member's access on his own initiative.[23] In any case, both Bundy and Rostow usually had a daily morning meeting with the president, anyway.[24]

Bundy's "paper access" to the president differed from Rostow's. Whereas Bundy often sent memoranda through another aide, Rostow sent his directly to the president.[25] This was probably because Rostow developed a closer personal relationship with Johnson.

Johnson's confidence in Rostow was also evident when other aides appealed to the national security assistant to present something to the president when their White House stature was diminishing. For instance, in September 1966, Rostow was informed by Moyers about a speech he had been writing on European policy. Moyers noted that such a speech would "go a long way to counter the charges that he [Johnson] is exclusively obsessed with Vietnam

and Asia" and asked if Rostow could "take it up with the President."[26]

Conversely, the president sometimes asked a political assistant to serve as a middleman for communications with Bundy. For instance, in April 1965, after Bundy, as well as some cabinet advisers, pressed for a presidential meeting with the Special Committee on U.S. Trade Relations with Eastern European Countries and the Soviet Union (known as the *Miller Committee*, after the Chairman J. Irwin Miller), Bundy wrote a memorandum to the president reading, in part: "Jack Valenti called me to say that you feel we are pushing you a little on this one."[27] On another occasion, after Bundy sent a memorandum to Johnson regarding the implications of the South East Asia Treaty of 1954 on contemporary U.S. involvement in Vietnam and allied responsibilities, Moyers wrote Bundy back:

The President asked me to tell you that this is not enough. He wants— "by the time I get up in the morning"—everything "that was pertinent in the SEATO debates, everything every Republican Senator and Congressman—and Democrats alike—said which indicates that SEATO requires us to give arms to SEATO countries or Protocol states. . . . Tell Mac to get that fellow [Director of Intelligence and Research] Tom Hughes out of bed over at State and make him do all this research tonight, and his people." And that, my unfortunate friend, is almost all verbatim.[28]

Johnson also sometimes asked Rostow to relay messages to the political aides. Once, after McPherson submitted a memorandum to Johnson advocating a halt to the bombing of North Vietnam on the basis of domestic politics, he received a call the next day from Rostow, who indicated that the president was aware of the various arguments in favor of a bombing pause, but had no intention of heeding McPherson's advice.[29]

One of the more significant questions about access during the Johnson administration is whether political assistants—especially Moyers—provided a "back door" for departmental officials, thereby detouring the national security assistant's allegedly biased filter of incoming information. Journalist David Halberstam has argued that Under Secretary of State George W. Ball sought the help of Moyers to get his memorandum "expressing his doubts" about the

diplomatic utility of bombing North Vietnam in the fall of 1964, since Bundy had not forwarded it. He futher noted that once Moyers did this, the president "encouraged it."[30] In fact, Ball did submit such a memorandum (entitled "How Valid Are the Assumptions Underlying our Viet-Nam Policies?") on October 5, 1964. But Johnson was busy campaigning and had left instructions that policy papers regarding the war were "not to reach his desk." It was on February 24, 1965—some five months later—that Ball revived the question of submitting the memorandum and appealed to Moyers. According to Ball, Moyers was "struck by it and insisted—as I assumed he would—on giving it to the President that afternoon."[31]

It would have been uncharacteristic for Bundy to have restricted a cabinet official's access. Indeed, he had forwarded a memorandum from Bell to Johnson on October 20, 1964, on another subject—the MultiLateral Force (MLF)—and noted in a cover memo that "Dean Rusk is signed on to it, and I have some reservations about it myself, especially as a proposal in light of the campaign. But I have an obligation to George to make sure you get it."[32]

So Bundy did not restrict Ball's access, the president did. Moyers did not serve as a "back door" for Ball. Instead, Ball sought to ally himself with Moyers since he knew they had similar views on the Vietnam War. Had it merely been a question of access, Bundy would probably have complied if Ball had asked him to resubmit the memorandum.

The legend of Moyers's "back door" was likewise alleged to have provided an information channel to the president while Rostow was national security assistant. The allegation was that Rostow, a staunch advocate of U.S. involvement in Vietnam, was filtering information, insulating the president from the "real story."[33] This notion was extended to other areas, particularly the Nuclear Non-Proliferation Treaty (NPT). According to journalist Patrick Anderson, Rostow, a supporter of the MLF, opposed the NPT. Anderson charged that officials who favored the NPT worked through Moyers, who "served as an alternative channel by which . . . [they] could get their ideas to the President."[34] In fact, by the time Rostow became national security assistant, he felt that the MLF was a dead proposal. Moreover, years later, when interviewed, he found it absolutely ridiculous that anyone would feel

that he prevented the president from seeing their position papers. He explained that he had, in fact, favored the NPT. However, he said that he did feel at the time that the NPT was something that could not be rushed or handled hastily since it posed constitutional questions for the non-nuclear weapons states that might sign and because the original demands of the Soviet Union could have been detrimental to the cohesion of the NATO alliance.[35] Hence, it seems that NPT advocates, who wanted to push the treaty faster than did Rostow, thought that it was prudent to ally themselves with Moyers. But it does not appear that Moyers was providing a heretofore nonexistent channel to Johnson.

THE TRANSITION PERIOD

Access to the president did become a problem during the interim between Bundy's resignation and Rostow's appointment (from February 28 to April 1, 1966). Moyers wanted Bundy's post, and Bundy had recommended to Johnson that Moyers become national security assistant. Shortly before he departed, Bundy advised the president that he should quickly appoint a successor, lest confusion develop, and that, until he did so, NSC staffer Robert Komer would serve as acting national security assistant.[36]

Johnson did not follow Bundy's advice. For one month there was no head of the NSC staff. When Rostow assumed the post, he found that Moyers and his aide, Hays Redman, had established a channel for foreign policy documents from the bureaucracy in addition to the regular NSC channel. It was at Secretary of State Dean Rusk's insistance, however, not Rostow's, that this channel was discontinued. According to Rostow, Rusk felt that numerous White House channels, for any executive department or agency documents, not just the State Department's, caused coordination problems.[37] But this channel was not established surreptitiously. The day after Bundy resigned, Moyers sent a memorandum to Bromley Smith, executive secretary of the NSC, which read: "The President wants me to receive a copy of all of the important memos, cables, etc., which pass to him in the international field. Will you take care of this?"[38]

During this transition period the question of Bundy's replacement resulted in appeals to various staff members by officials out-

side the White House. According to Valenti, after it became known that the president was considering the appointment of Rostow, Ambassador John Kenneth Galbraith called him for an "urgent appointment," during which he "cited a catalogue of laments about Rostow."[39] Nevertheless, Valenti recommended Rostow's appointment in a memorandum to the president on March 21, 1966, only days after Galbraith's appeal.[40]

FOREIGN AFFAIRS SPOKESMANSHIP AND DIPLOMACY

As he was during the Kennedy years, Bundy was asked by the president to be a public spokesman, particularly in defense of the administration's Indochina policy. Bundy's compliance in this regard was taken by Johnson as a sign of loyalty and did not create friction with the political aides. Perhaps one reason that was so was that Bundy regularly notified the press secretary about his media contacts.[41] Moreover, Bundy was considered a useful consultant for other White House staffers wondering how to handle foreign affairs journalists.[42]

But after Bundy left the administration, Johnson decided to downgrade the role of the national security assistant and shift toward a more State Department–centered foreign policy process. Accordingly, the president chose to have Press Secretary Moyers, rather than Rostow, be the administration's foreign policy spokesman.[43] However, within three months of his White House appointment, in the midst of Johnson's "credibility gap" and Moyers's fall from presidential grace, Johnson asked Rostow to appear at the Democratic Governor's Conference about the Vietnam War. Shortly thereafter he began appearing on shows like "Face the Nation" and "Issues and Answers."[44]

It was probably beneficial politically for the administration to have both a "hawk" and a "dove" appearing to have the president's ear, to serve as a "lightning rod" for criticism from both the left and right. It is likely that Moyers understood this; thus he was not annoyed when Rostow shared the foreign policy spokesmanship role. According to Rostow, he and Moyers had cordial relations the entire time they were in the White House together. Rostow's increased public visibility did not sour the relation-

ship.[45] After Moyers resigned Rostow did emerge as a more visible spokesman. But this probably reflected his attempt to fill the void created by Moyers's departure rather than an explicit attempt by Moyers to restrict Rostow's public spokesmanship while he was still in the White House.[46]

Accusations that Bundy was running foreign policy because of Johnson's alleged incompetence to do so prompted the president to demand that Rostow keep his diplomatic activities confidential and to a minimum, and Rostow complied.[47] Bundy departed before the question of who controlled foreign policy—the president or the national security assistant—became a major issue, thereby averting friction with political assistants. The mere hint that this could happen, and Rostow's awareness of it, probably helped to prevent tension within the White House while he was national security assistant.

INFLUENCE BECAUSE OF INTIMACY

Reportedly, Johnson once told Moyers and Bundy that he did not want them "ganging up" on him.[48] While not "ganging up," the two aides did ally themselves with one another on at least one occasion due to their common reading of domestic politics, national security considerations, and, most important, the president's personality. When Johnson was deciding how to explain to the public about U.S. military intervention in the Dominican Republic in April 1965, Moyers's and Bundy's mutual advice apparently prevailed over Secretary of State Rusk's.

After Ambassador W. Tapley Bennet, Jr., sent a cable to Washington saying that the lives of U.S. citizens were in danger because of a violent uprising in the Dominican Republic, both cabinet and White House advisers were unanimously behind the decision to send troops. Moyers and Bundy apparently told the president to refrain from alluding to a communist threat when he announced the intervention, mainly because they felt there was insufficient evidence to substantiate such an accusation. Rusk, on the other hand, felt the president needed to express his concern about the danger to "free institutions" as a veiled reference to the communist threat.[49]

Moyers and Bundy did this, as probably anyone else on the

White House staff would have, because they knew that Johnson tended to exaggerate and could quickly get himself into trouble. When asked about the advice of Moyers and Bundy during the Dominican intervention, Cater said: "I think in general all of us [on the White House staff] felt a certain degree of concern about the hyperbolic language of the president. . . . Johnson came from a storytelling background where he would exaggerate and add more to the next story."[50] McPherson, likewise, referred to Johnson as being a "hyperbolic sort of person."[51] Rusk, in contrast, probably did not realize, at least to the extent that White House staffers did, how difficult it would have been for Johnson to maintain a *veiled* reference to communism.

Moyers's and Bundy's concern was well founded. In his first statement to the nation explaining the landing of U.S. troops, Johnson said he had done so "in order to give protection to hundreds of Americans who are still in the Dominican Republic and to escort them safely back to this country."[52] But four days later, after criticism about the intervention mounted, he explained it by saying: "What began as a popular democratic revolution, committed to democracy and social justice, very shortly moved and was taken over and really seized and placed into the hands of a band of Communist conspirators."[53] The subsequent inability of the administration to document substantial communist involvement made Johnson appear to have overstated his case, to have overreacted to criticism.[54]

When Rostow was national security assistant, he and McPherson allied themselves in a passive way after the president asked them to write a speech to justify escalation of the bombing in Vietnam above the Demilitarized Zone in late October 1967. McPherson has written: "Neither of us, I believe, had much appetite for that—Rostow because he had other fish to fry, I because I was hoping to write about its termination. We postponed it until it was forgotten."[55] When asked about this, McPherson explained how Johnson tended to rattle off commands, sometimes out of anger or frustration, which experienced members of the staff knew should not be followed since they would harm both the nation and the president. He said that Johnson realized his staff knew him well enough so that such orders were a means for him to ventilate his emotions, and nothing was said of them later.[56]

CONCLUSION

In some respects, the Kennedy and Johnson administrations appear quite similar. Both relied heavily on *ad hoc*, informal coordination mechanisms. Both presidents had some of the same key officials serving under them. However, unlike Kennedy, during the Indochina conflict Johnson had to face substantial, continuous dissent and questioning—both inside and outside the administration—about some of the most basic foreign policy assumptions. Hence, the pitfalls of *ad hoc* coordinating mechanisms grew more apparent. By 1966, departmental officials (often at the assistant secretary level) complained about not having input into and not being informed about the administration's policies. A perception developed that the president was insulated from their views, that the national security assistant was sifting information headed to the Oval Office, and that it had become necessary for these officials to reach Johnson through another White House staffer: Moyers. In fact, the president was not insulated by either Bundy or Rostow, and any attempts to reach Johnson through another White House staffer were done for persuasive, not merely communicative, reasons. In any case, Johnson, like Kennedy, was a "talking president"; it was unlikely that he would isolate himself from information.

The key officials Johnson retained from the Kennedy administration were not "Johnson's men." But they developed cordial relations with Johnson's longtime aides, despite the president's personal style. Johnson periodically used fear and intimidation to motivate his staff. He did not develop an air of easy collegiality and cooperation to the same degree as his predecessor. Despite this, two of Johnson's senior aides, Moyers and Rostow—who had divergent opinions on the foreign policy issue with the most dramatic domestic political repercussions (the Vietnam War)—had cordial, friendly relations.

One main reason for the relative absence of intra–White House friction was Bundy's and Rostow's deference to cabinet secretaries' prerogatives. Hence, an NSC-State rift did not develop and become a political issue. Another reason is that the national security assistants' public spokesmanship did not endanger the president's popularity. Bundy resigned before his growing public spot-

light became a political problem for Johnson. Rostow became a lightning rod for criticism, and hence, his public visibility was probably more of a political asset than a liability for the president. Therefore, as during the Kennedy administration, the White House staff had no reason to try to reduce the national security assistants' public exposure.

One main advantage that White House aides have over cabinet officials is a better understanding of the president's personality and emotions. White House staff members might be able to caution a president about saying something during a public address that he would find difficult not to exaggerate, as did Moyers and Bundy regarding the announcement of the landing of U.S. troops in the Dominican Republic. White House staffers might also know when *not* to follow presidential orders that were delivered during a period of intense frustration or anger. Whether this is entirely beneficial is an open question. It is possible that Johnson's seeming overreaction four days after he first announced U.S. intervention in the Dominican Republic was related to a sense of frustration that he had not alluded to the communist threat the first time. It is also possible that two aides could feel so strongly about not doing something that they could convince themselves that a presidential order was made in a fit of anger, only to find out later that the president had made a sincere request.

NOTES

1. Doris Kearns, *Lyndon Johnson and the American Dream* (New York: Harper and Row, 1976), p. 251. On Johnson's decision-making style and treatment of his staff, see, among others, Richard Tanner Johnson, *Managing the White House: An Intimate Study of the Presidency* (New York: Harper and Row, 1974), pp. 159–198, especially p. 160; Eric F. Goldman, *The Tragedy of Lyndon Johnson* (New York: Knopf, 1968), p. 102; Patrick Anderson, *The Presidents' Men* (Garden City, N.Y.: Doubleday, 1968), p. 273; David Halberstam, *The Best and the Brightest* (New York: Fawcett Crest, 1972), p. 642; and Jack Valenti, *A Very Human President* (New York: W. W. Norton, 1975), p. 54.

2. Telephone interview with George E. Christian, Jr., Austin, Tex., 9 November 1984. See also Kearns, *Lyndon Johnson and the American Dream*, p. 249; and Stephen Hess, *Organizing the Presidency* (Washington, D.C.: The Brookings Institution, 1976), p. 100.

3. Oral history interview with S. Douglass Cater, Jr., 8 May 1969, Johnson Library, Austin, Tex., p. 20.

4. George Christian, *The President Steps Down: A Personal Memoir of the Transfer of Power* (New York: Macmillan, 1970), p. 208; Johnson, *Managing the White House*, p. 176; Nelson Lichtenstein, ed., *Political Profiles: The Johnson Years* (New York: Facts on File, 1976), pp. 105, 442–443, 496; David C. Humphrey, "Tuesday Lunch at the Johnson White House: A Preliminary Assessment," *Diplomatic History* 8 (Winter 1984): 81–101, especially pp. 87, 89–90; Lyndon Baines Johnson, *The Vantage Point: Perspectives of the Presidency, 1963–1969* (New York: Holt, Rinehart and Winston, 1971), pp. 149, 181, 195, 532; W. W. Rostow, *The Diffusion of Power: An Essay in Recent History* (New York: Macmillan, 1972), p. 358; Hugh Sidney, *A Very Personal Presidency: Lyndon Johnson in the White House* (New York: Atheneum, 1968), pp. 204–205; and Henry F. Graff, *The Tuesday Cabinet: Deliberation and Decision on Peace and War under Lyndon Johnson* (Englewood Cliffs, N.J.: Prentice-Hall, 1970), pp. 3, 21.

5. Johnson, *Managing the White House*, p. 176; and Lichtenstein, ed., *Political Profiles: The Johnson Years*, pp. 635–636.

6. Humphrey, "Tuesday Lunch at the Johnson White House": 94; McGeorge Bundy, Memorandum to Mr. Jack Valenti, 28 June 1965, National Security File, Aide File: Bundy, Boxes 18, 19, Folder: Luncheons with the President, Vol. 1, Part 1, Johnson Library, Austin, Tex.; Michael Amrine, *The Awesome Challenge: The Hundred Days of Lyndon Johnson* (New York: G.P. Putnam's Sons, 1964), p. 78; Lichtenstein, ed., *Political Profiles: The Johnson Years*, p. 619; Valenti, *A Very Human President*, p. 131; Anderson, *The Presidents' Men*, p. 313; and Goldman, *The Tragedy of Lyndon Johnson*, pp. 115–116.

7. Anderson, *The Presidents' Men*, p. 299; Amrine, *The Awesome Challenge*, p. 98; and Goldman, *The Tragedy of Lyndon Johnson*, pp. 122–124.

8. Telephone interview with S. Douglass Cater, Jr., Chesterstown, Md., 8 November 1984; Johnson, *The Vantage Point*, pp. 209–210; Lichtenstein, ed., *Political Profiles: The Johnson Years*, pp. 95, 396–397; and Anderson, *The Presidents' Men*, pp. 374–376.

9. Good relations are reflected in Valenti, *A Very Human President*, pp. 80–81; Rostow, *The Diffusion of Power*, p. 507; interview with Walt W. Rostow, Austin, Tex., 25 October 1984; and telephone interviews with George E. Reedy, Milwaukee, Wis., 4 November 1984; with S. Douglass Cater, Jr., Chesterstown, Md.; 8 November 1984; with George E. Christian, Jr., Austin, Tex., 9 November 1984; and with Harry C. McPherson, Jr., Washington, D.C., 9 November 1984.

10. Interview with Walt W. Rostow, Austin, Tex., 25 October 1984; and telephone interview with George E. Christian, Jr., Austin, Tex., 9 November 1984.

11. Said Reedy: "Quite possibly the resolution was a surprise to everyone [on the White House staff] except Bundy." Telephone interview with George E. Reedy, Milwaukee, Wis., 4 November 1984. David Halberstam has implied that Bundy sought to prevent the involvement of other White House staff members in the background deliberations about the resolution. He wrote that after Bundy informed Cater about it, Cater asked whether such an action was "a little precipitous" and said "I haven't really thought it through," and that Bundy replied: "Don't." David Halberstam, "The Very Expensive Education of McGeorge Bundy," *Harper's* 239 (July 1969): 34. When asked about this, Cater said it was inaccurate. He mentioned that while the resolution was being considered, his office was in the Situation Room (since he had just started working in the White House and there was a lack of office space) and he therefore attended NSC staff meetings and worked closely with Bundy. Telephone interview with S. Douglass Cater, Jr., Chesterstown, Md., 8 November 1984. Cater's involvement is reflected in Douglass Cater, Memorandum for McGeorge Bundy, 23 May 1964, National Security File, Aide File: Bundy, Boxes 18, 19, Folder: Meetings on Southeast Asia, Vol. 1, Johnson Library, Austin, Tex. Moyers and Valenti also worked closely with Bundy on this matter. McGeorge Bundy, Memorandum for the President, 9 August 1964, National Security File, Aide File: Bundy, Memos for the President 6/64–2/65, Folder: Vol. 6, 7/1 to 9/30, 1964, Johnson Library, Austin, Tex.; and Valenti, *A Very Human President*, pp. 139–140.

12. According to Christian, Rostow notified him about "any sensitive foreign policy question." Telephone interview with George E. Christian, Jr., Austin, Tex., 9 November 1984. On the coordination between the press office and the NSC staff, see W. W. Rostow, Memorandum for the President, 17 January 1967, National Security File, Name File: Rostow, Boxes 7, 8, Johnson Library, Austin, Tex.; and Christian, *The President Steps Down*, pp. 208, 211.

13. Telephone interview with Harry C. McPherson, Jr., Washington, D.C., 9 November 1984.

14. Interviews with Walt W. Rostow, Austin, Tex., 25 October 1984 and 8 January 1985.

15. Telephone interview with George E. Reedy, Milwaukee, Wis., 4 November 1984.

16. Horace Busby, Memorandum for Mr. Bundy, 9 October 1964, Aide File: Busby, Box 18 (1301), Folder: Memos for McGeorge Bundy, Johnson Library, Austin, Tex.

17. Bill Moyers, Memorandum for McGeorge Bundy, 22 December 1965, Papers of LBJ, Office Files of Bill Moyers, Box 6 (1341), Folder: Bundy Memos, Johnson Library, Austin, Tex.

18. Bill Moyers, Memorandum to the President, 24 January 1966; and McGeorge Bundy, Memorandum to the President, 26 January 1966, National Security File, Aide File: Bundy, Box 6, Folder: Vol. 19, Jan. 19–Feb. 4, 1966, Johnson Library, Austin, Tex.

19. McGeorge Bundy, Memorandum for the President, 11 June 1964, National Security File, Aide File: Bundy, Memos for the President, 6/64–2/65, Box 2, Folder: Vol. 5, 6/1–30/64, Johnson Library, Austin, Tex.

20. McGeorge Bundy, Memorandum for the President, 3 October 1965, National Security File, Aide File: Bundy, Memos for the President, Box 5, Folder: Vol. 15, Sept. 23–Oct. 14, 1965, Johnson Library, Austin, Tex. Vietnam was indeed discussed by Johnson and the Pope during their meeting. Johnson, *The Vantage Point*, pp. 379–380. Since Rostow's file was not yet open during this research, memoranda of this nature were inaccessible.

21. FMB [Francis M. Bator], Memorandum to McG.B. [McGeorge Bundy], 28 September 1965, National Security File, Name File: Bator Memos, Boxes 1, 2, Johnson Library, Austin, Tex.

22. Johnson, *Managing the White House*, p. 176. On one occasion, when Bundy entered the Oval Office, Johnson reportedly said, "dammit, Bundy, I've told you that when I want you I'll call you." Quoted in Anderson, *The Presidents' Men*, p. 273. Apparently, periodic restriction of access was part of Johnson's tendency to, in Kearns' words, "keep each of his assistants off guard, giving praise one day and taking it back the next, drawing close and then pulling away." Kearns, *Lyndon Johnson and the American Dream*, p. 249. See also Goldman, *The Tragedy of Lyndon Johnson*, p. 102.

23. Telephone interview with Harry C. McPherson, Jr., Washington, D.C., 9 November 1984.

24. Michael Solliday, "The Special Assistant to the President for National Security Affairs and the National Security Council: A Comparative Study of Presidential Decision-Making" (Ph.D. diss., Southern Illinois University, 1975), p. 165; interview with Walt W. Rostow, Austin, Tex., 25 October 1984; telephone interview with George E. Christian, Jr., Austin, Tex., 9 November 1984; W. W. Rostow, Memorandum for the President, 24 July 1968, National Security File, Name File: Rostow, Boxes 7, 8, Johnson Library, Austin, Tex.; and Thomas B. Morgan, "The Most Happy Fella in the White House," *Life* 63 (1 December 1967): 80A.

25. See, for instance, McGeorge Bundy, Memorandum to Valenti for the President, 27 November 1964, National Security File, Aide File: Bundy,

Memos to the President, 6/64–2/65, Folder: Vol. 7, 10/1 to 12/31 1964; W. W. Rostow, Memorandum for the President, 24 July 1968, National Security File, Name File: Rostow, Boxes 7, 8, Johnson Library, Austin, Tex.; and Morgan, "The Most Happy Fella in the White House," p. 80B. When the president was away from Washington, Bundy sent his daily summary of international events to the president via Valenti, who, Bundy noted in a memorandum to Johnson, "will not bother you with it unless you ask for it or unless there is a crisis." McGeorge Bundy, Memorandum for the President, 6 October 1964, National Security File, Aide File: Bundy, Memos for the President, Box 2, 6/64–2/65, Folder: Vol. 7, 10/1 to 12/31, 1964, Johnson Library, Austin, Tex. According to Valenti, he felt that one of his responsibilities was "to keep the Oval Office gate swinging open on easy hinges so that LBJ's men could freely express themselves to the president." Valenti, *A Very Human President*, p. 69.

26. Bill Moyers, Memorandum for Walt Rostow, 30 September 1966, National Security File, Name File: Moyers, Boxes 7, 8, Johnson Library, Austin, Tex.

27. McGeorge Bundy, Memorandum for the President, 28 April 1965, National Security File, Aide File; Bundy, Memos for the President, Box 3, Folder: Vol 10, April 15 May 31, 1965, Johnson Library, Austin, Tex. Johnson apparently felt besieged by conservatives on the matter of East-West trade. See Johnson, *The Vantage Point*, p. 471.

28. Bill Moyers, Note to "Mac," 8/19/65, National Security File, Aide File: Bundy, Box 4, Folder: Vol. 13, August 1965, Johnson Library, Austin, Tex.

29. Townsend Hoopes, *The Limits of Intervention: An Inside Account of How the Johnson Policy of Escalation Was Reversed* (New York: David McKay, 1969), p. 148. When asked why the president did not tell him this directly, McPherson said it was probably because Johnson was angry about this or something else. Telephone interview with Harry C. McPherson, Jr., Washington, D.C., 9 November 1984.

30. Halberstam, *The Best and the Brightest*, p. 603. See also p. 777.

31. Quoted in Larry Berman, *Planning a Tragedy: The Americanization of the War in Vietnam* (New York: W. W. Norton, 1982), p. 48.

32. McGeorge Bundy, Memorandum for the President, 20 October 1964, National Security File, Aide File: Bundy, Memos for the President, 6/64–2/65, Folder: Vol. 7, 10/7 to 12/31, 1964, Johnson Library, Austin, Tex.

33. See, for instance, Louis W. Keonig, "The Invisible Presidency," in *The Presidential Office*, eds. Sidney Wise and Richard F. Schier (New York: Thomas Y. Crowell, 1968), p. 36; and Kearns, *Lyndon Johnson and the American Dream*, p. 335.

34. Anderson, *The Presidents' Men*, p. 345.

35. Interview with Walt W. Rostow, Austin, Tex., 25 October 1984. On Rostow's views about the MLF and NPT, see Rostow, *The Diffusion of Power*, pp. 250, 377–384. Evidence that Rostow was not the information screen he has sometimes been accused of being is apparent in his own conception of his role. See ibid., pp. 364–366; and Morgan, "The Most Happy Fella in the White House": 80B. David K. Hall, referring to the basic theory that Rostow screened Johnson's information about the Vietnam War, has noted: "Conversations with NSC staff members who worked with Rostow, including those who had responsibilities for the war, suggest that he was hardly the systematic distorter of others' data and views which was painted at the time by many opponents of the war. There is no tangible proof that Rostow ever withheld from the President information on the war which challenged Rostow's views." David K. Hall, "The National Security Assistant as Policy Spokesman, 1947–1981" (Paper prepared for the American Political Science Association Convention, New York, 3 September 1981), p. 53.

36. Moyers's desire for the NSC post is reported in Valenti, *A Very Human President*, pp. 250–251; and Anderson, *The Presidents' Men*, p. 347. Bundy's suggestion that Moyers replace him is noted in McGeorge Bundy, Memorandum for the President, 2 February 1965, National Security File, Aide File: Bundy, Memos for the President, Box 2, Folder: Vol. 8, 1/1 to 2/28, 1965, Johnson Library, Austin, Tex. His advice that Komer should act in his place temporarily is noted in McGeorge Bundy, Memorandum for the President, 19 February 1966, National Security File, Aide File: Bundy, Box 6, Folder: Vol. 20, February 5–28, 1966, Johnson Library, Austin, Tex.

37. Interview with Walt W. Rostow, Austin, Tex., 25 October 1984. See also Hall, "Implementing Multiple Advocacy," p. 613; and Carroll Kilpatrick, "Johnson's 'Little State Dept.' Fades," *Washington Post*, 2 April 1966, p. A6.

38. Bill Moyers, Memorandum for Bromely Smith, 1 March 1966, National Security File, Name File: Moyers, Boxes 7, 8, Johnson Library, Austin, Tex. At the bottom is typed: "CC: The President, Bob Komer."

39. Valenti, *A Very Human President*, p. 251.

40. Ibid., p. 252.

41. Hall, "The National Security Assistant as Policy Spokesman," pp. 23–25; Anderson, *The Presidents' Men*, p. 272; and McGeorge Bundy, Memorandum for Mr. Moyers, 9 September 1965, National Security File, Aide File: Bundy, Box 4, Folder: Vol. 14, Sept. 1–22, 1965, Johnson Library, Austin, Tex.

42. See, for instance, [Horace] Busby, Note to "Mac," 11-10-64, Na-

tional Security File, Aide File: Bundy, Memos for the President, Box 2, Folder: Vol. 7, 10/1 to 12/31, 1964, Johnson Library, Austin, Tex.

43. Symbolically, Rostow was given the formal title "Special Assistant to the President" without "for National Security Affairs" at the end. This was meant to show how Rostow did not outrank other presidential assistants in international affairs. Hall, "Implementing Multiple Advocacy," p. 611. See also "Transcript of President's News Conference on Foreign and Domestic Matters," *New York Times*, 1 April 1966, p. 18.

44. Hall, "The National Security Assistant as Policy Spokesman," pp. 25–27.

45. Interview with Walt W. Rostow, Austin, Tex., 25 October 1984. See also Morgan, "The Most Happy Fella in the White House": 84.

46. For an alternative view, see David K. Hall, "The 'Custodian-Manager' of the Policymaking Process," *Report of the Commission on the Organization of the Government for the Conduct of Foreign Policy* [commonly referred to as the *Murphy Commission*], Appendix E, Vol. 2, Ch. XII (Washington, D.C.: Government Printing Office, 1975), pp. 100–119, especially p. 111; Hall, "Implementing Multiple Advocacy," p. 618; and Solliday, "The Special Assistant," p. 169.

47. Rostow, *The Diffusion of Power*, pp. 509–525; Hall, "Implementing Multiple Advocacy," p. 620; and Solliday, "The Special Assistant," p. 166.

48. Anderson, *The Presidents' Men*, p. 273.

49. Charles Roberts, *LBJ's Inner Circle* (New York: Delacorte, 1965), pp. 76, 207–211; Johnson, *Managing the White House*, p. 606; and Johnson, *The Vantage Point*, pp. 194–195. According to Anderson, after the violence came under control, Moyers and Bundy persuaded Johnson "to resist advice that he install a pro-U.S. military regime there." Anderson, *The Presidents' Men*, p. 336. McPherson did not consider this accurate. Telephone interview with Harry C. McPherson, Jr., Washington, D.C., 9 November 1984.

50. Telephone interview with S. Douglass Cater, Jr., Chesterstown, Md., 8 November 1984.

51. Telephone interview with Harry C. McPherson, Jr., Washington, D.C., 9 November 1984.

52. Quoted in Johnson, *The Vantage Point*, p. 196.

53. Quoted in Roberts, *LBJ's Inner Circle*, p. 210.

54. Ibid., 76, 204–205, 210–211. The extent to which Bundy allied himself with other members of the White House staff is, of course, difficult to decipher. On at least one occasion, a number of political assistants solicited Bundy's support, but to no avail. In early August 1964, after the Gulf of Tonkin incident, a number of White House aides asked

Bundy to side with them in their attempt to dissuade Johnson from justifying the first U.S. air strikes against North Vietnam on the basis of vague accounts of a night attack against U.S. destroyers. According to the president's military aide, Chester V. Clifton, Jr., Bundy's response to them was that he "couldn't fight the President any more." David K. Hall's interview with Chester V. Clifton, Jr., 25 October 1979, as reported in Hall, "Implementing Multiple Advocacy," p. 601.

55. Harry McPherson, *A Political Education* (Boston: Little, Brown, 1972), p. 423.

56. Telephone interview with Harry C. McPherson, Jr., Washington, D.C., 9 November 1984.

6

The Nixon Administration

Two aspects of Richard M. Nixon's background and personality are suggestive of how he organized his White House staff. First, he disliked interpersonal conflict. Although he could handle it in the broad public arena, face-to-face confrontation pulled at his emotions and made him uncomfortable. Hence, rather than establishing a national security policy system in which he listened to his advisers debate, he preferred to receive recommendations on paper and developed an elaborate "formal options" NSC system.[1] Second, as an avid reader of history, Nixon had developed strong ideas about the role of the United States in world affairs and the president's essential areas of influence in the U.S. political system. Frank Gannon, a White House Fellow in the Nixon administration, related that Nixon felt the chief executive "had to make a difference in foreign policy and that domestic policy would pretty much handle itself."[2] Nixon believed that key foreign policy initiatives—some of which were hazardous politically, such as rapprochement with the People's Republic of China—could be directed only by him. Hence, from the outset of the administration, he planned, in his own words, to "direct foreign policy from the White House."[3] This had implications for the duties assigned to his national security assistant and the behavior of the rest of the White House staff. For Nixon, a White House-centered foreign policy meant heavy reliance on the national security assistant, who was required to perform substantial diplomatic functions.[4] But as

the national security assistant's role was elevated, other White House aides sought to ensure that he did not receive undue credit for the administration's foreign policy successes lest the president's public image and political support be jeopardized.

NIXON'S STAFF

Nixon chose Henry A. Kissinger, a Harvard professor and consultant to the NSC during previous administrations, to be his national security assistant. In Kissinger, he found someone with whom he agreed philosophically and substantively about foreign policy, whose views he had read and respected in the area of nuclear strategy. Kissinger had already displayed rudimentary loyalty by providing Nixon's campaign team with timely information about the Johnson administration's Vietnam Peace initiatives during the 1968 presidential race. In addition, because Kissinger was a professor, lacked a political base, and, as a native of Germany, spoke with a foreign accent, Nixon and his aides felt he would not attract attention and with it credit for foreign policy initiatives.[5]

Nixon's foremost political assistant was Harry Robbins ("H. R.") Haldeman, an advertising executive who had served as an advance man for Vice President Nixon during the 1956 campaign. Subsequently, Haldeman served as a key strategist for Nixon's unsuccessful 1960 presidential campaign and 1962 race for the California governorship. In 1968, he managed the successful presidential campaign.[6]

Ronald Ziegler, who also had worked in Nixon's unsuccessful 1962 gubernatorial campaign, was recruited by Haldeman to be the administration's press secretary. John Ehrlichman, a college friend of Haldeman's who had participated in Nixon's 1960, 1962, and 1968 campaigns, had been a legal expert in land use and thereby developed an understanding of local domestic political problems. The president appointed him to be a counselor, but made him Assistant to the President for Domestic Affairs in November 1969, to parallel Kissinger on the domestic side.[7]

BOUNDARIES OF RESPONSIBILITY BETWEEN THE STAFF

Boundaries of responsibility within the Nixon White House were drawn rather stringently. According to Kissinger, there was "an

almost total separation between the domestic and foreign policy sides," drawn so rigidly as to be comparable to "prisoners in adjoining cells."[8] This delineation extended throughout the White House. The NSC staff interacted very little with the general White House staff.[9] The political aides understood that Kissinger was the expert in foreign affairs, and he did not claim to be knowledgeable about domestic politics.[10] His foreign policy province was respected generally by the president, who allowed Kissinger to hire NSC staff members despite Haldeman's admonitions that some of them were too liberal.[11]

But there were some overlapping areas. Having worked as advance men, Ehrlichman and Haldeman frequently planned Nixon's foreign travel agenda with Kissinger. Moreover, Ehrlichman sometimes worked with Kissinger on matters for which the foreign policy–domestic policy distinction was not applicable, such as those regarding energy.[12]

But it was Haldeman, much more than Ehrlichman, who handled the White House public relations apparatus and kept informed about foreign policy developments. Although he and Bryce N. Harlow, who was recruited to handle congressional liaison, tried on numerous occasions to get Kissinger to attend general White House staff meetings, Kissinger only grudgingly attended a few, later dropping them altogether. Nixon did not insist that he attend.[13] However, national security information was transmitted by other means. Haldeman usually attended Kissinger's informal foreign policy briefings with the president, interjecting his ideas about the political consequences of new developments or various options. He also occasionally attended NSC meetings. Haldeman at times even sat in for the president during some critical national security planning sessions.[14]

But Haldeman's main role was public relations. In that capacity he was instructed to keep a watchful eye on Kissinger. Initially, Nixon and his aides did not expect this to be a major task. They thought it unlikely that the national security assistant would become a public figure. Nor, in 1968, did Kissinger consider it a likely, or even desirable, development. Mindful of the media's merciless treatment of Johnson's national security assistant, Walt W. Rostow, Kissinger informed the president-elect that as an NSC consultant during the Kennedy and Johnson administrations he had refused interviews with reporters and planned to continue that

practice. Nixon enthusiastically agreed since he fully intended to manage all press functions with the help of Haldeman and Ziegler.[15]

KISSINGER AS A PUBLIC FIGURE

Despite these original intentions, Kissinger did not, of course, remain an anonymous public servant. There are three apparent reasons for this. First, Ziegler, who started as press secretary at age twenty-nine, was not a particularly experienced public spokesman. Second, it was felt that the burden of foreign affairs spokesmanship could not be given to Secretary of State William P. Rogers since he was a foreign affairs novice. This was, in fact, one of the principle reasons Nixon selected him. Finally, Kissinger was masterful with the media. His rapport with reporters, in contrast to the president's and the political aides' disdain and distrust for them, proved usually, but not always, to be a domestic political asset. Leonard Garment, a senior White House assistant and legal adviser, stated that "Kissinger was instrumental in terms of domestic politics because he sold foreign policy to the public."[16]

In contrast to McGeorge Bundy and Walt Rostow, Kissinger's policy spokesmanship originally was restricted to anonymous background briefings. But when Kissinger came into the public spotlight the president and his aides monitored him closely lest he, not Nixon, receive credit for foreign policy successes.[17] In accordance with his tendency to avoid face-to-face confrontations, Nixon asked Haldeman and Ehrlichman to convey to Kissinger his restrictions on press exposure.[18]

THE POLITICAL AIDES AS MIDDLEMEN: THE EFFECT OF STAFF RELATIONS ON ACCESS TO THE PRESIDENT

In addition to relaying presidential instructions, the political aides sometimes served as a channel through which Kissinger communicated with Nixon. Generally, Kissinger had no difficulty seeing the president and normally had at least one private meeting with him daily. Usually he spoke with the president on the phone or in person six or more times a day.[19] But sometimes when Nixon was angry with him, Kissinger's only access to the president was

through Haldeman. Such restrictions were not always for short periods, sometimes they lasted as long as a week.[20]

Other reasons, in addition to presidential disfavor, accounted for Kissinger's periodically restricted access to Nixon. While the president was preparing messages to Congress or a major speech, he did not normally take calls from Kissinger, regardless of the importance of the messages (such as news of an imminent North Vietnamese offensive in Laos and the decision of whether to begin B-52 strikes there).[21]

Haldeman, on occasion, did restrict Kissinger's access to the president *on his own initiative*. But this occurred only when the president was sleeping and Haldeman felt that Kissinger had insufficient reason for waking him. For instance, one evening in April 1970, Kissinger wanted to wake the president to tell him about the mechanical difficulties of Apollo 13. Since Haldeman did not consider it a foreign policy–related problem but instead something to be handled by the public relations staff, he prevented Kissinger from seeing Nixon, apparently thinking that a presidential statement could wait until morning.[22] In September of the same year, Haldeman prevented Kissinger from waking Nixon to inform him of preliminary reports that Egyptian President Gamal Abdel Nasser had died from a heart attack. Once the reports were confirmed, however, Kissinger was allowed to wake the president.[23]

Haldeman exerted no control over Kissinger's written memoranda to the president. Despite claims to the contrary, Haldeman only screened papers related to domestic, not foreign, affairs.[24] In fact, it is probably most accurate to consider Nixon's political aides, particularly Haldeman, as *facilitating* Kissinger's access to the president. Kissinger himself has stressed how Haldeman was instrumental in carrying his views to Nixon "whenever personal persuasion failed."[25]

Kissinger apparently had substantial confidence in the reliability of the political assistants' communication channel. Reportedly, during Vietnam peace negotiations, Kissinger used it as a means to communicate with Nixon so that he would be able to say to the North Vietnamese negotiator that he had not yet "spoken" with the president about a given proposal. And, hence, he would be able to say so with a straight face, with no hint of lying.[26]

Nor was communication the only aspect of the political aides'

middlemen role. Given Kissinger's growing prominence in foreign affairs, it was almost inevitable that he and Secretary of State Rogers would clash. When they did, the political aides often served as a buffer—in Nixon's words, as "a sort of DMZ" (De-Militarized Zone)—between Kissinger and Rogers and between them and the president.[27]

So, in many ways, the senior aides served as communication links and as peacekeepers, rather than restrainers of Kissinger's access or originators of White House conflict. And their relations with Kissinger, although they included intermittent, issue-oriented friction, were usually friendly. It seems that it was not until the 1972 presidential election year that the atmosphere between them soured.[28]

THE EFFECT OF ISSUE-ORIENTED FRICTION ON INFORMATION EXCHANGE

Some of the squabbles during the Nixon administration were predictable, and perhaps desirable. Ehrlichman and Kissinger feuded a few times about the size of the defense budget. Ehrlichman felt that more resources should be devoted to social programs and advocated cutting Pentagon appropriations whereas Kissinger felt that such cuts would leave the United States vulnerable.[29] The two assistants also clashed during the president's 1969 trip to Europe; Kissinger was interested in diplomacy, Ehrlichman was concerned about how Nixon's appearances would, in his own words, "play on the evening news back home."[30]

Another source of friction among staff members was the Vietnam War. The friction stemmed not from disagreement over military strategy *per se* but from differing opinions on how to handle the domestic reaction once the strategy was implemented. In fact, Nixon had made it rather clear to Haldeman, Ehrlichman, and Kissinger that the political aides would handle domestic discontent. In the spring of 1969, Nixon insisted that Kissinger keep Haldeman informed about the secret B-52 attacks on North Vietnamese and Vietcong sanctuaries within Cambodia. He felt that if news of the bombings was leaked (which it was),[31] then Haldeman would need to handle the likely public outcry. Similarly, at Nixon's request, Kissinger kept Ehrlichman informed about the

U.S. and South Vietnamese ground invasion of Cambodia in April 1970.[32]

Kissinger did not seem to appreciate having the political aides privy to sensitive international matters.[33] But, in both instances, Kissinger complied with Nixon's request and apparently gave the aides more detailed briefings than even they thought necessary.[34] These details were probably given as a means to ensure that Haldeman and Ehrlichman understood the foreign policy imperatives associated with each military action, perhaps in the hope that their knowledge of the international conditions would prevent parochial political counsel about the likely domestic response. Nevertheless, after four student protesters were shot at Kent State University four days after the ground invasion of Cambodia, Ehrlichman clashed with Kissinger on how to handle the domestic unrest. Kissinger argued that it should not cause a change in U.S. posture, advising Nixon not to make a public gesture about the tragic killings. Any such sign, he seemed to have felt, would endanger the image of resolve that was intended to further the prospects for ending the war diplomatically. In contrast, Ehrlichman suggested that Nixon announce a "National Day of Prayer" as an indication of "tacit support" for the goal of peace. In anticipation of the national protest in Washington planned for May 9, Ehrlichman argued that the president "make whatever gestures of communication were possible" whereas Kissinger vehemently opposed any conciliatory moves until the Cambodian operation was completed, saying that foreign policy should not be "made by street protests." Nixon, in agreement with Ehrlichman, held a press conference on the evening of May 8 to try to quell the discontent.[35]

THE SOURING OF RELATIONS

Despite intermittent, issue-oriented friction, staff relations in the Nixon White House remained cordial until late 1971. Prior to the revelation of his secret visits to the People's Republic of China in July of that year, Kissinger had not been the subject of frequent media attention. His background briefings were usually devoid of information needed for exciting news stories.[36] But this revelation, plus the erosion of his background cover, meant that, hence-

forth, Kissinger would sometimes be allowed to brief the press *on the record* and *for quotation*. Moreover, Kissinger had difficulty maintaining his "high-level administration official" cover; his "ground rules" were sometimes violated.[37]

Therefore, at this point, U.S. foreign policy could be attributed to Kissinger whenever it was consistent with his public statements but different from Nixon's perceived policy stance. This meant that it might be advantageous for Nixon's critics to attribute popular policies to Kissinger. Conversely, it meant that it might be politically beneficial for the president if an unpopular policy were depicted as Kissinger's.[38]

But what evolved does not appear to have been the White House assault on his person that Kissinger has alleged occurred.[39] The White House staff did occasionally attribute unpopular policies to Kissinger. However, there was no active conspiracy against him. Instead, the staff simply made little effort to protect Kissinger's image.

The first occurrence of this kind of behavior was in December 1971, when the United States "tilted" toward Pakistan, after India, armed with Soviet weapons, attacked first East Pakistan, where a separatist revolt ignited a brushfire war, and then the West Pakistan border. Both Nixon and Kissinger felt that the dependability of U.S. support was at issue and decided there was no choice but to "discourage Indian aggression and Soviet adventurism."[40] Shortly after the meetings of the Washington Special Actions Group (WSAG—the NSC "crisis" committee) on December 2, 4, and 6, syndicated columnist Jack Anderson published excerpts of the meetings that documented Kissinger siding with the Pakistanis.[41] Since a number of State Department officials previously had made public statements in support of India, reporters had reason to believe that there was dissension at high government levels about the U.S. stance.[42] Perhaps sensing an opportunity to not bear the blame for the unpopular stance against India, Nixon cut off Kissinger's access to him. Moreover, according to Kissinger, Press Secretary Ziegler "made no statement of [the president's] support [of what was being cast as Kissinger's policy], nor did he deny press accounts that I was out of favor."[43] Hence, it appears that rather than being "out to get" Kissinger, Nixon and his aides were, instead, not "out to save" him.

Nor does it seem that White House actions during the Vietnam peace negotiations were the underhanded public relations assault against Kissinger that he perceived them to be.[44] Instead, Kissinger apparently misjudged both Nixon's and South Vietnamese President Nguyen Van Thieu's perceived political constraints and pushed for a settlement before they were ready. Nixon then made it clear—publically, not through leaks—that he was not going to rush into a settlement.

Kissinger believed that the North Vietnamese had a sincere desire to land a settlement in October 1971, before the 1972 presidential election since, he reasoned, they thought Nixon would be more bellicose in his second term than he was in his first. However, it was likely that Nixon would have difficulty pursuing a tough negotiating posture during his second term. Congress was scheduled to reconvene on January 3, and there was ample evidence that a legislative rather than a diplomatic end to the war was imminent.[45] Kissinger, sensing the North Vietnamese oversight, felt it prudent to seize upon their "self-imposed" pre-election deadline. He viewed this deadline as an "ultimatum" that afforded the United States the opportunity to improve on Hanoi's October 8 settlement offer. Kissinger also feared the likely domestic response if the United States rejected the October 8 proposal and Hanoi went public with it, since it was, in large part, the same as previous U.S. offers.[46]

In contrast, Nixon and his aides thought a pre-election peace would be a political liability. When Kissinger returned from Paris on October 12 and informed Nixon of substantial progress in the negotiations, the president informed him that he did not feel a settlement was necessary for his reelection.[47] Haldeman stressed that an agreement would be a liability, arguing that it would alienate the Republican right and, regardless, would not be effective in attracting doves.[48] Also at this time, the White House received an intelligence report from the Pentagon alleging a North Vietnamese and Vietcong plan for a "massive land-grabbing operation" in the South after the proclamation of a cease-fire, to be accompanied by a "murderous bloodbath" of all opponents in the areas they controlled. If this happened, it would have infuriated conservatives as well as moderates and invited criticism that the settlement had been made hastily.[49]

After Thieu's intransigence became evident, which made it politically difficult to agree to the October terms, some of Nixon's aides appear to have leaked stories suggesting that a dramatic change in the peace negotiations was unlikely to occur prior to the election.[50] Kissinger, then in Saigon attempting to satisfy Thieu, was shocked when he heard about these stories. He began to sense that he was being set up to bear the brunt of criticism that would follow a breakdown of the negotiations. He also was concerned that Nixon and his aides might attempt to preempt Hanoi's publicizing of the settlement text by denouncing the provision contained therein for an election commission in the South as a North Vietnamese attempt for a coalition government (which it was not). While en route to Washington from Saigon on October 23, Kissinger cabled Nixon and suggested that if Hanoi published the text, he would "give a press conference, acknowledge the agreement, indicate that it represented major progress, but insist that some details remained to be worked out free of any artificial deadline."[51]

Hanoi publicized the text of the agreement on October 25, strongly denouncing "the Nixon Administration's lack of good will and seriousness" and demanding that the agreement be signed by October 31 (seven days before the election).[52] Kissinger was allowed to hold a press conference, his first televised appearance, to explain the breakdown of negotiations and to discourage speculations about peace. But, much to the chagrin of Nixon and his aides, rather than trying to quell such speculation, Kissinger created more of it by telling the press and many receptive public ears that "peace is at hand."[53]

Both the Kalb brothers and Kissinger have alleged that White House aides leaked stories at this time that said Kissinger had exceeded his authority in the October round, did not keep Nixon fully informed, and that the president later found legal errors in the draft and was not satisfied with it.[54] But such stories did not need to be leaked for reporters to write about differences between Kissinger and Nixon on the negotiations. After publishing an article in the *New Republic* to that effect and then being told by Kissinger that "whoever told you this, you should never put any credence into again," White House Reporter Osborne responded

that "nobody planted the notion with me; it was my reading of his [Kissinger's] and Hanoi's accounts of the October negotiations."[55]

Nixon felt he had been backed into a corner by the "peace is at hand" statement. His response, however, was made publically, not through covert leaks. Shortly after Kissinger's press conference, Nixon gave a speech in Ashland, Kentucky, and stressed that the war would not be settled until he was satisfied that the agreement would "discourage aggression in the future rather than encourage it."[56] On October 31, Press Secretary Ziegler told the White House press corps that Nixon would not be rushed into an agreement that did not offer "the best hope for lasting peace."[57] And on November 2, Nixon declared, during a televised campaign address, that "we are not going to allow an election deadline or any other kind of deadline to force us into an agreement which would be only a temporary truce and not a lasting peace. We are going to sign the agreement when the agreement is right, not one day before."[58] With statements like these, it did not take any stretch of the imagination to conclude that Nixon did not feel that peace was necessarily at hand.

Peace did not come before the election. At the beginning of the second term, one of Nixon's major challenges was to work rapidly before Congress cut off funds and to get an "honorable peace" by bargaining with an infuriated Hanoi and making it agreeable (if not in fact, in appearance) to an intransigent Saigon. The challenge of his political aides was to ensure that Nixon, not Kissinger, got credit for the settlement.

Because the president felt that stern handling of Hanoi was the best way to satisfy Thieu and Republican conservatives and believed it was the best posture for acquiring a settlement before war funds were cut by Congress, Kissinger's friendly treatment of North Vietnamese negotiator Le Duc Tho in front of reporters in late November (when the peace talks resumed) was not well received. The president sent Kissinger a cable, advising him to tell the North Vietnamese that he would not hesitate to take "strong action." The cable was accompanied with a rebuke from Haldeman, suggesting that Kissinger present a "sterner appearance" when being photographed with Tho.[59] Moreover, it appears that a number of

stories may have been planted that painted the president as being tough with the North Vietnamese and Kissinger as being soft with them.[60]

Planted or not, the stories had their effect. The South Vietnamese, it seems, decided to make the most of the presumed split between Nixon and Kissinger. For instance, a Saigon radio commentary argued: "Perhaps he [Kissinger] overplayed his hand as an assistant . . . [and] took one or two steps beyond his power to the point of overlapping that of the President whom he is serving. . . . The South Vietnamese people resolutely express their determination to oppose any more moves in the coming period."[61]

At the same time, Hanoi changed its bargaining position. On November 23, Tho suddenly revived his demand for Thieu's ouster and denounced all of Saigon's revisions to the October agreement. And by December 4, Tho withdrew nine of the twelve changes he had accepted during the November sessions.[62]

At this point, Kissinger was certain that Hanoi was ready to break off the talks and wait for a legislated end to the war by the U.S. Congress. On December 5, he sent a cable to Nixon explaining Hanoi's change in posture, implying that the talks should be broken off and that military escalation should be forthcoming to shock the North Vietnamese from their patient mood as they waited for Congress to act before resuming serious negotiations. He also suggested that the president appear on national television to explain the breakdown of the talks so as to rally support for the resumption of massive bombing of the North.[63]

Nixon, on the other hand, feeling that expectations had been unduly raised in the United States because of Kissinger's "peace is at hand" announcement, argued through Haldeman that the talks had to be continued or, if broken off, only "recessed." Moreover, if this happened, the cable specified that Kissinger would explain the reasons why the talks were broken off in a "low-key" briefing. According to Kissinger, "Haldeman was deputized to overrule me."[64]

Kissinger stressed in his cable back to Haldeman on December 6 that, without the support of the public, a congressional cutoff would certainly be forthcoming as a result of the resumed bombing (that would make the escalation a futile exercise), and, in his

opinion, "only the President" could adequately rally such support.[65] But Nixon and his aides were little inclined to have the
president take the blame for the breakdown of negotiations.[66] Because the press had painted Kissinger as overly conciliatory and
the president as the hard-liner, any breakdown of the talks and
military escalation would likely be blamed on Nixon and only add
to Kissinger's popularity.[67]

Therefore, on December 16, the author of "peace is at hand,"
went on national television to state that negotiations had broken
off. But Kissinger took pains to identify Nixon as the key to a
future settlement, mentioning the president fourteen rather than
three times during his "peace is at hand" announcement. Kissinger stated: "We have not reached an agreement that the President
considers just and fair. If we can get an agreement that the President considers just, we will proceed with it."[68] He mentioned
nothing about the resumption of the bombing.

On December 17, the mines in Haiphong Harbor were reseeded
and B-52s resumed bombing of the North. Despite Kissinger's
support for and indeed suggestion of the escalation, the press
identified him as being in opposition to it.[69] Kissinger apparently
felt some satisfaction, however, in seeing the White House staff's
alleged media efforts to create the impression of a split between
the president and him backfire, since the backfire now added to
his popularity.[70] As a consequence, he apparently decided not to
quell press speculation about his opposition to the bombing, if
indeed he did not encourage it.[71]

It appears that Kissinger leaked at least one article to this effect.
On December 31, James Reston published an article in the *New
York Times*, which stated that Kissinger was probably "opposed
to the President's bombing offensive in North Vietnam . . . [and
that he] would be more willing than the President to take a chance
on signing the ambitious truce terms of Oct. 26."[72] Both Haldeman and Nixon felt certain that Reston's "inside information" could
only have come from Kissinger. And, according to Haldeman, he
later found out that Kissinger had spoken with Reston on the phone
shortly before the article was published.[73] Following this incident,
the president instructed Chuck Colson, another aide, to monitor
Kissinger's phone calls, epitomizing the lack of trust that had developed within the White House.[74]

Finally, on December 26, after a massive B-52 raid, the North Vietnamese cabled Washington and indicated their willingness to resume negotiations. Kissinger met with Tho on January 8 in Paris and initialed the final agreement on January 23. By this time, relations within the White House had soured to such an extent that, according to Kissinger, when he returned from Paris to pick up his deputy, Alexander M. Haig, Jr., to join the president at Key Biscayne, his plane was ordered by the control tower to a "distant corner" of the runway at Homestead Air Force Base, "out of range of even telescopic lenses" of onlooking journalists.[75] Even after the agreement was signed on January 27, Nixon instructed members of his staff to keep an eye on his national security assistant so that the credit for the end of the Vietnam War did not "settle on Kissinger."[76]

IMPLICATIONS OF SOUR RELATIONS

The sour inner–White House relations were apparently consequential in other areas, including staff purges and the Strategic Arms Limitation Talks (SALT). After defeating George McGovern, Nixon decided that a massive change in executive branch personnel was needed to reverse the "historic pattern" of "an administration . . . [running] out of steam after 4 years, and then to coast, and usually coast downhill."[77] The post-election purge between November 28 and December 22 included fifty-seven "resignations" and eighty-seven personnel changes.[78] While making these decisions, Nixon was at Camp David with Haldeman and, for a while, with Ehrlichman. Kissinger spoke with the president in person twice and only "occasionally" on the phone.[79]

Kissinger was apparently somewhat reluctant to challenge Haldeman's counsel about personnel changes at this time. Kissinger did not attempt to prevent the purges of Central Intelligence Agency Director Richard Helms, Commerce Secretary Peter Peterson, and Arms Control and Disarmament Agency (ACDA) Director Gerard Smith.[80] According to one White House official: "Kissinger didn't fight . . . [the purge] because he was scared to death of Haldeman and didn't want to cross him. . . . His reluctance to oppose the purge . . . made [the negotiation of] SALT

II a lot tougher than it would have been otherwise. It lost momentum."[81]

Seemingly, before the purge Kissinger had been able to guide arms control negotiations on a "middle course" by balancing "liberal" ACDA positions with the "conservative" stances of the Joint Chiefs of Staff. After more conservative officials were placed at ACDA, Kissinger no longer had the balance, and his middle positions, which frequently were similar to those of the State Department and the Office of the Secretary of Defense, now appeared liberal.[82] As a consequence, in contrast to the carefully managed SALT I deliberations, the negotiating team at the Moscow summit in June 1974 was without an agreed State-Defense position, which contributed to the failure to make progress on controlling offensive nuclear weapons, the primary objective.[83]

TWO DIFFERENT SENIOR STAFFERS

Under normal circumstances, sour relations among the White House staff and publicized divisions between the president and an assistant can be handled by a purge, albeit with a loss of political capital. Kissinger was spared, however, probably as a result of the already substantial loss of Nixon's political prestige due to the Watergate scandal.[84] Instead of Kissinger being asked to leave, President Nixon announced the resignations of both Haldeman and Ehrlichman in May 1973, because of their involvement in the Watergate affair. By replacing them with Alexander Haig, Jr., and Melvin Laird, both of whom had extensive national security expertise, the White House environment became somewhat different.

Haig had been Kissinger's deputy before becoming Vice Chief of Staff of the Army in January 1973. He had been one of the few, if not the only, member of the NSC staff who had developed a close relationship with the president, largely as a result of his comradery with Haldeman and Ehrlichman.[85] Therefore, not only did he understand Kissinger's work habits and foreign affairs philosophy, he also understood the president's. With this in mind, Haldeman recommended that Haig replace him, and Nixon enthusiastically agreed.[86] Kissinger, however, was originally against the appointment since, he felt, "Haig's interest in national security

matters . . . [meant] there was the potential for rivalry on substance."[87] But after discussing the appointment with Nixon and receiving assurances that his "paramount role in foreign policy-making" would not be threatened, Kissinger gave his approval.[88]

Haig maintained the role as communication link between Kissinger and Nixon, but, because he either was not asked or had refused, he did not perform the function of delivering presidential reprisals as had Haldeman. Nor did Haig obstruct Kissinger's access to Nixon although there were times when he suggested that the president not be disturbed in the middle of the night in light of his "distraught" condition. Haig's delivery of messages was apparently both reliable and essential, faithfully conveying Kissinger's cables as Nixon's periods of seclusion proliferated during the Watergate crisis.[89]

In addition, quite distinct from Haldeman's practices, Haig conveyed news of confidential presidential matters about which he felt Kissinger should be informed.[90] According to Kissinger, if Nixon had ever planned to link foreign policy to Watergate, Haig would have informed him of it and given him a chance to comment. Eventually, at Kissinger's request, it appears that Haig was instrumental in convincing the president to make no reference to the scandal in his foreign policy addresses.[91]

Haig apparently also informed Kissinger about confidential presidential actions that might influence Kissinger's diplomatic efforts. On December 13, 1973, the president had met with Soviet Ambassador Anatoly Dobrynin apparently in the hope of landing a spectacular foreign policy breakthrough that might override the effects of Watergate. The president wanted news of the meeting kept confidential as evidenced by his denial of Haig's request for information about its substance. However, realizing that any news of U.S.-Soviet collusion might make Egyptian President Anwar Sadat have second thoughts about terminating his country's friendship treaty with the Soviet Union, Haig sent a cable to inform Kissinger, who was in the Middle East, about the meeting.[92]

But Haig was not disloyal to the president. In other cables to Kissinger, he stressed the importance of attributing credit for foreign policy initiatives to Nixon, especially during times of dramatic domestic developments linked to Watergate.[93] At one point

Haig drew together nearly 250 subcabinet officials and spoke at great length about Nixon's diplomatic initiatives.[94]

Haig's foreign affairs expertise, it seems, made it less burdensome for Kissinger to convince the president of the advisability of certain foreign policy options. Whereas Haldeman may well have delivered Kissinger's advice faithfully, Haig, perhaps, delivered it faithfully and *convincingly*, mainly because he was intimately aware of the reasons for Kissinger's advice and apparently agreed with it. This was particularly evident during the Yom Kippur War, when Kissinger worked through Haig to stress the timely necessity of sending matériel to Israel via air transport. In addition, according to Kissinger, he asked Haig to suggest to Nixon that diplomatic measures should quickly follow when the fighting ceased.[95] The two assistants also worked together in convening a WSAG meeting regarding the U.S. reaction to the possible deployment of a Soviet military contingent to the Middle East during the war. Both briefed the president on WSAG actions the following morning.[96]

In contrast to Haig, Melvin Laird's White House tenure did not fare so well with Kissinger. Relations between the national security assistant and the former secretary of defense were strained while Laird was at the Pentagon, and Nixon's appointment of Laird in June 1973 to fill Ehrlichman's post was probably viewed with trepidation by Kissinger. His fear that Laird would become a White House contender for influence in foreign affairs was given credence by Ziegler's announcement that Laird would "sit in on the National Security Council," as his predecessor never had.[97]

In at least one instance, it appears that Laird was successful in convincing Nixon to do something that differed from Kissinger's advice. In the summer of 1973, when both chambers of Congress passed anti-bombing amendments aimed at ending U.S. military involvement in Indochina, Laird, a former congressman, urged a "compromise" bill, convinced that the president's veto would eventually be overridden. On June 29, such a bill was passed by both chambers. It permitted the bombing of Cambodia until August 15, but banned *all* military activity in Indochina thereafter. Kissinger urged a veto, since he felt the bill would endanger the maintenance of the Vietnam settlement. Laird, however, con-

vinced Nixon not to veto it, probably arguing that it was the best possible compromise, given the sentiment in Congress.[98]

Although Laird and Kissinger periodically clashed over foreign policy substance, they were, according to NSC staffer Winston Lord, "worthy adversaries" who respected each other.[99] In fact, rather than trying to diminish Kissinger's influence in foreign policy, Laird suggested that Kissinger be made secretary of state.[100] Haig apparently agreed with Laird's assessment and took his views to the president.[101] This action may have been decisive, leading to Kissinger's appointment as secretary of state while retaining his post as national security assistant in September 1973.[102]

In the final days of the Nixon administration, Haig kept Kissinger informed daily about Watergate developments. Both men felt that an impeachment trial would create problems for U.S. foreign relations, and both knew that it would be essential that contingency plans be made for the almost certain presidential resignation.[103]

CONCLUSION

The experience of the Nixon administration illustrates the hazards inherent in having the national security assistant serve extensively as a diplomatic operative. To the extent that he emerges as a public, and, more important, *popular*, figure, the president's political assistants are put into an untenable position. It is probable that they will feel impelled to take measures to ensure that the president's popularity not be reduced when the national security assistant becomes a popular figure. Furthermore, even if the political assistants do not take such measures, the media and the public will probably assume that they have, and stories about a rift between the president and his national security assistant will proliferate. Such stories radically reduce the effectiveness of the national security assistant's diplomacy since the extent to which he operates with presidential authority is put into question.

Political aides, obviously, can serve as important channels of communication between the president and the national security assistant. If the aide has national security expertise, as did Haig, this arrangement, it seems, can quickly result in the formation of alliances when the aide delivers the information *convincingly*. It is

possible, of course, that the opposite could happen if the two assistants disagree on policy substance.

Rigid boundaries of responsibility can contribute to friction among the White House staff. There probably would have been more friction in the Nixon White House had the president not insisted that Kissinger keep Haldeman and Ehrlichman informed about national security developments, for example, during the escalation of bombing during the Indochina conflict. But the assistants still clashed on the basis of their near-exclusive areas of responsibility, much like cabinet secretaries are prone to do, as when Kissinger clashed with Ehrlichman over budget priorities. Just as Truman White House staffer George M. Elsey mentioned, the choice appears to be whether the president will have his conflict between cabinet secretaries while maintaining a staff of generalists, or, instead, have a staff of specialists who will clash over substantive issues. Staff friction of this nature, *on its own*, is probably not harmful for presidential decision making; debate over substance can often lead to a more thorough consideration of options. It can, however, seep into other areas where the maintenance of cordial staff relations is essential, such as when the political assistants provide a vital communication link to the president for the national security assistant.

NOTES

1. For descriptions of Nixon's difficulty in handling interpersonal conflict and his decision-making style, see Richard T. Johnson, *Managing the White House: An Intimate Study of the Presidency* (New York: Harper and Row, 1974), pp. 201, 213–215; Alexander L. George, *Presidential Decisionmaking in Foreign Policy: The Effective Use of Information and Advice* (Boulder, Colo.: Westview, 1980), p. 155; and Henry A. Kissinger, *White House Years* (Boston: Little, Brown, 1979), p. 481.

2. Interview with Frank Gannon, Washington, D.C., 10 September 1984.

3. Richard M. Nixon, *RN: The Memoirs of Richard Nixon* (New York: Grosset and Dunlap, 1978), p. 340.

4. Symbolically, the assistant's office was eventually moved from the basement to the first floor of the White House.

5. Nixon, *RN*, p. 323; David K. Hall, "The National Security Assistant as Policy Spokesman, 1947–1981" (Paper prepared for the Amer-

ican Political Science Association Convention, New York, 3 September 1981), p. 28; H. R. Haldeman with Joseph DiMona, *The Ends of Power* (New York: Times Books, 1978), p. 84; Kissinger, *White House Years*, pp. 25–26; and Henry A. Kissinger, *Years of Upheaval*, (Boston: Little, Brown, 1982), pp. 414–415.

6. Eleanora W. Schoenebaum, ed., *Political Profiles: The Nixon/Ford Years* (New York: Facts on File, 1979), pp. 261–263; and Stephen Hess, *Organizing the Presidency* (Washington: The Brookings Institution, 1976), p. 117.

7. Schoenebaum, ed., *Political Profiles: The Nixon/Ford Years*, pp. 182–183, 689.

8. Kissinger, *Years of Upheaval*, p. 77.

9. Telephone interview with Winston Lord, an NSC staff member, New York, N.Y., 27 September 1984.

10. Kissinger, *Years of Upheaval*, p. 78; and Dan Rather and Gary Paul Gates, *The Palace Guard* (New York: Harper and Row, 1974), p. 177.

11. Marvin Kalb and Bernard Kalb, *Kissinger* (Boston: Little, Brown, 1974), p. 81; David K. Hall, "Implementing Multiple Advocacy in the National Security Council, 1947–1980" (Ph.D. diss., Stanford University, 1982), p. 633; and Kissinger, *White House Years*, p. 12.

12. John Ehrlichman, *Witness to Power: The Nixon Years* (New York: Simon and Schuster, 1982), p. 290; and Kissinger, *Years of Upheaval*, p. 869.

13. Telephone interview with Bryce N. Harlow, Washington, D.C., 7 September 1984.

14. Telephone interview with John Ehrlichman, Santa Fe, N.M., 3 August 1983; John Osborne, *The Fifth Year of the Nixon Watch* (New York: Liveright, 1974), pp. 104–105; Kissinger, *White House Years*, p. 243; Ehrlichman, *Witness to Power*, p. 80; Haldeman with DiMona, *The Ends of Power*, p. 80; Nixon, *RN*, p. 451; Johnson, *Managing the White House*, p. 218; and Seymour M. Hersh, *The Price of Power: Kissinger in the Nixon White House* (New York: Summit Books, 1983), p. 372n. The book by Hersh will be used supplementally throughout the rest of this chapter and will not be used as a primary source since its reliability is a matter of considerable controversy, even more so than most memoirs.

15. Hall, "The National Security Assistant as Policy Spokesman," p. 28. According to Harlow, Kissinger told him at the beginning of the administration that he intended to fill the NSC position in a similar way as Eisenhower's National Security Assistant Robert Cutler had filled it. Telephone interview with Bryce N. Harlow, Washington, D.C., 7 September 1984.

16. Interview with Leonard Garment, Washington, D.C., 2 October 1984. As aptly put by the Kalb brothers, even though "the White House

inner-circle men did not join in the Kissinger boom, they were professional enough to recognize its political usefulness." Kalb and Kalb, *Kissinger*, p. 147.

17. Apparently, the monitoring of Kissinger's media exposure became so stringent that Haldeman and Ziegler counted the number of times
he mentioned Nixon's name when he spoke to the press. Herbert G.
Klein, *Making It Perfectly Clear* (Garden City, N.Y.: Doubleday, 1980),
pp. 309–310; Kissinger, *White House Years*, p. 1451; and Kissinger, *Years
of Upheaval*, p. 1078.

18. According to Ehrlichman: "Over the years I conveyed my instructions from the President to Kissinger forbidding Henry to appear on
television, to grant interviews on various subjects or to attend press functions." Haldeman likewise did the same, since, when Nixon "outspok-
ingly disapproved of Henry's self-aggrandizing leaks and posturing . . .
he almost never spoke to Henry about his unhappiness. Instead, he told
Bob Haldeman to chastise Henry." Ehrlichman, *Witness to Power*, pp. 310,
274–275. See also Kissinger, *White House Years*, pp. 21–22; Kissinger, *Years
of Upheaval*, p. 415; and Hersh, *The Price of Power*, p. 44.

19. Stephen R. Gaubard, *Kissinger: Portrait of a Mind* (New York: W.
W. Norton, 1974), p. 287; Hersh, *The Price of Power*, p. 44; and interview
with anonymous source, Washington, D.C., 7 July 1983.

20. Kissinger, *White House Years*, p. 456; Hersh, *The Price of Power*,
pp. 170–171; Roger Morris, *Uncertain Greatness: Henry Kissinger and
American Foreign Policy* (New York: Harper and Row, 1981), pp. 144–
145; John Schell, *The Time of Illusion* (New York: Knopf, 1976), p. 162;
and *Time* (8 June 1970):18.

Bob Woodward and Carl Bernstein argued that this restriction of access was usually presidentially directed. Bob Woodward and Carl Bernstein, *The Final Days* (New York: Simon and Schuster, 1976), p. 31. According to Kissinger, this restriction of access was used to keep him "in
the state of insecurity . . . [which Nixon felt] was essential to my sense
of proportion." Kissinger, *Years of Upheaval*, p. 415. In support of this
assessment, see Haldeman and DiMona, *The Ends of Power*, pp. 94–97;
and Bill Gully and Mary Ellen Reese, *Breaking Cover* (New York: Simon
and Schuster, 1980), pp. 133, 251.

21. Kissinger, *White House Years*, pp. 451–452. That Kissinger believed Nixon's isolation was his own doing, not Haldeman's, is indicated
on p. 48 of *White House Years*.

22. Kissinger, *White House Years*, p. 483.

23. Ibid., p. 927.

24. Those who have indicated that Haldeman had *complete* control over
the paper flow, including Kissinger's, include Michael Medved, *The Shadow*

Presidents (New York: Times Books, 1979), p. 322; and Woodward and Bernstein, *The Final Days*, p. 187. See also Hersh, *The Price of Power*, p. 103. In contrast, when interviewed, those who were in the White House considered this a ridiculous claim. Telephone interview with Bryce N. Harlow, Washington, D.C., 7 September 1984; with Winston Lord, New York, N.Y., 27 September 1984; and with Leonard Garment, Washington, D.C., 2 October 1984. The only influence Haldeman might have had on Kissinger's memoranda was relaying Nixon's request that they be kept brief. According to Frank Gannon: "The system reflected both Nixon's personality and desires. . . . One of the reasons Kissinger did so well is that he cooperated with Haldeman's system. . . . Kissinger . . . understood that that was the way to get Nixon's attention." Interview with Frank Gannon, Washington, D.C., 10 September 1984.

25. Kissinger, *White House Years*, p. 642. Apparently, Kissinger sometimes did the same with Ehrlichman, who said in an interview that if Kissinger "had something that he needed our help on, he would come to us [Ehrlichman and Haldeman] and ask that we go talk with the president about it." Telephone interview with John Ehrlichman, Santa Fe, N.M., 3 August 1983.

26. Haldeman with DiMona, *The Ends of Power*, p. 173. Another instance of Haldeman's role as a communications link, under other circumstances, during the peace negotiations is reported in Nixon, *RN*, pp. 746–747.

27. Nixon, *RN*, p. 433. Kissinger's similar perception of their role is reported in Kissinger, *Years of Upheaval*, p. 419; and Haldeman's in Haldeman with DiMona, *The Ends of Power*, pp. 175–179. Kissinger, who apparently thought that the aides were usually instructed by Nixon to side with him, asked them at one point for their cooperation in convincing the president to limit Rogers's freedom in the foreign policy arena. Kissinger, *Years of Upheaval*, p. 98; and Ehrlichman, *Witness to Power*, pp. 297–299.

28. Kissinger's generally friendly relations with the political aides is reflected in Kissinger, *Years of Upheaval*, pp. 94, 97, 970; Haldeman with DiMona, *The Ends of Power*, p. 84; Ehrlichman, *Witness to Power*, pp. 288–289; Medved, *The Shadow Presidents*, p. 322; and indicated during a telephone interview with John Ehrlichman, Santa Fe, N.M., 3 August 1983; Frank Gannon, Washington, D.C., 10 September 1984; and with Leonard Garment, Washington, D.C., 2 October 1984. When asked whether relations between the political advisers and Kissinger were generally cordial before the election year, when just before it Kissinger emerged as a *popular*, public figure, Winston Lord said that "it is fair to say [that relations soured around that time] . . . when Kissinger became a public figure.

I'm sure there were some in the White House, out of loyalty to the president, who resented Kissinger's publicity." Telephone interview with Winston Lord, New York, N.Y., 27 September 1984.

29. Kissinger, *White House Years*, p. 213; and Kissinger, *Years of Upheaval*, p. 93.

30. Ehrlichman, *Witness to Power*, p. 291.

31. *New York Times*, 9 May 1969, pp. A1, A6.

32. Kalb and Kalb, *Kissinger*, pp. 131, 159; Roger Morris, *Haig: The General's Progress* (New York: Playboy Press, 1982), p. 138; and Hersh, *The Price of Power*, p. 60.

33. When asked whether he did, Ehrlichman replied: "I'm sure he would rather not have done so, primarily because Henry really didn't want others involved in his work." Telephone interview with John Ehrlichman, Santa Fe, N.M., 15 May 1984. On Kissinger's sensitivity to being in control of national security information, see John Osborne, *White House Watch: The Ford Years* (Washington: New Republic Books, 1977), p. 127; Woodward and Bernstein, *The Final Days*, pp. 192–193; and Ehrlichman, *Witness to Power*, p. 295.

34. Kalb and Kalb, *Kissinger*, pp. 131, 159; and Hersh, *The Price of Power*, p. 60.

35. Nixon, *RN*, pp. 403, 458–459.

36. Gaubard, *Kissinger: Portrait of a Mind*, pp. 280–281.

37. In December 1971, Senator Barry Goldwater placed one of Kissinger's "anonymous" press transcripts in the *Congressional Record*, and the *Washington Post* refused to honor Kissinger's anonymity rule. As a result, according to John Osborne, "any attempt to continue . . . [the "a high-administration official" cover] as a regular practice would . . . [have been] futile and silly." John Osborne, *The Third Year of the Nixon Watch* (New York: Liveright, 1972), p. 187.

38. With the benefit of hindsight, Kissinger realized this. Kissinger, *Years of Upheaval*, p. 7.

39. For instance, Kissinger wrote that after his "secret trip to China in 1971 had destroyed my previous anonymity . . . the White House missed few opportunities to cut me down to size." Kissinger, *Years of Upheaval*, p. 7. See also p. 415.

40. Nixon, *RN*, pp. 526–527.

41. Apparently, Anderson got the WSAG minutes from a Navy yeoman assigned to the NSC. Ibid., pp. 531–532. However, in Osborne's judgment, the person who leaked the minutes "was shooting at Henry Kissinger. . . . It is this *official* whom I take to be a *high-ranking* rat." John Osborne, *The Fourth Year of the Nixon Watch* (New York: Liveright, 1973), pp. 2–3 (emphasis added). If this was true, then it completely dis-

proves the argument presented herein. This was Osborne's opinion. He reported no evidence to substantiate it.

42. On the official statements at State, see Nixon, *RN*, pp. 531–532.

43. Kissinger, *White House Years*, p. 918. In his memoirs, where he mentioned the press attacks against Kissinger surrounding the Indo-Pakistani war, Ehrlichman did not indicate that there was any presidential guidance to plant or deny them. Ehrlichman, *Witness to Power*, p. 307. According to the Kalb brothers, Kissinger felt that Ehrlichman and Haldeman "were then engaged in an intensive effort to undermine his position in the White House." Kalb and Kalb, *Kissinger*, p. 263.

44. Kissinger, *White House Years*, pp. 900, 918, 1424.

45. The Vietnam Disengagement Act, which would have required the withdrawal of all U.S. troops by Dec. 31, 1971, is but one example. See Kissinger, *White House Years*, pp. 1000, 1012, 1307.

46. Ibid., pp. 1305, 1312, 1324, 1348.

47. Ibid., p. 1362. Ehrlichman recalled that Nixon felt a pre-election peace would hurt him politically. Ehrlichman, *Witness to Power*, p. 312. In an interview with Hersh, Charles Colson, another political aide, said that: "Our great fear was that a settlement would let people say 'Well, we will elect a Democrat because Democrats always do more in peacetime.' The one thing was that we didn't want to appear to be exploiting, as Johnson had done in '68 with the bombing pause, which was so blatantly and transparently political." Hersh, *The Price of Power*, p. 591.

48. Kissinger, *White House Years*, pp. 1349, 1362.

49. Kalb and Kalb, *Kissinger*, p. 388; and Hersh, *The Price of Power*, p. 596.

50. See, for instance, Robert C. Toth, "U.S. Sources Deny Viet Breakthrough," *Los Angeles Times*, 19 October 1972, pp. 1, 8.

51. Kissinger, *White House Years*, p. 1394. See also pp. 1377–1378.

52. Ibid., p. 1397.

53. According to Ehrlichman, shortly thereafter, Kissinger "mounted a furious media blitz for several days . . . [which] described the course of the negotiations and repeated his prediction that one more negotiating session should wrap up the whole thing." Ehrlichman, *Witness to Power*, p. 312. Kissinger may have wanted the text published so as to force an agreement. Osborne was rather certain that Kissinger had provided some of the October agreement text to the *New York Times*. Osborne, *The Fourth Year of the Nixon Watch*, pp. 176–177. This is inconsistent, however, with what Kissinger wrote about his thoughts in anticipation of the consequences of the text being made public. Kissinger, *White House Years*, p. 1348.

54. Kalb and Kalb, *Kissinger*, p. 388; and Kissinger, *White House Years*,

pp. 1409, 1423. On page 1455, Kissinger indicated he felt that the political aides had done this on their own initiative, not at Nixon's direction.

55. Osborne, *The Fourth Year of the Nixon Watch*, p. 200. Inconsistently, Osborne later stressed that the impression of differences between Nixon and Kissinger were fostered by White House leaks at the direction of Haldeman and Ehrlichman. John Osborne, *The Fifth Year of the Nixon Watch* (New York: Liveright, 1974), p. 37. The important point, however, is that such stories did not need to be planted; they probably would have grown by themselves, regardless of the White House staff's actions.

56. Quoted in Hersh, *The Price of Power*, p. 608. For Nixon's feelings about the "peace is at hand" statement and his discussion with Kissinger about the Ashland speech, see Nixon, *RN*, pp. 705–707.

57. Quoted in Hersh, *The Price of Power*, p. 608.

58. Quoted in Nixon, *RN*, p. 707.

59. Kissinger, *White House Years*, pp. 1419, 1440; and Kalb and Kalb, *Kissinger*, p. 397.

60. See, for instance, "Last Chance for Tough Viet Agreement," *Human Events* (25 November 1972): 1, which quoted unidentified sources "in the highest councils of the government" as saying that "the President is irritated with Dr. Kissinger for having virtually concluded an agreement that the Communists—in the words of one critical observer—'can drive several thousand tanks through.' " See also Stewart Alsop, "Facts Hard and Soft," *Newsweek* (18 December 1972): 112.

61. Quoted in Kalb and Kalb, *Kissinger*, p. 398.

62. Kalb and Kalb, *Kissinger*, pp. 395, 400; and Kissinger, *White House Years*, pp. 1427–1429.

63. Kissinger, *White House Years*, pp. 1430–1431, 1446–1448.

64. Ibid., p. 1431.

65. Ibid., pp. 1431–1432; and Kalb and Kalb, *Kissinger*, p. 413.

66. According to Ehrlichman, when Haldeman asked him if the president should make an announcement about the deadlock in negotiations, he replied negatively, saying that "the president should explain successes. The staff explains failures." Apparently Treasury Secretary John Connelly, White House aide Chuck Colson, and Ziegler felt also that the President should not make the announcement. Ehrlichman, *Witness to Power*, p. 314.

67. On December 6, 1972, Nixon spoke with Haldeman and Ehrlichman about the possibility of appearing on television to announce the bombing and the breakdown of the talks. According to Ehrlichman, Nixon said, "Maybe he [Kissinger] just wants people to associate me with the failure." Ehrlichman agreed. *Witness to Power*, p. 315. See also Kalb and Kalb, *Kissinger*, pp. 413, 417.

68. Quoted in Kalb and Kalb, *Kissinger*, pp. 413–414; and Osborne, *The Fourth Year of the Nixon Watch*, p. 203.

69. Charles Colson decided to set the record straight shortly after getting out of prison for Watergate-related crimes. See Douglas Watson, "Colson Allegation Links Kissinger to Bombing," *Washington Post*, 8 February 1975, pp. A1, A6. Both Kalb and Kalb, *Kissinger*, p. 414; and Morris, *Uncertain Greatness*, pp. 190–191; suggested that Kissinger had spread "hints" that he disagreed with the bombing escalation.

70. William Safire, *Before the Fall: An Inside View of the Pre-Watergate White House* (Garden City, N.Y.: Doubleday, 1975), pp. 667–668.

71. Although he argued that he did not suggest to any journalist that he opposed the so-called Christmas bombs, Kissinger admitted that he "did little to dampen the speculation, partly in reaction to the harassment of the previous weeks, partly out of a not very heroic desire to deflect the assault from my person." Kissinger, *White House Years*, pp. 1423–1456. On page 1423, Kissinger indicated that he tried to warn Haldeman and Ziegler that their efforts to dissociate him from the president would eventually backfire.

72. James Reston, "Nixon and Kissinger," *New York Times*, 31 December 1972, p. E9.

73. Haldeman with DiMona, *The Ends of Power*, p. 95. This account is in agreement with the one provided by Safire, *Before the Fall*, pp. 667–668.

74. Charles W. Colson, *Born Again* (Old Tappan, N.J.: Chosen Books, 1976), pp. 79–80. The sourness of relations was also apparent in the feeling among the NSC staff, to quote Osborne, that "if anything good could come of Watergate it was the removal of Bob Haldeman and his California crowd from power in the White House." Osborne, *The Fifth Year of the Nixon Watch*, p. 83.

75. Kissinger, *White House Years*, p. 1468.

76. Klein, *Making It Perfectly Clear*, p. 391. Nixon's infuriation at the popularity of Kissinger's Vietnam peace diplomacy was evidenced in the president's angry reaction to the national security assistant's receipt of the Nobel Peace Prize and his and the president's *joint* nomination to be *Time* Magazine's "Men of the Year." Haldeman with DiMona, *The Ends of Power*, p. 84; and Kissinger, *Years of Upheaval*, p. 1455.

77. Quoted in Hess, *Organizing the Presidency*, p. 134.

78. Ibid., p. 135.

79. Kissinger, *White House Years*, p. 1408.

80. Hall, "Implementing Multiple Advocacy," p. 632; and interview with anonymous source, Washington, D.C., 7 July 1983.

81. Interview with anonymous source, Washington, D.C., 7 July 1983.

Contrary to this explanation, when asked about it, Ehrlichman said: "I am not aware of any reluctance on Henry's part to approach Nixon." Telephone interview with John Ehrlichman, Santa Fe, N.M., 3 August 1983.

82. Interview with anonymous source, Washington, D.C., 7 July 1983.

83. *New York Times*, 29 June 1974, pp. 1, 10, and 4 July 1974, pp. 1–3; and Hall, "Implementing Multiple Advocacy," p. 640.

84. Kissinger conceded as much in *Years of Upheaval*, p. 415. Consideration of Kissinger's purge within the White House is noted by William Safire, "Puppet as Prince," *Harper's* 250 (March 1975): 17.

85. Morris, *Haig: The General's Progress*, pp. 123–124; Kissinger, *Years of Upheaval*, p. 107; and interview with anonymous source, Washington, D.C., 7 July 1983.

86. Nixon, *RN*, p. 856; and Woodward and Bernstein, *The Final Days*, pp. 31–32.

87. Kissinger, *Years of Upheaval*, p. 108. That this was in fact Kissinger's concern rather than any dislike for Haig, as some writers have suggested (e.g., Woodward and Bernstein in *The Final Days*), is supported by Osborne's argument against the "loathing thesis" in Osborne, *White House Watch: The Ford Years*, p. 313.

88. Kissinger, *Years of Upheaval*, pp. 109–110, 415.

89. Kissinger, *Years of Upheaval*, pp. 415, 454, 480, 585–586, 804. Winston Lord indicated that Haig did not obstruct Kissinger's access. Telephone interview with Winston Lord, New York, N.Y., 27 September 1984.

90. Sharing his knowledge of the Oval Office taping system is but one example. Kissinger, *Years of Upheaval*, p. 110.

91. Ibid., pp. 110, 416–417, 543, 599. Both Presidential Assistant Leonard Garment and Special Counsel Alan Wright were instrumental also in this regard.

92. Ibid., pp. 771–772.

93. Ibid., pp. 567, 657.

94. Apparently, some of the officials who attended interpreted Haig's statements to be a "denigration" of Kissinger. Jules Witcover, "Nixon Directing Foreign Policy, Haig Reassures U.S. Aides," *Washington Post*, 25 May 1974, p. A11; and Morris, *Haig: The General's Progress*, p. 285.

95. Kissinger, *Years of Upheaval*, pp. 468, 479–480.

96. During the WSAG meeting, it was decided to give a firm indication of how strongly the United States opposed the potential Soviet move. United States strategic forces were moved from Defense Condition V ("Def Con V"—the lowest stage of nuclear alert) to Def Con III (the medium range). Nixon, *RN*, pp. 938–939; and Kissinger, *Years of*

Upheaval, pp. 582–593. See also p. 915, where another instance of Haig's advocacy of Kissinger's advice is reported.

97. Osborne, *The Fifth Year of the Nixon Watch*, pp. 104–105.

98. Kissinger, *Years of Upheaval*, pp. 356–359. Leonard Garment vaguely remembered the friction between Kissinger and Laird regarding this matter. Interview with Leonard Garment, Washington, D.C., 2 October 1984.

99. Telephone interview with Winston Lord, New York, N.Y., 27 September 1984.

100. Laird apparently told this to Kissinger (who did not know whether Laird told the same to Nixon) because he felt that Kissinger's position would soon become "untenable," given the dissatisfaction with his prominence—while merely a presidential assistant—among the executive bureaucracy and the Congress. Kissinger, *Years of Upheaval*, p. 420.

101. Ibid., pp. 4, 420.

102. The influence of Haig's advocacy is, of course, difficult to decipher. If Kissinger had no desire for the State Department post, as Haldeman has argued, then Haig's advocacy would seem to have been influential indeed. Haldeman with DiMona, *The Ends of Power*, p. 176. Nixon's recounting of his decision to appoint Kissinger as secretary of state is reported in *New York Times*, 13 May 1977, p. A8.

103. Tad Szulc, *The Illusion of Peace*, (New York: Viking, 1978), p. 789; Theodore H. White, *Breach of Faith: The Fall of Richard Nixon* (New York: Atheneum, 1975), pp. 11–12; and Kissinger, *Years of Upheaval*, pp. 1197–1198, 1205.

7

The Ford Administration

Having served in the House of Representatives for more than two decades, Gerald R. Ford knew the art of compromise and was comfortable with face-to-face debate. Although he retained the NSC machinery of his predecessor, he relied less on formal policy papers than on direct interaction with his advisers. His decision-making style did not require the long periods of solitude so characteristic of President Nixon.[1]

Nor did Ford search for spectacular foreign policy initiatives. He saw his role as bringing stability, honesty, and confidence in the wake of Watergate. And while he certainly had some knowledge about national security matters by virtue of his past membership on the House Defense Appropriations and Foreign Operations Subcommittees, he felt that his expertise was domestic politics, not foreign policy.

After President Nixon informed his vice president of his decision to resign, Ford immediately contacted Henry Kissinger, asking him to remain secretary of state and national security assistant.[2] But Kissinger was not to retain the preeminence he enjoyed in the Nixon administration. In addition to Kissinger's counsel, the president sought the foreign policy views of his political assistants and his "kitchen cabinet" of seven former congressmen and corporate leaders.[3]

FORD'S STAFF

Robert T. Hartmann—former minority sergeant at arms of the U.S. House of Representatives, Ford's foremost aide since 1969, and his first chief of staff during his vice presidency—was appointed presidential counselor, with cabinet rank, at the beginning of the administration. Hartmann headed the speech-writing staff and served as a senior political adviser.[4]

Donald Rumsfeld, a member of Ford's transition team, headed the White House staff. A former Illinois congressman, Rumsfeld had been instrumental in the transfer of House minority leadership from Representative Charles W. Halleck to Representative Gerald R. Ford in 1965. He served as director of the Office of Economic Opportunity and then as NATO ambassador during the Nixon administration. He replaced Haig as assistant to the president in September 1974.

Rumsfeld brought a trusted assistant, Richard B. Cheney, with him to the White House. Cheney had been an aide to both Governor Warren Knowles and Congressman William Steiger of Wisconsin before he worked under Rumsfeld during the Nixon administration. Within the Ford White House, he served as Rumsfeld's deputy.

John O. Marsh, Jr., like Rumsfeld, had once been a congressman and had served on Ford's transition team. He had also worked on Ford's vice-presidential staff. He headed Ford's office of congressional liaison during the administration.[5]

Ford's first press secretary, Jerald terHorst, resigned only a month into the administration, after Ford granted Nixon a pardon from criminal proceedings. To replace him, the president chose Ron Nessen, a former Vietnam War reporter and NBC correspondent who had covered Ford during his vice presidency.[6]

BOUNDARIES OF RESPONSIBILITY, INFORMATION SHARING, AND ACCESS TO THE PRESIDENT

Ford wanted his political advisers to participate actively in foreign policy-making. For instance, Rumsfeld regularly attended NSC meetings and did not hesitate to offer his advice on foreign policy

at such meetings or at other times.[7] At "crisis" NSC meetings—such as those concerning the seizure of the U.S. cargo ship *Mayaguez* on May 12, 1975—Rumsfeld, Hartmann, Marsh, Nessen, and the president's legal counselor, Philip W. Buchen, attended.[8]

Nessen was determined to improve the bitter relationship between the White House and the press corps that had evolved during the Watergate affair. He insisted that he be kept informed about both domestic and international matters and that it be his responsibility to decide what information would be kept from the press. Ford promised Nessen that he would be able to attend all but "private talks with individuals" and highly sensitive NSC meetings. Nessen was told that he would be regularly supplied with foreign affairs information.[9]

But Kissinger was neither accustomed to nor fond of sharing national security information with other members of the White House staff. Nor did he appreciate the fluid boundaries of responsibility in the Ford White House. He resisted having to clear NSC staff policy statements with Marsh's congressional liaison office or with Hartmann for "final editing" and did not like aides "dabbling" in presidential foreign policy speeches. Kissinger did not consider it necessary to seek the advice of the political aides or explain diplomatic strategy to them.[10]

The political aides objected to Kissinger's insistence on retaining his accustomed exclusivity in foreign affairs. Hartmann quoted Rumsfeld as stating at a White House staff meeting, referring to Kissinger as well as a number of other cabinet advisers: "Some people seem to think it's to their private advantage not to work with others. . . . Nobody should covet a particular area and keep others in the dark."[11]

Kissinger's reluctant disclosure of information particularly bothered Nessen, who not only had Ford's promise that he would be privy to national security matters, but also thought an inadequate flow of information hurt his effectiveness as a press secretary.[12] The press apparently agreed. According to John Osborne of the *New Republic*, the tight hold on information by Kissinger and his staff contributed to Nessen's "appearance of uncertainty in dealing with foreign affairs."[13]

Kissinger had a daily, private, often hour-long meeting with Ford. There is no evidence that other members of the White House

staff reduced the frequency of these private meetings or otherwise impeded Kissinger's open access to the president.[14] But some political aides were jealous of Kissinger's hold on Ford's time. More significant, however, was their concern that these private discussions jeopardized an effective policy process; that "snap decisions" made in such meetings were less enlightened than they would have been had other advisers attended.[15] Ford's aides were also concerned that Kissinger's policy papers contained one-sided views. According to journalist Laurence Leaman, "Rumsfeld told James Connor, the Cabinet Secretary, to balance Kissinger's . . . [position papers] with information and arguments from other senior White House assistants. Only then did he [Rumsfeld] send the documents to the president."[16] However, one former Ford aide doubted that Rumsfeld did this. In any case, given Ford's respect for Kissinger's opinions, the former aide said that additional opinions noted next to Kissinger's would have had little influence on presidential decisions.[17]

DISAGREEMENTS OVER INTELLIGENCE INVESTIGATIONS AND REFORMS

As occurred during the Nixon administration, there was disagreement in the Ford White House about how to handle public criticism. Much of the early public scrutiny focused on the intelligence community as a result of allegations of vast domestic civil liberties abuses and foreign covert activities. On December 22, 1974, Seymour Hersh wrote a piece in the *New York Times* asserting that the Central Intelligence Agency (CIA) had in the past engaged in pervasive domestic intelligence operations of dubious propriety and legality in the United States. Kissinger, apparently concerned that these assertions would cause a wave of congressional investigations that could leak sensitive information, sent a memorandum to Ford (who was in Colorado) suggesting that the administration not respond "in such a way as to give credence to the allegations."[18] According to one senior Ford assistant, the president was being urged by a number of the political advisers to become " 'Mr. Knight-in-Shining-Armor.' . . . The overall issue at that time was really sleaziness in government. The political types said that if the president defended the CIA he would be tarred

with a Watergate brush." The former aide said that the political assistants wanted Ford to separate himself from past CIA misdeeds. However, he said Kissinger and other NSC staffers convinced Ford that any attempt to make such a separation would probably be detrimental to the national security.[19] Rather than releasing the sensitive information, Ford decided to try to contain the political uproar by establishing a blue-ribbon commission to investigate the CIA's past activities, chaired by Vice President Nelson Rockefeller.[20]

Meanwhile, the disclosure of sensitive information by Hersh and others at this time resulted in demands by Republican conservatives to prosecute reporters who published articles containing top secret information. Because of the growing publicity about intelligence-related problems, Ford created a committee to coordinate investigations, the Intelligence Coordinating Group (ICG), headed by Mike Duval, a former Nixon staffer. Nessen was informed by Duval that the ICG was seriously considering the prosecution of three reporters for violation of the Signals Intelligence Act, which prohibits the publication of classified information obtained by use of electronic eavesdropping equipment. Nessen was concerned that any such prosecution would be disastrous to the president's reputation for openness with the press and would invite accusations that Ford was using the Act to cover CIA misdeeds. Hence, Nessen disagreed with Kissinger, NSC deputy Brent Scowcroft, and Secretary of Defense James Schlesinger, who favored prosecution of the reporters. As a consequence, Nessen, with the help of Duval, attempted to protect the president politically by keeping him insulated from the matter and posing it as merely a legal question. Nessen and Duval did not inform Ford of the proposed prosecution and forwarded the evidence to Attorney General Edward Levi, who concluded that too much sensitive information would be disclosed during a trial to justify prosecution. Levi therefore brought no charges against the reporters.[21]

Later in the administration, Rumsfeld, Marsh, Buchen, and CIA Director William E. Colby, as well as Ford's congressional colleagues, convinced the president to provide sensitive information to House and Senate committees investigating past CIA misdeeds since, they reasoned, holding it back would only prolong and exacerbate the domestic and international costs of the investigations.

Kissinger, as well as Scowcroft and Secretary of Defense James Schlesinger, were against the disclosure.[22]

FRICTION OVER DÉTENTE

The struggle within the White House over East-West relations began in early July 1975, after Ford declined an invitation to attend an AFL-CIO dinner in honor of Aleksandr I. Solzhenitsyn, a popular Soviet dissident. Subsequently, North Carolina Senator Jesse Helms wrote a letter to Marsh requesting an appointment to bring Solzhenitsyn to the Oval Office. Scowcroft, speaking on behalf of Kissinger (who was out of town), argued that a meeting with Solzhenitsyn, a foe of détente, would not be taken well by the Soviets and would endanger chances of achieving a second Strategic Arms Limitation agreement (SALT II). Ford decided, in his own words, "to subordinate political gains to foreign policy considerations," and asked Marsh to tell Helms that his schedule was "too tight" to meet with Solzhenitsyn.[23]

At least some members of the White House staff felt that they had not been consulted adequately prior to this decision, which turned out to be politically costly for the president. Some of them felt that Kissinger had failed to consider the domestic political implications when he advised that Ford not meet with the Soviet dissident.[24]

In any case, some of the political assistants subsequently sought to protect the president from accusations of being "soft" on the Soviets. A few weeks after Ford's refusal to meet with Solzhenitsyn, the president was scheduled to attend the Conference on Security and Cooperation in Europe, held in Helsinki, Finland. A number of U.S. ethnic groups and conservatives argued that Ford's attendance would constitute a "betrayal" of the "captive nations" of Eastern Europe. Therefore, in preparation for the president's address at the conference, speech writer Paul A. Theis asked his co-worker, John J. Casserly, to "fix up" Kissinger's draft and rewrite sections that left Ford open to domestic criticism. After doing so, Casserly contacted Dennis Clift of the NSC staff and informed him of the changes. According to Casserly, Clift became irritated and said that Kissinger's draft was "exact and precise for reasons."[25] As a consequence, Casserly confided in Theis, who spoke

with Hartmann, who not only retained Casserly's revisions but also invited Congressman Edward Derwinski, an outspoken opponent of Soviet domination of Eastern Europe, to add his ideas to the draft. This draft was revised substantially, however, in Helsinki by Hartmann and his assistant, Milton A. Freidman, just prior to the president's address.[26]

Just before the Helsinki conference, Hartmann refused to submit the draft of the president's departure address to the NSC staff. Anticipating that the speech would put the conference in an unfavorable light, Scowcroft drafted an entirely different speech and, in a cover memo, informed the president about his reservations of what he expected Hartmann's draft to say. Ford used Scowcroft's draft, not Hartmann's.[27]

During the Helsinki conference, somebody leaked stories to the press that Ford had been dragged to it by Kissinger. Ford himself wrote that members of his staff "intimated that it was 'another Kissinger deal that was forced down the President's throat'; they started making excuses for it, and this furthered speculation that the journey was ill-conceived."[28] One former staffer said that this may well have been the case, but added that he was certain that the "principle leaker" had been "one of Kissinger's lieutenants," who himself had strong views about Soviet domination of Eastern Europe.[29]

PORTRAYING PRESIDENTIAL CONTROL OF FOREIGN POLICY

The political assistants' concern about the image of Kissinger's primacy in foreign affairs was evident from the very beginning of the Ford administration. They advised, as "part of transition symbolism," that Ford convene the National Security Council during his second day in office. Kissinger, on the other hand, apparently felt an NSC meeting would send the wrong signal abroad and convinced Ford to call it off. Ford's advisers—Rumsfeld and Hartmann among them—saw this as a "symbolic danger of its own" and reversed the president's decision.[30]

But the objective of some members of the White House staff throughout the rest of 1974 was mainly to publicly emphasize Ford's *ability* to handle foreign policy. During the summit with Soviet

leaders at Vladivostok in November 1974, Nessen did not hesitate to inform reporters that Kissinger, during a casual conversation, had told him that Ford had a better negotiating style than Nixon.[31] And after Ford, without the assistance of Kissinger, briefed congressional leaders about the Vladivostok summit, John Osborne of the *New Republic* wrote that a number of Ford's aides were "pathetically proud" of how well the president handled it in Kissinger's absence.[32]

But by 1975, an attempt to project Ford's *control* of foreign policy began, often centering on the content of speeches. White House speech writers apparently resented Kissinger's dominant hand in writing the president's April 10, 1975, State of the World message. They felt that Kissinger had prevented Ford from including statements about the "disarray" and "mistakes" made during the Nixon administration and that Kissinger was "literally writing his own history."[33] Two days later, after meeting with Kissinger about their joint address at the American Society of Newspaper Editors, Ford felt impelled to tell his speech writers: "I don't want people to try to split us [Ford and Kissinger] apart or to allow it to seem that we might be apart on anything. Our policy statements have to be the same. We have got to coordinate the two speeches."[34] Therefore, the aides were asked to get Kissinger's comments on the president's draft, and Hartmann was reportedly told to take out a joke chiding Kissinger in an upcoming presidential speech for a House and Senate Republican fund-raising dinner.[35]

What particularly angered Ford were efforts by the White House staff, in an attempt to project the president's control of foreign policy, to make it appear that he and Kissinger *differed on policy substance.* He felt that the staff was attempting to do so both through his speeches and by planting stories in the press. As Ford has written:

In a well-meaning but misguided attempt to establish my credentials as a President who was knowledgeable about foreign policy, some members of my staff leaked stories to the effect that I had overruled Kissinger on several decisions. Reading such nonsense in the press upset me enormously. The stories were totally inaccurate—there was never a conflict of any significance between us.[36]

However, when asked about this, one senior White House staff member said:

I don't really quite understand that passage of his [Ford's] book. . . . There were a number of occasions in which Kissinger was overruled by the president and these stories were leaked to the press. But Ford did not reveal his dissatisfaction at the time. I can say that I participated in the so-called leaks very frequently and only once without the prior knowledge of the President of the United States.[37]

Political assistants were not alone in planting these stories. People outside the White House were leaking some of them. State Department Counselor Helmut Sonnenfelt reportedly did this at least once.[38] Furthermore, according to Casserly, some members of the White House staff believed that *Kissinger* promoted some of these stories, on the theory that they compelled Ford to praise Kissinger publicly (which he sometimes did) and that, at other times, Kissinger desired "to put some daylight" between himself and the administration's policy.[39]

In any case, continued media coverage of this topic did not require sustained effort by anybody: Once "planted" it tended to "grow" on its own. As aptly put by Osborne:

The Ford-Kissinger story is largely a media creation. It persists in print and in broadcasts mainly because journalists and commentators continue to be fascinated and to assume that their readers and listeners are fascinated with the supposition that Gerald Ford is taking charge of foreign policy in ways and to an extend that he didn't even attempt when he succeeded to the presidency and that Richard Nixon never attempted, either.[40]

But when the White House staff did plant stories about Ford's primacy, it was only a problem when aides leaked stories of substantive disagreements as a means to demonstrate the president's ultimate control. The approach Ford apparently preferred, and one that would have been infinitely better for foreign policy coherence, was to merely say that the president was in control and leave it at that. There was no need, Ford felt, to invent policy incoherence to project his primacy.[41]

Although Ford did not always emphasize his foreign policy control when the opportunity presented itself, he was rather clear about it to reporters, giving on-the-record answers, even early in the administration. For instance, on February 9, 1975, when asked by a *Chicago Tribune* reporter whether he had ever considered "what would happen to foreign policy if something should happen to Dr. Kissinger," Ford tensed up and answered with unusual emphasis: "I think first we are lucky to have a man of that outstanding capability available during this very critical period. I don't know just how the decisions were made before I became President, but I can tell you that the final decisions in these cases today are made by me." [42]

Usually, the White House staff sought to further this notion. For instance, according to Nessen, after hearing that Ford had been overheard saying that "in a short period of time I'm going to take over foreign policy myself," and then being asked by a reporter whether the president was "pulling away from Kissinger a little," the press secretary nodded his head affirmatively. [43]

But at least once, precisely the opposite happened: Ford asserted his primacy and an aide softened the message. On April 24, 1975, while en route to New Orleans to address students at Tulane University, Kissinger was bypassed in drafting some critical passages of the president's speech on the Vietnam War. The final lines, which included the statement that Vietnam is "a war that is finished as far as America is concerned," were typed while aboard the plane, on which Kissinger was not a passenger. [44] Afterward, while flying back to Washington, when reporters asked the president whether Kissinger had prepared or approved the speech in advance, Ford answered with an abrupt "No!" [45] Immediately thereafter, with Kissinger's probable reaction in mind and knowing that "there'd be hell to pay," Hartmann said, "Mr. President, I think you should explain that a draft of this text went through the regular system, including the NSC office, so we assume Dr. Kissinger or his deputy saw it." [46] Hartmann was correct that the text, except the last few lines, had been approved by Scowcroft. What he did not say was that those last lines had been left out, at Ford's request, and added later, since the president felt Kissinger would not have approved them if they had been included. [47]

Shortly thereafter, Rumsfeld reportedly convinced Ford to con-

vene two staff meetings to give Kissinger instructions about the content of several speeches the national security assistant was soon to deliver at international conferences.[48] In addition, during preparations for the NATO meeting in Brussels in May 1975, Rumsfeld proposed that *only* Ford, not Kissinger, conduct media briefings and that Kissinger be excluded from press photographs of the president and other NATO leaders.[49] But Ford did not always cooperate with the efforts of his aides to project his foreign policy primacy. Despite Rumsfeld's efforts about handling the media, Ford did not, to any substantial degree, downplay Kissinger during the NATO summit. According to Osborne:

> There is in truth a substantial, fairly widespread belief among some of the President's closest assistants that Mr. Ford *ought* to diminish his reliance upon and identification with Henry Kissinger. Where reports based upon private information to this effect go wrong is in jumping to the conclusion that the President is doing what some of his people think he should do. He just isn't. At the NATO summit sessions . . . and in press conferences there and elsewhere explaining the Ford purpose and performance, Kissinger figured as prominently as he ever has.[50]

On at least one occasion, when Ford did not cooperate with his political assistants in this regard, *Kissinger did*. After the national security assistant negotiated the Sinai agreement between Israel and Egypt in September 1975, some White House staffers thought it would be a good idea to televise Ford at Camp David in a phone conversation with Israeli Prime Minister Yitzhak Rabin and Kissinger in Jerusalem. Ford was given a statement to read, which looked to Osborne "as if it were something he [Ford] had nothing to do with," which stated that "I have constantly worked for this outcome" and only mentioned Kissinger's "tireless efforts" in the last sentence.[51] However, after reading the statement, Ford "evened matters" by saying: "Well, let me say, Henry, very very deep, very deeply, how very grateful I am for the tremendous effort you have made in this last round of negotiations. I know how long and hard and devotedly you have spent many, many hours not only with me but with Prime Minister Rabin and [Egyptian] President [Anwar] Sadat."[52]

Kissinger, who in Osborne's opinion was aware of the political

assistants' objective as well as Ford's own desire to be seen as in command of foreign policy, responded: "I appreciate this very much, Mr. President, and of course we have spent more time on the Middle East, you and I, than on any other problem." He later closed the conversation by saying: "Well Mr. President, we have worked together on this and your strong support and your leadership in your talks [in Salzburg and Washington] with Sadat and Rabin made this possible."[53]

KISSINGER'S LOSS OF THE NSC POST

Given Ford's desire to project his command of foreign policy, one obvious signal would have been to ask Kissinger to give up his NSC post. Instead of doing this immediately upon taking office, Ford waited fourteen months. At that point he apparently felt that enough time had elapsed, that the uproar surrounding Nixon's resignation had settled, and that asking Kissinger to step down would not hurt stability and continuity in U.S. foreign relations. Ford may also have weighed the persistent criticism of Kissinger's dual role by members of the Senate, although he later denied that congressional pressure was a decisive reason for his decision to ask Kissinger to resign from the NSC post.[54]

In any case, Kissinger's loss of one of his two hats does not appear to have been a "coup" by the White House staff. Had Rumsfeld been the one who convinced Ford to take away Kissinger's NSC post (as was alleged by some at the time) the president would probably not have called both him and Kissinger into the Oval Office at the same time on October 25, 1975, to tell them about Kissinger's changed status and Rumsfeld's appointment as secretary of defense.[55] According to one senior Ford aide, Kissinger's move from the NSC post had nothing to do with the White House staff. Instead, he said: "What happened is that Ford reached a point that he wanted to make the changes. It was sort of the end of the transition. It would have happened sooner if he would have come in [to the presidency] under different circumstances [i.e., without Watergate]."[56]

SCOWCROFT AS NATIONAL SECURITY ASSISTANT

Ford chose Brent Scowcroft to replace Kissinger as national security assistant. One difficulty Scowcroft encountered was handling the political advisers' apparent insistence that Ford not be seen as being dominated by Secretary of State Kissinger. In fact, a number of White House staff members—Nessen and Marsh among them—reportedly advised Ford to postpone announcing Scowcroft's appointment to the NSC post at the same time that Kissinger left it since Scowcroft "would appear to be Henry's handpicked successor."[57] Nevertheless, on November 3, 1975, Ford simultaneously announced Kissinger's resignation and his replacement by Scowcroft.

There was little danger that Scowcroft would overshadow the president in foreign affairs. Kissinger retained substantial clout and, at least as important, Scowcroft had a "careerist" perception of his job. He kept his contact with the media on an off-the-record basis and had no inclination to become a public figure.[58] However Cheney (who replaced Rumsfeld as chief of staff) and Nessen thought that one way to show that Scowcroft was not a "tool of Kissinger" would be to have him appear on a number of television programs. Neither Scowcroft nor Ford favored the idea. As Scowcroft later said: "Ford played an important role in keeping away from an NSC-State rift. If he had told me to go on 'Meet the Press' I would, of course, have done it."[59]

As with Kissinger, Scowcroft's personal access to the president was not obstructed by other presidential assistants. On the whole, it seems that Scowcroft's relations with the White House staff were better than Kissinger's had been, since he tended to grant them more active participation in the foreign policy decision-making process and to share sensitive information with them.[60]

There was one instance, however, when Scowcroft's failure to disclose sensitive information caused a clash with Nessen. After former President Nixon returned from his trip to the People's Republic of China in February 1976, he sent a report on U.S.-Chinese relations to Scowcroft, who read it, passed it to Ford, let CIA Director George Bush read it while at the White House, and then

sent it promptly back to Nixon. Since the White House press corps had daily asked Nessen about the trip, he was embarrassed to first read about the report in *Time* magazine and angrily left the White House with the thought of resigning. He had not been informed because both Cheney and Scowcroft felt that Nixon's trip would bring back memories of his pardon right before the New Hampshire primary.[61] An additional explanation, by a senior aide, is that Scowcroft

had researched it very carefully and had determined that, since Nixon was a private citizen, we would be liable to a Freedom of Information request. Therefore, if Nessen saw it they [the press] could get it. . . . [This] would have been extremely awkward, not only politically, but with what it revealed about the Chinese. But Nessen took it personally. This was a position of if he [Nessen] knew it, he either had to lie or give it away. He couldn't lie because sooner or later they [the press] would have found out and he would have been utterly destroyed as a press secretary. So, in a sense, it was to protect him, but he didn't see it that way at the time.[62]

Eventually, Cheney called Nessen and convinced him to return to the White House. Thereafter, Ford met with them and Scowcroft and reemphasized that Nessen was to be kept fully informed on all foreign policy matters.[63]

The presidential election caused friction on another occasion as well. In May 1976, some of Ford's political advisers were upset with Scowcroft for not persuading Kissinger to postpone his tour of South Africa. During the trip, Kissinger denounced apartheid, an unpopular stance among conservatives. The trip immediately preceded Republican primaries in several conservative Southern states.[64]

In one instance, Scowcroft cooperated with the political assistants, albeit passively, in convincing Ford not to do something that Kissinger, among others, thought he should do. At the Republican National Convention in Kansas City, Ford's aides sought Scowcroft's support in convincing the president not to fight the "Morality in Foreign Policy" plank introduced by Ronald Reagan. Among other things, the plank commended Aleksandr Solzhenitsyn for his "human courage and morality," described the Helsinki Agreement as "taking from those who do not have free-

dom the hope of one day getting it," and committed the Republican party to a foreign policy "in which secret agreements, hidden from our people, will have no part."[65] The plank obviously attacked the administration's foreign policy and the secretary of state's diplomatic style. It infuriated Ford, Rockefeller, Kissinger, and Scowcroft, all of whom felt that the president should fight it.[66] Nessen and Cheney, on the other hand, thought it would be politically damaging if it was opposed and was then passed by a convention vote. They felt that, if the plank was welcomed, "Reagan's effort to provide a test of strength would evaporate."[67] Eventually, Cheney and Nessen got Scowcroft to agree that it would not be damaging for Ford to *postpone* making a statement about the plank. When the president was told by Nessen that he, Cheney, and Scowcroft all agreed in taking some time to "sift through the political implications" before making a statement, Ford agreed, "grudgingly." In the end, Ford accepted the plank to avoid a floor battle.[68]

Finally, in the last days before the election, Scowcroft worked with both Cheney and Nessen in trying to persuade the president to retract the statement that he had made during his debate with presidential candidate Jimmy Carter that: "There is no Soviet domination of Eastern Europe and there never will be during a Ford administration."[69] Scowcroft, of course, instantly recognized the mistake and tried to "clarify" Ford's statement during a press briefing held immediately after the debate. But Cheney told Scowcroft that it would be unwise to interpret the president before talking with him.[70] The resulting delay meant that the mistake became front-page news, and it took five days before the aides could get Ford to acknowledge it.[71]

CONCLUSION

Even though Ford's aides were critical of how Kissinger handled his advisory role, without presidential backing they were powerless to do anything about it. The aides felt that policy should not be made in private meetings between the president and Kissinger. But those meetings persisted because that was what Ford wanted. Similarly, even if Rumsfeld "balanced" Kissinger's position papers by including the views of other advisers, it probably

had little effect on presidential decisions since Ford gave great weight to Kissinger's advice. Nonetheless, it is significant that Ford's aides considered ways to improve the decision-making process.

Because of Kissinger's prominence, Ford's control of foreign policy was questioned in the press. To counter this perception, Ford and his political assistants sought to project presidential command of foreign policy. However, despite Ford's specific instructions to the contrary, some aides leaked stories about disagreements between the president and Kissinger on foreign policy substance as a way of demonstrating ultimate presidential control.

Two apparent problems resulted because of Kissinger's retention of the position of national security assistant. First, Ford's aides were uneasy about Kissinger's attempt to retain the kind of exclusive reign over foreign affairs that he had enjoyed during the Nixon administration. Second, when Ford's aides thought it would be politically beneficial to criticize the foreign policies of the previous administration, Kissinger—who, of course, had a distinct "investment" in those policies—sought to prevent criticism of them. The resentment of this by members of Ford's speech-writing staff strengthened their inclination to project substantive differences between the president and Kissinger on foreign policy.

Scowcroft's sharing of national security information with other aides was more generous than was Kissinger's. However, as discussed above, on at least one occasion, he held back information from Nessen. Some of Ford's political aides wanted Scowcroft to become a public figure to counteract Secretary of State Kissinger's pervasive media visibility. Scowcroft resisted and Ford backed him.

NOTES

1. Ford's decision-making style is discussed in R. Gordon Hoxie, "Staffing the Ford and Carter Presidencies," in *Organizing and Staffing the Presidency*, ed. Bradley D. Nash (New York: Center for the Study of the Presidency, 1980), pp. 44–85, especially pp. 52–55; and Michael Medved, *The Shadow Presidents* (New York: Times Books, 1979), pp. 338–340.

2. Gerald R. Ford, *A Time to Heal* (New York: Harper and Row, 1979), pp. 30, 128–129; and David K. Hall, "Implementing Multiple Advocacy in the National Security Council, 1947–1980" (Ph.D. diss., Stanford University, 1982), pp. 641–642.

3. Robert T. Hartmann, *Palace Politics: An Inside Account of the Ford Years* (New York: McGraw-Hill, 1980), pp. 360–365; and Hall, "Implementing Multiple Advocacy," p. 643.

4. Ford, *A Time to Heal*, pp. 184–185; and Hoxie, "Staffing the Ford and Carter Presidencies," pp. 46, 51–52.

5. Hoxie, "Staffing the Ford and Carter Presidencies," pp. 48–49, 52; Eleanora W. Schoenebaum, ed., *Political Profiles: The Nixon/Ford Years* (New York: Facts on File, 1979) pp. 552–553; Ford, *A Time to Heal*, pp. 38, 147, 149, 186, 342; Lawrence Leamen, "Playing for Keeps: The Long Distance Race of Donald Rumsfeld," *Washingtonian* 12 (February 1977): 96; and Hartmann, *Palace Politics*, pp. 109–110.

6. Jerald F. terHorst, *Gerald Ford and the Future of the Presidency* (New York: The Third Press, 1974), pp. 183–184; Hartmann, *Palace Politics*, p. 288; Ford, *A Time to Heal*, p. 184; and Schoenebaum, ed., *Political Profiles: The Nixon/Ford Years*, p. 464.

7. After Cheney replaced Rumsfeld as chief of staff in November 1975, he, too, attended NSC meetings regularly. Interview with anonymous source, Washington, D.C., 25 July 1983; and John Osborne, *White House Watch: The Ford Years* (Washington: New Republic Books, 1977), p. 145.

8. Ford, *A Time to Heal*, pp. 282–283; Hartmann, *Palace Politics*, p. 325; and Ron Nessen, *It Sure Looks Different from the Inside* (New York: Playboy Press, 1978), pp. 127–128.

9. Ford, *A Time to Heal*, p. 184; and David K. Hall, "The National Security Assistant as Policy Spokesman, 1947–1981" (Paper prepared for the American Political Science Association Convention, New York, 3 September 1981), p. 37.

10. Hartmann, *Palace Politics*, p. 361; John J. Casserly, *The Ford White House: The Diary of a Speechwriter* (Boulder: Colorado Associated University Press, 1977), p. 42; and interviews with anonymous sources, 3 October and 17 October 1984.

11. Hartmann, *Palace Politics*, p. 361. See also pp. 329, 374.

12. Nessen wrote: "I frequently had run-ins with Kissinger because he believed that the truth should be shaded or withheld if that would advance his foreign policy objectives." Nessen, *It Sure Looks Different from the Inside*, p. 132. See also p. 352.

13. Osborne, *White House Watch: The Ford Years*, p. 185. As a consequence, wrote Hartmann, Rumsfeld and Nessen "tangled repeatedly with Kissinger about his fetish of witholding vital information from everyone except Ford himself." Hartmann, *Palace Politics*, p. 341.

14. Telephone interview with Donald Rumsfeld, Skokie, Ill., 13 July 1983; personal interviews with anonymous sources, Washington, D.C., 25 July 1983 and 17 October 1984; Hartmann, *Palace Politics*, pp. 201,

277, 362; Osborne, *White House Watch: The Ford Years*, p. 144; Ford, *A Time to Heal*, p. 150; and Casserly, *The Ford White House*, p. 42.

15. Hartmann, *Palace Politics*, p. 341; Osborne, *White House Watch: The Ford Years*, p. 144; and John Hersey, "The President," *New York Times Magazine* (20 April 1975): 108–109.

16. Leaman, "Playing for Keeps," p. 98. John Casserly, a White House speech writer, also noted Rumsfeld's dissatisfaction with Kissinger's lack of "giving Mr. Ford a balanced and objective picture of world events." Casserly, *The Ford White House*, p. 73. Nessen reported that he agreed with Rumsfeld's assessment that Ford "should seek advice on foreign-policy matters from a wider group than just Kissinger and the NSC." Nessen, *It Sure Looks Different from the Inside*, p. 132. Hartmann wrote that he "agreed with Rumsfeld, [Melvin] Laird [a member of Ford's "kitchen cabinet"] and others that a President needs foreign-policy input from a variety of sources." Hartmann, *Palace Politics*, p. 288.

17. Interview with anonymous source, Washington, D.C., 17 October 1984.

18. Quoted in Nessen, *It Sure Looks Different from the Inside*, pp. 54–56. See also William Colby and Peter Forbath, *Honorable Men: My Life in the CIA* (New York: Simon and Schuster, 1978), p. 16.

19. Interview with anonymous source, Washington, D.C., 17 October 1984.

20. Nessen, *It Sure Looks Different from the Inside*, p. 56; Ford, *A Time to Heal*, p. 230; and Colby and Forbath, *Honorable Men*, pp. 16–17.

21. Nessen, *It Sure Looks Different from the Inside*, pp. 66–67; interview with anonymous source, Washington, D.C. 17 October 1984; and Hartmann, *Palace Politics*, pp. 309, 399.

22. Colby and Forbath, *Honorable Men*, pp. 436–437, 450; and Hall, "Implementing Multiple Advocacy," p. 652.

23. Ford, *A Time to Heal*, p. 298. According to Casserly, the initial invitation was declined because "Kissinger wrote at least one (and perhaps more) memorandum to the President indicating that detente might suffer if Mr. Ford were to attend the AFL-CIO dinner honoring Solzhenitsyn." Casserly, *The Ford White House*, p. 126. Hartmann, in contrast, wrote that Ford declined the dinner invitation "for good and sufficient reasons unrelated to the Russians." Hartmann, *Palace Politics*, p. 338.

24. Interview with Paul A. Theis, a speech writer who worked immediately under Hartmann, Washington, D.C., 3 October 1984; and Casserly, *The Ford White House*, p. 126. In his memoirs, Hartmann's statement that he, too, urged the president not to see Solzhenitsyn is somewhat misleading in that he had merely opposed a meeting for July 3 or 4—the only days the Soviet dissident, according to the letter from

Helms, could see Ford—since the president had already planned to be away from Washington then. Hartmann felt, as a matter of principle, that Solzhenitsyn should have been able to conform his schedule to the president's. Hartmann, *Palace Politics*, pp. 337–338; and telephone interview with anonymous source, Bethesda, Md., 15 November 1984.

25. Casserly, *The Ford White House*, p. 131.

26. Ibid., pp. 130–133; Hartmann, *Palace Politics*, p. 339; and telephone interview with anonymous source, Bethesda, Md., 15 November 1984.

27. Interview with anonymous source, Washington, D.C., 17 October 1984.

28. Ford, *A Time to Heal*, p. 301. See also Hartmann, *Palace Politics*, p. 340.

29. Telephone interview with anonymous source, Bethesda, Md., 15 November 1984.

30. Hartmann, *Palace Politics*, pp. 185–186; and Richard Reeves, *A Ford Not a Lincoln* (New York: Harcourt Brace Jovanovich, 1975), p. 72.

31. Nessen, *It Sure Looks Different from the Inside*, p. 48.

32. Osborne, *White House Watch: The Ford Years*, p. 43.

33. Casserly, *The Ford White House*, p. 68. See also p. 60 for friction over an earlier speech. According to Hartmann, he once told Ford that the "Nixon guys" remaining in his administration were "understandably more dedicated to the vindication of their own records and provision for their futures than they are to *you*." Hartmann, *Palace Politics*, p. 389. Emphasis in original. Theis said: "There was always friction between Kissinger and the speech-writing staff. He [Kissinger] had his own ideas about what he wanted to say." Telephone interview with Paul A. Theis, Washington, D.C., 3 October 1984.

34. Quoted in Casserly, *The Ford White House*, p. 69.

35. Ibid., p. 70.

36. Ford, *A Time to Heal*, p. 355.

37. Telephone interview with anonymous source, Bethesda, Md., 15 November 1984. This is consistent with what Nessen has written: "I sensed that he [Ford] was not unhappy at all about the stories describing Ford's control of foreign policy as getting stronger and Kissinger's as getting weaker." Nessen, *It Sure Looks Different from the Inside*, p. 135.

38. Hartmann, *Palace Politics*, pp. 346–347.

39. Casserly, *The Ford White House*, pp. 38, 75. An example of Ford praising Kissinger subsequent to a wave of these stories is reported in Osborne, *White House Watch: The Ford Years*, pp. 110–111.

40. Osborne, *White House Watch: The Ford Years*, p. 142.

41. According to one senior staffer: "It was Ford [who was] in ultimate control. Ford did not mind when the political assistants emphasized

that he was in control of foreign policy. He had an ego, and it hurt him when people said Kissinger was running foreign policy instead of him." Interview with anonymous source, Washington, D.C., 17 October 1984.

42. Quoted in Osborne, *White House Watch: The Ford Years*, p. 104.

43. Nessen, *It Sure Looks Different from the Inside*, p. 133.

44. Ibid., pp. 107–108; and Casserly, *The Ford White House*, pp. 80–81.

45. Hartmann, *Palace Politics*, p. 322; and Osborne, *White House Watch: The Ford Years*, pp. 123–124.

46. Quoted in Hartmann, *Palace Politics*, p. 322. This account was confirmed by an anonymous former staffer in a telephone interview, Washington, D.C., 3 October 1984.

47. Hartmann, *Palace Politics*, pp. 321–323; Casserly, *The Ford White House*, pp. 80–81; and Osborne, *White House Watch: The Ford Years*, pp. 123–124.

48. According to Nessen, before then "Kissinger would have decided himself what to say in the speeches." Nessen, *It Sure Looks Different from the Inside*, p. 134. When asked about this, one senior Ford staff member said: "I have no recollection of that. Kissinger did not have to clear his statements through the White House staff." Telephone interview with anonymous source, Bethesda, Md., 15 November 1984.

49. Nessen, *It Sure Looks Different from the Inside*, p. 134. One former staffer said about this: "I can only say it does not sound untrue. . . . I know Rumsfeld and Kissinger had pretty much of a knockdown dragout [fight] during that [summit] . . . I know they had been at considerable loggerheads at that time. Part of it was that Rumsfeld was very seriously concerned that the president was taking a backseat to Kissinger. I supported him [Rumsfeld]." Telephone interview with anonymous source, Bethesda, Md., 15 November 1984. On the plane en route to the summit Nessen jokingly told reporters that Rumsfeld, who was experienced in NATO matters, would take the title of "senior American official" in place of Kissinger (who was not aboard the plane) when Rumsfeld spoke with them. Much to the chagrin of Rumsfeld, several reporters took Nessen seriously and wrote stories that Rumsfeld "was trying to cut in on Henry's turf." Nessen, *It Sure Looks Different from the Inside* , pp. 134–135. Hartmann, *Palace Politics*, pp. 341–342; Osborne, *White House Watch: The Ford Years*, pp. 143, 146; and Casserly, *The Ford White House*, p. 158.

50. Osborne, *White House Watch: The Ford Years*, p. 144. Emphasis in original.

51. Quoted in ibid., p. 183.

52. Ibid.

53. Ibid., p. 184.

54. Ibid., p. xxviii. Also see p. 218.

55. Ford, *A Time to Heal*, p. 326. According to Nessen, "Rumsfeld was often named as the one who secretly put Ford up to [having Kissinger give up his NSC post]. . . . Ford and Rumsfeld repeatedly denied this speculation." Nessen, *It Sure Looks Different from the Inside*, p. 160. *Newsweek* correspondent Russel Watson reported that one reason for Kissinger's loss of the NSC position may have been that "some presidential advisers complained that Kissinger was not responsive enough to domestic political needs, particularly in the demands he was making on Ford's travel time." Russel Watson et al., "Signs of a Big Shake-up," *Newsweek* (10 November 1975): 17. Apparently, Vice President Rockefeller felt that Rumsfeld was behind Kissinger's loss of the NSC post. Osborne, *White House Watch: The Ford Years*, p. xxiv. It is probably accurate that Rumsfeld continued to feel, as was the transition team recommendation, that Kissinger should give up his NSC position. This is reflected in Casserly, *The Ford White House*, p. 73. But this does not mean that he had a decisive influence in Ford's decision to do so in October. Although two senior officials contended that Rumsfeld might have had a hand in Kissinger's move from the White House, neither of them were certain of it. Both of them said also that Ford had always been slightly uncomfortable with Kissinger's "two hats." Interview with anonymous source, Washington, D.C., 19 October 1984; and telephone interview with anonymous source, Bethesda, Md., 15 November 1984.

56. Interview with anonymous source, Washington, D.C., 25 July 1983. This is consistent with what Ford told Osborne, that the reason was "that we had come to the point where there had to be an overall reorganization." Quoted in Osborne, *White House Watch: The Ford Years*, p. xxviii.

57. Nessen, *It Sure Looks Different from the Inside*, p. 158. See also Hall, "The National Security Assistant as Policy Spokesman," pp. 37–38.

58. Occasionally, Scowcroft gave presentations on national security policy in public forums that were unlikely to attract media attention. Hall, "The National Security Assistant as Policy Spokesman," pp. 36–40; Alexander L. George, *Presidential Decisionmaking in Foreign Policy: The Effective Use of Information and Advice* (Boulder, Colo.: Westview, 1980), p. 200.

59. Interview with Brent Scowcroft, Washington, D.C., 17 October 1984. See also Hall, "The National Security Assistant as Policy Spokesman," p. 40. One other senior administration official who had a vague recollection of this said: "Ford would not have stood for anyone pressuring Scowcroft to make public statements." Interview with anonymous source, Washington, D.C., 25 July 1983.

60. Interviews with anonymous sources, Washington, D.C., 25 July

1983 and 17 October 1984; and Hall, "Implementing Multiple Advocacy," p. 650. Hall claimed that there was friction between Scowcroft and the president's speech writers when Scowcroft resisted their attempts to insert phrases that made Ford appear to be taking a different stance than Secretary of State Kissinger. This was said to be inaccurate by an informed source. Referring to meetings regarding speeches with the president, Scowcroft, and senior speech writers in attendance, the former aide said: "I don't remember that being a part of our discussions." Interview with anonymous source, Washington, D.C., 17 October 1984. See Hall, "The National Security Assistant as Policy Spokesman," p. 38.

61. Osborne, *White House Watch: The Ford Years*, pp. 293, 310; Nessen, *It Sure Looks Different from the Inside*, pp. 201–202; and Ford, *A Time to Heal*, p. 360.

62. Interview with anonymous source, Washington, D.C., 17 October 1984. See also Nessen, *It Sure Looks Different from the Inside*, p. 202.

63. Ibid., p. 203; Osborne, *White House Watch: The Ford Years*, p. 302.

64. Philip Shabecoff, "Ford's Primary Losses Divide White House Staff as Factions Trade Charges of Laxity," *New York Times*, 24 May 1976, p. 18. One senior aide said that some members of the staff "thought it was a Kissinger ego trip" and criticized Scowcroft for supporting him. Interview with anonymous source, Washington, D.C., 17 October 1984.

65. Quoted in Ford, *A Time to Heal*, p. 398.

66. Ibid.

67. Nessen, *It Sure Looks Different from the Inside*, p. 230.

68. Ibid., pp. 230, 234; Hall, "The National Security Assistant as Policy Spokesman," p. 41; and interview with anonymous source, Washington, D.C., 25 July 1983.

69. Quoted in Osborne, *White House Watch: The Ford Years*, p. 416.

70. Interview with anonymous source, Washington, D.C., 17 October 1984. According to Nessen, after the debate Scowcroft said: "I think what the president was trying to say is that we do not recognize Soviet dominance of Europe," to which a reporter asked Scowcroft if he thought he should "issue a clarification on that," with Cheney responding: "No. I thought he [Ford] was clear in terms of what he meant." Nessen, *It Sure Looks Different from the Inside*, p. 271.

71. Ibid., pp. 271–272; Osborne, *White House Watch: The Ford Years*, p. 416; and Hartmann, *Palace Politics*, pp. 412–413.

8

The Carter Administration

Aside from six years in the Navy following his graduation from the U.S. Naval Academy in 1947, James E. Carter, Jr., had no experience in international affairs before he was elected president in 1976. However, while governor of Georgia, Carter acquired some knowledge of foreign affairs through his efforts to promote trade with the European Common Market and Japan. This made him a candidate for membership in the Trilateral Commission, whose distinguished political, business, and intellectual members sought to promote better economic and political ties between Western Europe, Japan, and the United States. Several of his Commission colleagues later provided him with foreign policy advice during his presidential campaign and subsequently filled numerous high-level posts within his administration.[1]

Trilateral Commission members Zbigniew Brzezinski and Cyrus Vance became, respectively, Carter's national security assistant and secretary of state. Brzezinski was a Polish émigré who headed Columbia University's Research Institute on Communist Affairs. A strong advocate for curbing Soviet influence in the world, Brzezinski became Carter's foremost foreign affairs adviser during the presidential campaign, and he prepared Carter for major speeches and debates on national security policy.[2]

Vance had also served as a Carter foreign affairs adviser during the 1976 presidential campaign. He had been secretary of the Army under President Kennedy and deputy secretary of defense under

President Johnson. Vance also had strong views about U.S.-Soviet relations, but he leaned toward a more cooperative approach than did Brzezinski.[3]

Differences between Vance and Brzezinski concerned Carter's transition advisers. They saw the potential for a State-NSC struggle similar to the one that plagued the Nixon administration.[4] Partly because of this, candidate Carter expressed his intention to rely less for foreign affairs policy on his national security assistant than on his secretary of state.[5] Likewise, after the announcement of his appointment as national security assistant, Brzezinski quickly and publicly stated that his responsibility would be "enhancing the decision-making process" and that the secretary of state would be the "primary adviser in foreign affairs."[6]

But Carter's decision-making style required what he called a "team approach," by which he sought a wide range of opinions from both his White House staff and cabinet secretaries. This approach was inconsistent with a rigid delineation of responsibilities between his secretary of state and national security assistant. Hence, despite initial declarations to the contrary, it was evident even at the outset of the administration that the national security assistant was unlikely to be relegated to the role of policy process custodian.[7]

Brzezinski, of course, soon assumed responsibilities far beyond "enhancing the decision-making process." Given Carter's inexperience in foreign affairs, he appreciated and encouraged Brzezinski's "tutorials." And the strong-willed former professor eagerly obliged. As international events, particularly those relating to Soviet behavior, seemed to Carter to substantiate Brzezinski's views of the U.S.S.R, the president relied increasingly on the advice of his national security assistant. Moreover, Brzezinski eventually became a key foreign policy spokesman for the administration to the public and to the media. Vance's disinclination to rebut administration critics made this role, in the president's eyes, even more imperative.[8]

As Carter's transition team had anticipated, the public visibility of the national security assistant created a political problem for the president just as it had for Nixon and Ford.[9] However, the response of Carter's White House staff to this problem was somewhat different than that of the two previous administrations.

CARTER'S STAFF: INTRA—WHITE HOUSE RELATIONS AND ACCESS TO THE PRESIDENT

Two of Carter's longtime assistants, Hamilton Jordan and Jody Powell, became particularly influential. Jordan, Governor Carter's executive secretary, managed the president's successful 1970 gubernatorial and 1976 presidential campaigns. At the beginning of the administration, he was appointed assistant to the president and served as a key political adviser. After Carter's "crisis of confidence" address in July 1979, Jordan was appointed chief of staff, a post he retained until June 1980, when he began working on the president's reelection campaign.

Powell had been an aide to Carter when he was a Georgia State Senator. He and Jordan had worked together during Carter's gubernatorial campaign. Powell then became the governor's press secretary, the same position he assumed during the presidential administration.[10]

Jordan initially resisted Brzezinski's appointment. He felt the professor's "establishment image" was inconsistent with Carter's grass-roots campaign image. But the two eventually became close friends. Likewise, Powell and Brzezinski developed cordial relations.[11]

Stuart E. Eisenstat was a much more seasoned political assistant than either Jordan or Powell. Eisenstat had worked on legislative proposals for President Johnson, Vice President Humphrey, and the Democratic National Committee. He had also advised Carter on state matters during his governorship and, then, helped coordinate his presidential campaign. Carter appointed him assistant for domestic affairs and policy, paralleling the post filled by John Ehrlichman in the Nixon administration.[12]

Much like Ehrlichman and Kissinger, Eisenstat clashed periodically with Brzezinski over budgetary matters, especially those related to the perennial trade-off between domestic and defense programs. Moreover, with a concern for domestic constituencies and a sensitivity to the Jewish lobby, Eisenstat and the national security assistant sometimes clashed when Brzezinski favored a strong U.S. response to continued Israeli settlements on the West Bank of the Jordan River.[13] But such occasional tensions did not result

in attempts by White House staff members to restrict Brzezinski's access to the president. In addition to his regularly scheduled morning briefing with Carter, Brzezinski was among the few—Jordan and Powell also among them—with open access to the Oval Office. The only slight influence other assistants exerted on Brzezinski's access was to shift the sequence of memoranda on the president's desk, putting theirs before his.[14]

MOVEMENT TOWARD INTEGRATION OF FOREIGN POLICY WITH DOMESTIC POLITICS

Consistent with his "team approach" to foreign policy decision-making, Carter eventually took measures to ensure that his political advisers were included in all foreign policy deliberations. Brzezinski might have resented this at first, but not later. At the beginning of the Carter administration, Brzezinski was of the opinion that foreign policy should not be tainted by domestic political considerations. But as the administration evolved and encountered a number of difficult political roadblocks to foreign policy initiatives, Brzezinski developed, in his own words, "a much higher awareness of the importance of domestic politics to our effectiveness."[15]

Likewise, the political assistants developed an awareness of the importance of anticipating and responding to domestic political repercussions of foreign policy actions. After witnessing vigorous senatorial reactions during the Panama Canal Treaty ratification process, Jordan, Powell, and other domestic advisers concluded from that point on that a concerted effort would be made to mobilize domestic support for the administration's foreign policy initiatives. Jordan warned Carter that too many foreign policy decisions were being made in a "political vacuum."[16]

Brzezinski not only considered domestic repercussions of foreign policy decisions; he often cooperated with the political assistants in mobilizing domestic support for these decisions. Jack Watson, who served as assistant to the president for intergovernmental affairs and eventually replaced Jordan as chief of staff, mentioned how Brzezinski, during the final stages of the Panama Canal Treaty ratification process, "worked very hard with all of us in getting the public and Congress behind it."[17] Brzezinski also

worked closely with Powell to ensure that the media gave Carter credit during the signing of the Camp David accords in September 1978.[18]

Brzezinski also became more cooperative with the speech-writing staff as the administration unfolded. Although initially both the speech-writing and the NSC staffs drafted foreign policy statements for the president, by October 1977, the two staffs worked on drafts together, albeit with the NSC having the final word.[19]

But it took a major foreign policy embarrassment before the administration actively sought the opinions of the political advisers *before* decisions were made. In October 1977, after first hearing on television about a proposed joint U.S.-Soviet peace initiative for the Middle East, which had been initiated by the State Department and approved by Brzezinski, a proposal that caused a furor throughout the Jewish community, Jordan persuaded the president to write Brzezinski a memorandum reminding him to coordinate foreign policy matters with the political advisers.[20] As Brzezinski later wrote, he had "erred in not consulting our domestic political advisers about . . . [the peace initiative's] likely internal impact."[21] Internationally, the initiative was not well received in either Egypt or Israel, and the Soviet Union complained about the subsequent move away from it by the United States.[22]

Yet after this political embarrassment Brzezinski still declined invitations by the political advisers to attend general White House staff meetings, and Carter did not insist that he attend.[23] Brzezinski reportedly said at the time: "There was a definite absence of coordination [within the White House]. People who want everything coordinated in advance may avoid domestic flak, but they run the risk of having nothing accomplished."[24]

In January 1978, Carter issued a written order that insisted that Jordan be privy to *all* significant national security developments and that Jordan would be expected to pay particular attention to the likely political impact of international events and foreign policy actions.[25] Moreover, Carter made Jordan a regular member of NSC meetings and Friday breakfasts. The latter were held exclusively for sensitive foreign policy matters. The only other regular breakfast attendees were Vance, Brzezinski, Vice President Walter F. Mondale, and Secretary of Defense Harold Brown. Powell sat in occasionally.[26]

PERSONAL VERSUS PRESIDENTIAL AGENDAS

Consistent with his "team approach," Carter delegated diplomatic responsibilities not only to his national security assistant but also to a number of political assistants. Brzezinski was supportive of the president's confidential emissaries as long as he felt they were in compliance with the administration's policy. For example, Jordan was involved heavily in the final Panama Canal Treaty negotiations and served as a confidential emissary in an effort to release the U.S. hostages taken captive in Tehran, Iran, in November 1979. In both instances, Brzezinski was supportive of Jordan and cooperated with him fully.[27]

In contrast, another presidential emissary, Robert Strauss, once clashed with Brzezinski. Strauss, a Texas lawyer and former Democratic party chairman, had served as Carter's special trade representative until being appointed special negotiator for the Middle East in March 1979. Apparently, Strauss thought Carter had given him carte blanche authority prior to his Middle East trip in August 1979. However, while en route to Israel, Strauss was handed an envelope by his traveling companion, NSC staffer Robert Hunter, which included detailed instructions for negotiating a settlement for Palestinian "autonomy" on the West Bank. Although the instructions were signed by Carter, Strauss was infuriated that Brzezinski had drafted them and, hence, in his judgment, was restricting his freedom to negotiate. Strauss did not hide his outrage to reporters on the plane, and the story drew wide publicity. The formula, as specified in the instructions, was rejected by both Israeli Prime Minister Menachem Begin and Egyptian President Anwar Sadat, perhaps due in part to the two leaders' awareness of Strauss's anger with his portfolio.[28]

The potential problem, from Brzezinski's point of view, was that Strauss might not have adhered to the administration's firm line with Israel on the settlement issue. In fact, when given the Middle East assignment, Strauss had stressed how pressuring Israel would be politically damaging for Carter. When interviewed, two former high-level officials in the Carter White House mentioned that the president, as well as Brzezinski, felt that Strauss needed to be reminded of the administration's position before

meeting with Israeli and Egyptian officials.[29] However, it seems that Brzezinski also wanted to push his views a bit since the message was given to Strauss while in flight because Brzezinski feared that otherwise, in his own words, "Strauss would phone the President to try to obtain alternative instructions."[30]

The dissemination of sensitive information was also a point of contention when Brzezinski questioned a political assistant's objectives for acquiring it. At one point Brzezinski prevented Eisenstat and other members of the domestic policy staff from entering the Situation Room to see sensitive cables about the Middle East. When interviewed, Brzezinski explained why he felt this had been necessary. He said that the domestic policy advisers often need information because they genuinely want to help the president attain his objectives. However, there are other times when they want to know certain things because they sympathize with a particular interest group. When this is the case, he explained, they do not want to *help* the president, but want to *influence* him. He agreed with NSC Middle East specialist William B. Quandt's distinction in this regard between "need to know" information and "want to know" information, as it is commonly referred to in the intelligence community.[31]

Eisenstat saw it differently. Although he did not question Brzezinski's *authority* to restrict his access to the Situation Room (nor did he appeal to the president about the matter), he did question the *advisability* of cutting off his information. He said that it was "on a highly irregular basis" that he needed to see the cable traffic, only during "sensitive political times."[32]

INFLUENTIAL ALLIANCES

Brzezinski was able to increase his influence vis-à-vis the secretary of state partly because he acquired the help of the president's political advisers. The following quote from Brzezinski's memoirs is revealing:

Secretaries of State frequently have difficulties with . . . [the president's political advisers]. During my service in the White House, I initially tried to resist their involvement in truly sensitive matters, but as the months went on, I discovered that it was actually helpful to forge an alliance with

. . . [them]. More attuned to domestic sentiment, they tended to be more "hard-nosed" than the foreign affairs experts produced by academia or diplomacy, and certainly better able to judge what was both feasible and desirable from the standpoint of domestic political support. On more than one occasion I would note in my journal that on key issues both Jody Powell and Ham Jordan were willing to urge the President to adopt a firmer line.[33]

Indeed, according to Watson: "I think that Zbig got along well with Jody and Hamilton and had their confidence. . . . Had that not been the case, I think Zbig would have had problems."[34]

On numerous occasions, Brzezinski added weight to his advice via these alliances. For instance, in July 1978, after the Soviet Union decided to put two of its most prominent dissidents on trial, Alexander Ginzburg and Anatoly Shcharansky, Brzezinski and some other presidential assistants proposed that selected U.S. technology transfers to the Soviet Union be restricted. Eventually, Secretary of Defense Brown also sided with Brzezinski. In contrast, Vance insisted that public criticism would suffice. On July 18, Carter decided to reestablish controls on exports to the Soviet Union on oil production technology, to defer decision about licence applications for an electron-beam welder and drill-bit factory, and to prevent the export of an advanced computer to Moscow for the 1980 Olympics. According to Brzezinski, he had "no doubt" that he and Brown "would have lost the argument if it were not for the very decisive intervention by our domestic advisers."[35] Apparently, both Powell and Public Relations Aide Gerald Rafshoon convinced the president that his credibility would suffer unless he took a strong stand. And indeed, when Carter informed congressional leaders about his decision, they responded favorably.[36]

Similarly, Brzezinski sought Jordan's support in advocating that General George Seignious, a member of the SALT delegation, replace Paul Warnke when he resigned as director of the Arms Control and Disarmament Agency in late 1978. Vance opposed the appointment of Seignious. After Brzezinski "worked quietly to mobilize support" on behalf of Seignious, Jordan, Brown, and Mondale eventually supported him. But it appears that Jordan had the most decisive impact on the president's decision. According to Brzezinski:

Ham succeeded in persuading the President to send a message to Vance [who was in Moscow] notifying him that Seignious was his choice unless Vance had serious objections. Cy's response was negative. . . . Two hours later Ham came into my office looking rather pleased and told me that the President had just phoned Seignious to offer him the job.[37]

However, whereas Jordan and Powell frequently added to Brzezinski's influence on the president's decisions, this was not the case with all presidential assistants. Carter's circle of aides expanded after the ten-day "domestic summit" at Camp David in July 1979, when nearly one hundred and thirty experienced executive branch officials were asked to offer their advice about how to improve the administration's performance and buttress its public support.[38] As he was advised, Carter asked Lloyd N. Cutler and Hedley W. Donovan to join his White House staff.

Cutler, a close friend of Vance and an experienced and respected Washington lawyer, became Carter's chief legal counsel and worked extensively on executive-legislative relations. Donovan, an experienced Washington journalist, became an adviser on both domestic and international issues. Both Cutler and Donovan attended NSC meetings and Friday breakfasts.[39] Cutler sided with Vance on most issues; Donovan, less frequently.

A debate within the White House evolved in August 1979 after intelligence reports indicated a Soviet brigade was based in Cuba. Brzezinski, who felt that SALT II needed to be linked to increased U.S. pressure on Cuba and the Soviet Union, saw the brigade as an impetus to make a statement about *overall* Cuban-Soviet behavior, including their involvement in the African Horn. Vance and Cutler, on the other hand, felt that general accusations would cause the Soviets to balk at SALT II and that any response needed to be directed *specifically* at the brigade. In the meantime, speculation about Soviet troops in Cuba became a domestic political issue.[40]

On September 4, a Policy Review Committee meeting headed by Vance was convened to discuss potential U.S. responses to the brigade.[41] According to Brzezinski, both Vance and Cutler argued during the meeting that if a brigade existed the president should insist that it be withdrawn. Brzezinski thought Cutler had been invited to the meeting by Vance "as an ally." In response, he in-

vited Donovan, whom he felt "had a distinctively more hawkish outlook," to subsequent meetings about the brigade. Although this alliance did not bear fruit since "Donovan would not say a word," Brzezinski eventually gained the support of Jordan and Powell and felt "increasingly encouraged."[42]

In late September Cutler and Donovan, supported by Vance but strongly opposed by Brzezinski, advised the president to appoint a panel of senior statesmen to recommend an appropriate U.S. response.[43] Carter took Cutler's and Donovan's advice and convened a panel that concluded that the brigade was not significantly different than the one in Cuba since 1962, that it posed no threat to the United States, and that any response should be "measured." Thereafter, both Vance and Cutler again advocated treating the brigade in isolation from other Soviet behavior to get the issue "behind us quickly and move on to the ratification of SALT."[44]

The panel's recommendation, along with a rebuke by Soviet Ambassador Anatoly Dobrynin that the brigade question was "phoney," apparently convinced Carter to address the nation on October 1 and attempt to disengage the United States from the issue, as well as from any broad-range response. Although Brown and Brzezinski sought to put "tougher lines" into the speech, much to Brzezinski's annoyance Culter successfully extracted the phrase "Soviet adventurism" from it.[45]

But Cutler did not always oppose Brzezinski. The background discussions of how to respond to the captivity of U.S. citizens taken hostage in Iran on November 4, 1979, are illustrative of how alliances might be viewed as permanent when they actually change, depending on the issue. Brzezinski wrote in his diary four days after the seizure of the hostages that he

huddled several times today with Ham and Jody. We all agreed that for political reasons as well as for substantive reasons the President should be tough on the Iranian issue. Ham is pressing to bring [Carter's close friend Charles] Kirbo up here [from Georgia] because he thinks that Kirbo will stiffen the President's back and cancel the weak advice likely to be given by Vance and Cutler.[46]

But, in fact, Cutler did not side with Vance on this issue. When interviewed, he stated that: "It is true that in general I tended to

side more with Vance than Brzezinski. But [in terms of] being tough on the Iranians, I think I was even tougher than Brzezinski."[47]

Vance was aware of the influence of these alliances on the president's decisions. After an NSC meeting about the hostages in Iran on November 5, Vance met privately with Jordan and Powell in Jordan's office and emphasized that Carter would ultimately be judged on whether the lives of the hostages were saved. However, almost immediately after Vance left, Brzezinski countered Vance's advice by stressing to Jordan and Powell that the hostage incident provided an opportunity for the president to show he could handle an international crisis and exhibit U.S. resolve.[48]

Later that month, according to Brzezinski, he was successful, with the help of Powell, Jordan, and Cutler, in convincing the president, despite the protests by State, Treasury, and Justice Department officials, to adopt measures to increase pressure for the deportation of Iranians residing illegally in the United States, discontinue purchasing Iranian oil, and freeze official Iranian assets held by U.S. banks. Shortly thereafter, in response to threats by emerging leader Ayatollah Ruhollah Khomeini that the hostages might be put on trial, Brzezinski, again with the help of Jordan and Powell, prevailed in persuading Carter to issue a public warning that any such trials would result in retaliatory action. Apparently, Vance, Brown, and Mondale were against making a public statement on the grounds that it "might polarize the situation." Vance, in particular, thought that Khomeini was trying to bait the United States into taking drastic action, which would only rally the Iranian public behind the regime he sought to erect.[49]

Nevertheless, the influence of Brzezinski, Jordan, and Powell vis-à-vis Vance and others on Carter's decision making about how to handle the hostage incident should not be exaggerated. Not only was Carter infuriated by Khomeini's statements about putting the hostages on trial, he also became increasingly impatient with diplomatic measures as time went on.[50] Nor was the president alone in his impatience. Apparently, Brown, Mondale, and Director of Central Intelligence Stansfield Turner joined Brzezinski, Jordan, Powell, and Cutler in telling the president at a meeting on April 11, 1980, that they favored, with some reservations, an attempt to rescue the hostages.[51] His awareness that the presi-

dent planned to proceed with the rescue attempt, of which he adamantly disapproved, was one reason Vance drafted a letter of resignation three days before the unsuccessful mission was executed on April 24.[52]

There were other reasons behind the secretary of state's resignation. Vance had become increasingly upset by Brzezinski's public pronouncements that conflicted with his own. In May 1978, while Brzezinski was on an official visit to the People's Republic of China, the national security assistant made what appeared to Vance (and to many others) to be "provocative comments" about Soviet international behavior.[53] And after the Soviet invasion of Afghanistan on December 17, 1979, U.S.-Soviet relations were dominated by Brzezinski, who publicly advocated strong sanctions against Moscow, including "playing the China card." Brzezinski, apparently with the support of Brown and Donovan, argued that the invasion provided a justification for opening a U.S.-Chinese defense relationship. Both Vance and Cutler opposed the proposition, arguing that it would substantially set back U.S.-Soviet relations. Eventually, the president asked Brown, who was about to make an official visit to Beijing, to inform the Chinese leaders that the United States was willing to sell them over-the-horizon radar, but not arms.[54]

Disagreements between Vance and Brzezinski on U.S.-Soviet relations continued during 1980, as did their alliances with White House staff members. In January Brzezinski granted an interview to a *Wall Street Journal* reporter and expounded a "regional security framework" response to the Afghanistan invasion. Afterward, he gave Carter a memorandum that spelled out the proposal in detail, including the suggestion to promote strategic cooperation between Egypt, Pakistan, Saudi Arabia, and Turkey. The president later told Brzezinski that he planned to use the idea in his upcoming State of the Union message and asked him to write a speech draft. Only hours before the president was to present the speech, Vance and Cutler were able to get the words "regional security framework" struck from the text. When Brzezinski found out, he alerted Powell, who penciled the three words back into the speech.[55]

THE WHITE HOUSE STAFF'S RESPONSE TO BRZEZINSKI'S ASCENDANCY

Toward the latter part of the Carter administration, many foreign affairs specialists and members of Congress expressed concern about the influence of Brzezinski relative to Vance. Given the reaction of both the Nixon and Ford White House staffs to Kissinger when his actions or prominence became a political liability for the president, one might have expected Carter's assistants to have done something to reduce the public perception that Brzezinski's influence on presidential decisions exceeded Vance's.[56] However, the political assistants, with a few notable exceptions, did nothing to reduce Brzezinski's public visibility. And they often helped him increase, not decrease, his private influence on the president's decisions.

The political assistants' behavior in this regard is explainable in part by Carter's decision-making style. The president considered it necessary to promote diversity to ensure that all options were presented and no information suppressed.[57] In addition, the White House environment under Carter did not include the basic operational tenet that existed, say, during the Eisenhower presidency, which made opposing a cabinet secretary's advice unthinkable. Therefore, for the president's aides to join Brzezinski in *privately* advocating certain foreign policy positions, which varied from Vance's, was quite understandable, especially when Brzezinski presented his positions as though they were in the president's political interests, as he often did.[58] And even amidst congressional concern about "two secretaries of state," the political assistants probably assumed that there was no obvious link between Brzezinski's private influence and the influence he was perceived to have by the public and the Congress.

When the political advisers felt that Brzezinski's foreign policy spokesmanship was harming the administration's public standing, they did, in fact, take action. Even though Carter both approved of and promoted Brzezinski's spokesmanship, there is evidence that the political assistants—Jordan, Powell, Rafshoon, and Assistant for Congressional Liaison Frank Moore, among them—sought to prevent future incongruities between Brzezinski's and Vance's

public statements. They did so subsequent to Brzezinski's trip to the People's Republic of China in May 1978, when he made statements about the Soviet Union sharply at variance with Vance's.[59] However, this effort to foster congruency was short-lived, for four apparent reasons. First, the assistants came to see Brzezinski's "hardline" position as a political asset following international events—particularly the taking of the U.S. embassy in Tehran, Cuban-Soviet involvement in Africa, and the Soviet Union's invasion of Afghanistan—that made the public less patient with diplomacy and weary of détente.[60] As early as May 30, 1978, an editorial in the *Washington Post* noted:

In a sense the Administration is arriving collectively at a point not far from where Zbigniew Brzezinski has been all along. It is a point consistent with the heightened apprehensions raised in the last year or so by Soviet power plays in Africa, and by Soviet strategic programs. It also happens to be a point consistent with the political mood of the country as we sense it.[61]

Second, by this time Carter had made a shift in his thinking about the Soviet Union. According to Cutler, after the Soviets invaded Afghanistan "Carter went through a metamorphosis. . . . As the staff began taking Brzezinski's side, they were reflecting how Carter had shifted."[62]

Third, the president and his political advisers thought Brzezinski's spokesmanship was useful as a lightning rod for criticism.[63] Furthermore, given that the administration asserted that it was challenging some basic, but outworn, tenets of U.S. foreign policy, criticism directed at Brzezinski was thought to be inevitable, since, as Powell once said about Brzezinski, "when you question old assumptions, you're going to ruffle feathers."[64]

Finally, it appears that some members of the White House staff underestimated the intensity of concern in the foreign policy community and the Congress about the so-called Vance-Brzezinski split. Referring to a visit by W. Averell Harriman during which he complained about Brzezinski's public spokesmanship, Jordan wrote: "I listened but respectfully disagreed, saying that the stories about Vance and Brzezinski were greatly exaggerated."[65] Cutler mentioned that he was rather startled when Brzezinski drew boos when he was introduced at the 1980 Democratic National Convention.[66]

Looking back, Brzezinski himself admitted that his spokesmanship probably hurt the administration more than it helped. But when Donovan told Brzezinski in late 1979 that he thought the "Vance-ZB split" presented the president with a serious political problem, Brzezinski was, in his own words, "genuinely surprised."[67] In Brzezinski's opinion, officials in the lower echelons of the State Department were responsible for amplifying the differences between him and Vance. He stressed, as did both Cutler and Jordan, how he and Vance agreed on many issues and that they always had cordial personal relations. Hence, the exaggerated press accounts about the alleged split were easily discounted.[68]

Eisenstat felt that he had not underestimated how politically damaging these stories were for Carter. But he also felt that it was up to the president to do something about it; that it was out of his control. Watson indicated how he differed with Carter on the proper role of the national security assistant, but said it was the "president's call," not his. Cutler had a similar feeling, although he said that, on a number of occasions, he did speak with Vance, Jordan, and Powell about Brzezinski's spokesmanship.[69]

CONCLUSION

The experiences of the Carter administration show how alliances between the national security assistant and the White House staff can be influential in presidential decision making. They show also that when this happens, cabinet secretaries will likely seek to form alliances of their own. However, the alliances tend to be issue-specific, not permanent.

Unlike President Ford's political assistants, who went to considerable lengths to try to reduce Kissinger's public stature, Carter's aides did not attempt on any consistent, systematic basis to undermine the perception of Brzezinski's dominance in the president's decision making. It was obvious to Ford's staff that Kissinger's public stature was a political problem for the president. Carter's political aides, in contrast, either underestimated the problem, viewed it as a political asset rather than a liability, or both. In any case, they had no presidential mandate to make it appear as if Brzezinski's stature was diminishing, as did Ford's staff regarding Kissinger.

The Carter administration, like others, eventually developed a means to integrate foreign policy with domestic politics. This became one of Jordan's main responsibilities. But it took a major domestic embarrassment almost a year into the administration (the announcement of the joint U.S.-Soviet Middle East peace initiative) before Jordan and other political advisers were included in the foreign policy decision-making process.

NOTES

1. Hamilton Jordan, *Crisis: The Last Year of the Carter Presidency* (New York: Berkley Books, 1983), p. 37. See also Jeremiah Novak, "The Trilateral Connection," *The Atlantic Monthly* (July 1977): 57–59; and Robert Shogan, *Promises to Keep: Carter's First Hundred Days* (New York: Thomas Y. Crowell, 1977), p. 86.

2. Zbigniew Brzezinski, *Power and Principle: Memoirs of the National Security Adviser, 1977–1981* (New York: Farrar, Straus & Giroux, 1983), pp. 3–13.

3. Jimmy Carter, *Keeping Faith: Memoirs of a President* (New York: Bantam, 1982), p. 50; and Jordan, *Crisis*, pp. 37–38.

4. The "Kissinger legacy," in this regard, was a negative one for the incoming administration.

5. See, for instance, Carter's statements in Jimmy Carter, "Making Foreign and Defense Policy: Openness, Coherence and Efficiency," *National Journal* 8 (23 October 1976): 1528–1529. On the concern of the transition advisers, see David K. Hall, "Implementing Multiple Advocacy in the National Security Council, 1947–1980" (Ph.D. diss., Stanford University, 1982), p. 656; and Carter, *Keeping Faith*, p. 52.

6. Quoted in the *New York Times*, 17 December 1976, p. B4.

7. On Carter's decision-making style and his conception of how he would work with his advisers, see Alexander L. George, *Presidential Decisionmaking in Foreign Policy: The Effective Use of Information and Advice* (Boulder, Colo.: Westview, 1980), pp. 159–164; Cyrus Vance, *Hard Choices: Critical Years in America's Foreign Policy* (New York: Simon and Schuster, 1983), p. 35; Brzezinski, *Power and Principle*, pp. 10–11, 514; and Robert H. Hunter, *Presidential Control of Foreign Policy* (New York: Praeger, 1982).

8. According to Jerrold Schector, the NSC press spokesman during most of the administration: "The public perception is that Brzezinski operated on his own [when he assumed the role of foreign policy spokesman] but in fact he was operating at the direction of the president." In-

terview with Jerrold Schector, Washington, D.C., 17 October 1984. See also Carter, *Keeping Faith*, pp. 53–54; Brzezinski, *Power and Principle*, p. 524; and Jordan *Crisis*, p. 40. This is at variance with Vance's recollection that "in spite of repeated instructions from the president, Brzezinski would attempt increasingly to take over the role as policy spokesman." Vance, *Hard Choices*, p. 35.

9. Hall, "Implementing Multiple Advocacy," pp. 656, 675–676; and Brzezinski, *Power and Principle*, pp. 30, 414–515, 523.

10. R. Gordon Hoxie, "Staffing the Ford and Carter Presidencies," in *Organizing and Staffing the Presidency*, ed. Bradley D. Nash (New York: Center for the Study of the Presidency, 1980), pp. 44–85, especially pp. 61–62, 75–78.

11. Jordan, *Crisis*, pp. 40–45, 50, 110; Brzezinski, *Power and Principle*, pp. 4, 73–74, 254; and Shogan, *Promises to Keep*, pp. 83–84.

12. Hoxie, "Staffing the Ford and Carter Presidencies," p. 62; and Carter, *Keeping Faith*, pp. 45–46.

13. Brzezinski, *Power and Principle*, pp. 45, 110, 345.

14. Carter, *Keeping Faith*, p. 56; Brzezinski, *Power and Principle*, p. 63; Jordan, *Crisis*, p. 34; Shogan, *Promises to Keep*, pp. 262, 269; and Dom Bonafede, "How the White House Helps Carter Make Up His Mind," *National Journal* 10 (15 April 1978): 586. At one point, Carter's personal secretary, Susan Clough, was quoted in the *Washington Post* as saying she controlled access to the president. Osborne contended that she had probably been misquoted, and, in any case, did not control the door to the Oval Office. John Osborne, "White House Watch: Tennis, Folks?" *The New Republic* 177 (26 November 1977): 12.

15. Brzezinski, *Power and Principle*, p. 35.

16. It was at this time that three of Jordan's subordinates, Landon Butler, Betty Rainwater, and Joseph Aragon, were assigned, respectively, to organize support for SALT II, U.S.-P.R.C. rapprochement, and Panama Canal Treaty ratification. John Osborne, "White House Watch: Dumping Bert," *The New Republic* 177 (17 September 1977): 10. See also Shogan, *Promises to Keep*, pp. 199–201.

17. Telephone interview with Jack Watson, Atlanta, Ga., 12 October 1984.

18. Victor Lasky, *Jimmy Carter: The Man and the Myth* (New York: Richard Marek, 1979), pp. 382–383; and John Osborne, "White House Watch: Carter's Summit," *The New Republic* 179 (30 September 1978): 16.

19. According to Brzezinski, at one point Alonzo McDonald, Jordan's deputy, "tried to gain control over the speech-writing process, but I made it very clear that as far as foreign policy was concerned the NSC re-

mained in charge." Brzezinski, *Power and Principle*, p. 72. See also John Osborne, "White House Watch: Ringing the Changes," *The New Republic* 176 (25 June 1977): 11. Apparently, the speech writers found the NSC drafts difficult to "translate into understandable English"—a statement made by one of them that Brzezinski did not find amusing. John Osborne, "White House Watch: At Jimmy's Place," *The New Republic* 177 (29 October 1977): 9.

20. Interview with Zbigniew Brzezinski, Washington, D.C., 2 November 1984; Tom Mathews et al., "Zeroing in on Zbig," *Newsweek* (30 January 1978): 50. Osborne reported some two months later: "Powell and Jordan in particular, and the others [on the White House staff] to a lesser extent, have been insisting for months that Brzezinski . . . provide opportunities to evaluate and anticipate the domestic political impacts of foreign policy positions and actions before they are set and announced. . . . An earlier complaint was that the joint U.S.-Soviet statement of Middle East purpose . . . ignored political realities." John Osborne, "White House Watch: Chasing Symbols," *The New Republic* 178 (21 January 1978): 9.

21. Brzezinski, *Power and Principle*, p. 110.

22. Ibid., p. 175.

23. Interview with Stuart E. Eisenstat, Washington, D.C., 5 November 1984.

24. Quoted in Mathews et al., "Zeroing in on Zbig," p. 50.

25. John Osborne, "White House Watch: After One Year," *The New Republic* 178 (11 February 1978): 10–12, especially p. 11. On Jordan's increased involvement in foreign affairs, see also Bonafede, "How the White House Helps Carter Make Up His Mind," p. 585; and John Osborne, "White House Watch: News from Cloud 9," *The New Republic* 179 (4 November 1978): 11.

26. Carter, *Keeping Faith*, pp. 55–56. According to Brzezinski, Jordan joined the breakfast group "on the grounds that he could help us by injecting political judgements into the discussions." Brzezinski, *Power and Principle*, p. 68. Similarly, Vance wrote that during these breakfasts, "we were able to consider the interaction between domestic and foreign policy matters." Vance, *Hard Choices*, p. 39.

27. Jordan quoted Brzezinski as saying: "Hamilton, Panama and the Shah are your specialty. I'm in charge of current leaders and big countries—you're in charge of former leaders and small countries." Jordan, *Crisis*, p. 185. Brzezinski's lack of resentment about Jordan's diplomatic activities is reflected also in Brzezinski, *Power and Principle*, pp. 477–506.

28. John Osborne, "White House Watch: Two Stories," *The New Republic* 181 (15 September 1979): 8–10; and John Osborne, "White House Watch: Moving On," *The New Republic* 181 (17 November 1979): 6, 8, 10. On the president's perception of Strauss's mission, see Carter *Keeping Faith*, pp. 490–492.

29. Interview with anonymous source, Washington, D.C., 17 October 1984; and telephone interview with NSC Middle East specialist William B. Quandt, Washington, D.C., 15 October 1984.

30. Brzezinski, *Power and Principle*, p. 439.

31. Interview with Zbigniew Brzezinski, Washington, D.C., 2 November 1984; and telephone interview with William B. Quandt, Washington, D.C., 25 October 1984. See also Brzezinski, *Power and Principle*, p. 239. On Eisenstat's advocacy on behalf of the Israeli lobby, see, for instance, Bonafede, "How the White House Helps Carter Make Up His Mind," p. 588.

This restriction of access to the Situation Room was apparently only regarding Middle East cable traffic. According to NSC Latin American specialist Robert Pastor, cables about Panama and Nicaragua—two "hot" areas during the administration—were shared freely with the political assistants. Telephone interview with Robert Pastor, College Park, Md., 29 October 1984.

32. Interview with Stuart E. Eisenstat, Washington, D.C., 5 November 1984.

33. Brzezinski, *Power and Principle*, p. 535. See also p. 73.

34. Telephone interview with Jack Watson, Atlanta, Ga., 12 October 1984.

35. Brzezinski, *Power and Principle*, p. 322.

36. Ibid., p. 323. For Carter's view on the trial of the dissidents, see Carter, *Keeping Faith*, pp. 222, 260.

37. Brzezinski, *Power and Principle*, p. 337. The influence of Jordan should not be overstated. Carter apparently had been impressed with Seignious when Brzezinski introduced the two.

38. The impetus for the domestic summit was, in large part, the shockingly low public opinion approval ratings of the administration's performance during this period. Hoxie, "Staffing the Ford and Carter Presidencies," p. 84.

39. Vance, *Hard Choices*, pp. 39, 358; Hoxie, "Staffing the Ford and Carter Presidencies," pp. 73–77; Hedley Donovan, "Advising a President," in *The Virginia Papers on the Presidency*, Vol. 6, ed. Kenneth Thompson (Washington: University Press of America, 1981), pp. 27, 32–33; and Brzezinski, *Power and Principle*, pp. 67–68.

40. Brzezinski, *Power and Principle*, pp. 346–350; and Vance, *Hard Choices*, pp. 360–364.

41. Under President Carter, there were two sub-NSC bodies: The Policy Review Committee (PRC) was headed by Vance, Brown, or Director of Central Intelligence Stansfield Turner when foreign policy, defense policy, or intelligence matters were being dealt with, respectively. The other group, the Special Coordination Committee (SCC), was headed by Brzezinski and handled crises as well as several other issues. See Brzezinski, *Power and Principle*, pp. 48–74.

42. Ibid., pp. 348–349.

43. Brzezinski's recollection was that only Cutler advocated the appointment of a panel. Ibid., p. 350. Vance, however, indicated that both Cutler and Donovan made the suggestion. Vance, *Hard Choices*, p. 363.

44. Vance, *Hard Choices*, pp. 363–364.

45. Brzezinski, *Power and Principle*, p. 351. When interviewed, Cutler remembered that he had requested that these words be taken from the text. He said that such phrases "have the same effect as President Reagan's statement of 'evil empire.' It would have created problems . . . [by fortifying] the opponents of SALT II." Interview with Lloyd N. Cutler, Washington, D.C., 5 November 1984.

46. Quoted in Brzezinski, *Power and Principle*, pp. 535–536.

47. Interview with Lloyd N. Cutler, Washington, D.C., 5 November 1984.

48. Jordan, *Crisis*, pp. 36–37, 44. Brzezinski's sentiments, in agreement with Jordan's, about how the hostage crisis influenced Carter's reelection prospects, are reported in Brzezinski, *Power and Principle*, pp. 508–509.

49. Brzezinski, *Power and Principle*, pp. 479, 483–484; Jordan, *Crisis*, p. 56; and Carter, *Keeping Faith*, pp. 465–466.

50. Jordan, *Crisis*, pp. 55–60, 113; and Brzezinski, *Power and Principle*, p. 486.

51. Jordan, *Crisis*, pp. 233–234; and interview with Lloyd N. Culter, Washington, D.C., 5 November 1984.

52. Vance, *Hard Choices*, pp. 409–413; *New York Times*, 29 April 1980, p. A1; and *Newsweek* (3 March 1980): 21.

53. Vance, *Hard Choices*, p. 116. See also Brzezinski, *Power and Principle*, p. 220. On Carter's reasons for sending Brzezinski to Beijing, see Carter, *Keeping Faith*, p. 194. On the "Vance-Brzezinski rift" and its impact on the foreign policy process see, among others, George, *Presidential Decisionmaking*, pp. 162–164; I. M. Destler, "A Job That Doesn't Work," *Foreign Policy* (Spring 1980): 84; and David K. Hall, "The National Se-

curity Assistant as Policy Spokesman, 1947–1981" (Paper prepared for the American Political Science Association Convention, New York, 3 September 1981), pp. 42–49.

54. Brzezinski, *Power and Principle*, p. 431; and Vance, *Hard Choices*, p. 78.

55. Brzezinski, *Power and Principle*, pp. 444–445. When asked about this, Cutler said: "My recollection is that we [Cutler and Vance] did not think it [the proposed "Regional Security Framework"] was much of an answer." Interview with Lloyd N. Cutler, Washington, D.C., 5 November 1984.

56. By 1979, an opinion poll indicated Vance trailing Brzezinski in the perception of who had more influence. "Who Runs America," *U.S. News and World Report* (16 April 1979): 33. The concerns of Congress are reflected in U.S., Congress, Senate, Committee on Foreign Relations, *The National Security Adviser: Role and Accountability*, Hearings (Washington: U.S. Government Printing Office, 1980), passim. See also Destler, "A Job That Doesn't Work," p. 87.

57. Vance, *Hard Choices*, p. 35; and Brzezinski, *Power and Principle*, p. 523.

58. See, for example, Brzezinski, *Power and Principle*, p. 535.

59. John Osborne, "White House Watch: Under Pressure," *The New Republic* 178 (24 June 1978): 10, 14; and telephone interview with Jack Watson, Atlanta, Ga., 12 October 1984.

60. For instance, Brzezinski has written that his reputation as a "hard-liner" was one reason he was asked by Anne Wexler, one of Carter's assistants, to become the principle administration briefer on SALT. Brzezinski, *Power and Principle*, p. 344.

61. Quoted in ibid., p. 518.

62. Interview with Lloyd N. Cutler, Washington, D.C., 5 November 1984. See also Brzezinski, *Power and Principle*, p. 31.

63. Carter, *Keeping Faith*, p. 54; and Brzezinski, *Power and Principle*, pp. 41, 97–98. The lightning-rod idea is also apparent in Carter's statement to Edmund Muskie, Vance's successor: "I need Zbig to speak out publicly. . . . He can protect my flanks." Quoted in Leslie H. Gelb, "Muskie and Brzezinski: The Struggle Over Foreign Policy," *New York Times Magazine* (20 July 1980): 26.

64. Quoted in Mathews et al., "Zeroing in on Zbig," p. 50.

65. Jordan, *Crisis*, p. 39.

66. Interview with Lloyd N. Cutler, Washington, D.C., 5 November 1984.

67. Brzezinski, *Power and Principle*, p. 523. See also pp. 30, 514–515.

68. Interviews with Zbigniew Brzezinski, Washington, D.C., 2 November 1984; with Lloyd N. Cutler, Washington, D.C., 5 November 1984; Jordan, *Crisis*, p. 39; and Brzezinski, *Power and Principle*, p. 38.

69. Interviews with Stuart E. Eisenstat, Washington, D.C., 5 November 1984; with Lloyd N. Cutler, Washington, D.C., 5 November 1984; and telephone interview with Jack Watson, Atlanta, Ga., 12 October 1984.

9

The Reagan Administration

This chapter, which deals with the first term of the Reagan presidency, must be read with particular caution. Administration officials declined to grant interviews, for understandable reasons. This made it impossible to check the accuracy of written accounts about the White House staff. Future scholarship will, no doubt, build substantially on what is contained herein.

Presidential scholar Fred I. Greenstein has labeled Reagan's decision-making style "ideology informed policy-making," meaning that he relys heavily on political abstractions as a guide to policy formation.[1] In his first term, at least, this was accompanied by a lack of personal presidential attention to critical aspects of the policy-making process. Indeed, the first year of the Reagan administration was nearly devoid of any systematic foreign policy review machinery.[2]

Partly because the ascendancy of previous national security assistants relative to the secretary of state had been a campaign issue in 1980, Reagan was certain about one aspect of his policy process: He directed that his national security assistant maintain a low profile and pledged to end the State Department–NSC disputes so apparent during the Nixon and Carter administrations. Accordingly, the national security assistant's office was moved from the first floor to the basement of the White House, back to the place McGeorge Bundy and Walt W. Rostow had occupied when they held the post.[3]

REAGAN'S STAFF

The political sentiment to reduce State-NSC friction was only one reason why President Reagan reduced the status of the national security assistant. Richard V. Allen, Reagan's first national security assistant, had recommended a downgrading of the position. Allen had worked as a foreign policy consultant for Nixon during his successful 1968 campaign and was a primary national security adviser for Reagan during the 1980 presidential race. After his appointment, Allen told reporters: "You're seeing a disappearing act." He persistently emphasized his intention to maintain a low profile, obviously with the approval of Reagan's political assistants.[4]

However, despite his participation in the 1980 presidential race, Allen, in the words of foreign policy scholar I. M. Destler, "never really penetrated the Reagan inner circle."[5] This limited the president's exposure to another viewpoint. In addition to the president's reliance on abstract principles for policy guidance, he also relied on close aides who shared similar political ideas, to whom he delegated extensive responsibility.[6]

During the first Reagan administration, one's influence on presidential decisions hinged largely on having a personal relationship with the president. To be sure, this is true in any administration. But it was especially the case in the first Reagan administration, particularly in 1981, when there was virtually no systematic, presidentially sanctioned procedures or mechanisms for national security decision making at senior levels.

It quickly became apparent that Secretary of State Alexander M. Haig, Jr., had to rely on a longtime Reagan aide housed in the State Department, Deputy Secretary of State William P. Clark, for a liaison to the president and his inner circle. Clark had served for two years as Governor Reagan's chief of staff before being appointed to California's Supreme Court.[7]

Reagan's senior political advisers, the "troika," as they came to be called, included Edwin Meese III, James Baker III, and Michael Deaver. Meese had worked as Governor Reagan's legal affairs secretary until he replaced Clark as chief of staff in 1967. He was appointed presidential counselor in 1981. His responsibilities included, among other things, overseeing the domestic policy staff,

running cabinet meetings, and reducing policy memoranda to a succinct list of options for presidential choice. Meese, in addition, had been instrumental in Allen's appointment.

Baker was chief of the White House staff.[8] Baker had been a campaign aide to Congressman George Bush during his unsuccessful senatorial campaign in 1970. He directed Nixon's 1972 campaign in Texas and later served as undersecretary of commerce during the Ford administration. In 1979 he managed Bush's unsuccessful campaign for the Republican presidential nomination. After Bush dropped out of the race, Baker helped Reagan prepare for his debates with President Carter and John Anderson. As chief of staff, Baker was responsible for White House press operations and shared administrative tasks with Meese.

Deaver was deputy chief of staff. He had worked with Meese during Reagan's 1976 and 1980 presidential campaigns and had a closer personal relationship with the president than either Meese or Baker. His White House responsibilities included handling the president's schedule and overseeing the office of the military liaison.[9]

Meese, Baker, and Deaver tended to get involved in foreign affairs selectively, that is, when issues had obvious domestic political implications. They were invited to all NSC meetings and attended regularly. Baker and Meese, in particular, sometimes had a decisive influence in foreign policy decisions. Among other things, Baker was instrumental in persuading Reagan to lift the Soviet grain embargo, and Meese was a primary architect of the compromise with Japan on limiting auto exports to the United States.[10]

THE STAFF'S INFLUENCE ON ALLEN'S AUTHORITY

For the most part, Allen adhered to his pledge to maintain a low profile. His contact with the press remained on a background basis, with only occasional on-the-record appearances. If the press happened to speculate that Allen's authority was on the rise, the president's aides downplayed Allen's influence. For instance, Baker impressed upon reporters that Haig's high standing in foreign policy remained even after it became known that Allen had opposed one of Haig's State Department nominations.[11]

However, later in the administration, Allen and Baker, at least once, responded to a key issue without consulting Haig, who strongly disagreed with their position. After Saudi Arabia balked at a proposal for restricted use of the airborne warning and control systems (AWACs) being sold to them by the United States, Allen and Baker reportedly suggested that Reagan request that a congressional delegation be sent to negotiate with Saudi leaders. After hearing about the plan for a congressional visit and Saudi Arabia's anger about it, Haig appealed to Reagan to kill the plan. The congressional delegation did not go to Riyadh, but Haig was clearly annoyed about Allen's and Baker's suggestion that such a visit be made and, especially, that he had not been consulted.[12]

Baker's collaboration with Allen on this matter was not a staff alliance specifically created to supersede Haig. Originally, Allen had been given the job of buttressing public support for the AWACs sale to Saudi Arabia. Baker intervened only later, reportedly because he felt that Allen was doing a poor job.[13]

ALLEN'S LACK OF ACCESS TO THE PRESIDENT

Allen's inability to "crack" the inner circle did not go unnoticed. Eventually, a numer of subcabinet State Department officials and presidential assistants began to criticize Allen for his failure to win the confidence of Reagan's top assistants (except, perhaps, for Meese) and complained about his lack of assertiveness. There was a widespread feeling, even at senior levels, that Allen was doing an inadequate job. According to reporters Lou Cannon and Lee Lescaze, some White House officials worried that the idea of a national security assistant with a low-profile had "succeeded beyond their wildest dreams."[14]

It seems that Deaver and Baker, in particular, became dissatisfied with Allen's performance. Prior to Reagan's visit to Canada in March 1981, Deaver felt compelled to call a high-level meeting with White House staff and State Department officials to discuss the reasons for inadequate preparations for the trip. While it was felt by some attendees of the meeting that the State Department had not provided briefing papers for the president in a timely fashion, others pointed out that State had sent the briefing mate-

rial days before and that the "logjam" was Allen's fault. In addition, Deaver and Baker apparently felt that Allen was deficient in his administrative abilities, that Allen's staff was of mediocre quality, and that he failed to provide the analytical information needed for daily intelligence briefings. This White House staff scrutiny is probably one reason why Allen sometimes refrained from asserting his own substantive views on policy issues, even when he felt strongly about them.[15]

Clearly, a critical obstacle to Allen's effectiveness was his restricted access to the Oval Office. Since Allen had to report to Meese, he did not have direct, easy access to the president.[16]

Departmental officials, some of whom apparently had a difficult time getting an appointment with the president, found Allen incapable of facilitating their access. According to Haig, a National Security Decision Directive (NSDD-1), which had been drafted by him, Secretary of Defense Caspar Weinberger, CIA Director William Casey, and Allen, had been given to Meese for the president's signature on January 20, 1981. But the document, which set forth plans to organize the administration's national security policy machinery, did not reach Reagan for over a year. Evidently, Meese did not find it satisfactory. According to Haig, he repeatedly tried to get Allen to forward the document, but found him unable to do so. Frustrated by their inability to get presidential authorization, Haig and Weinberger established policy review committees, in Haig's words, "as if the document *had* been signed."[17]

Six months into the administration, reportedly because Reagan and two of his aides were dissatisfied with Allen's performance, intelligence briefings—which had hitherto been a daily responsibility of the national security assistant—were canceled. Thereafter, Allen provided the president with only a written brief.[18]

ALLEN'S DEPARTURE AND REPLACEMENT BY CLARK

In November 1981, after it was discovered that Allen had received a $1,000 gratuity for arranging an interview with the president's wife for a Japanese journalist, the opportunity arose to release Allen in a relatively face-saving way. After merciless press

scrutiny about the financial transaction, Allen took a leave of absence. According to journalist Laurence I. Barrett, who interviewed numerous White House officials, after an investigation of the case began, "Deaver told Reagan that Allen should not be taken back, regardless of how the investigation turned out."[19] In January 1982, reportedly on the advice of Deaver and Baker, Reagan moved Clark from the State Department to the NSC post after accepting Allen's "resignation" and appointing him a consultant to the President's Foreign Intelligence Advisory Board.[20]

Allen's restricted access to the president had become such an irritant within the executive bureaucracy that Reagan stated publicly that Clark would take papers directly to the president; Meese did not control Clark's access. Clearly a member of the inner circle, Clark attended informal brainstorming sessions with Reagan and his other three close aides. Daily intelligence briefings resumed, attended by Meese, Baker, and Deaver, as well as Bush and Clark's deputy, Robert C. McFarlane.[21]

Unlike Allen, Clark was not hesitant to assert himself. After the president complained about leaks of sensitive national security information, Clark proposed a directive requiring that "a senior official" approve contacts between administrative personnel and journalists on NSC and intelligence matters. Baker, concerned about the press's reaction to such a directive, asked Clark to delay its issuance. Clark disregarded Baker's plea, saying, "Press considerations should not be involved in this."[22]

Another instance when Clark overruled the political aides occurred during the war between Argentina and Great Britain over the Falkland Islands in June 1982. According to Haig, White House assistants decided to prevent journalists from taking pictures of Reagan's meeting with British Prime Minister Margaret Thatcher in an attempt to downplay the U.S. tilt toward Britain. After hearing about the decision, Haig appealed to Clark, saying that the Argentine officials might take the ban on photography as a sign of U.S. sympathy and, hence, prolong the war in the hope of a U.S. tilt in their direction. The decision was reversed and picture taking was allowed.[23]

COLLABORATION BY MEMBERS OF THE
WHITE HOUSE STAFF

Clark did not always side with Haig in opposition to the president's other assistants. For instance, he joined Meese, as well as Weinberger, in persuading Reagan to place sanctions on European firms using technology under U.S. licenses and U.S. firms operating abroad that were cooperating with the Soviet Union in the construction of a transnational natural gas pipeline. Reagan made the decision during an NSC meeting where Haig was absent, though it was known that he adamantly opposed the measure. The European allies were unanimous in their denunciation of the sanctions and sought to protect their firms through legal action. The unilateral U.S. move probably hindered NATO cohesion and was later substantially rescinded.[24]

In the spring and early summer of 1982 Clark clashed with Haig on a number of policy process issues. Clark insisted that Reagan be put "into the loop" of foreign affairs and that other advisers besides the secretary of state be included in major national security decisions. In late June, Haig, sensitive about infringement on his prerogatives, told Clark that he might soon resign, due to Clark's deep involvement in the foreign policy process, among other things. By this time Clark had apparently found Haig a difficult person with whom to deal. Hence, whereas before he had shrugged off Haig's threats to resign, Clark now informed Reagan of the possibility. Subsequently, Clark and Deaver began looking for a new secretary of state.

On June 24, after Haig met with Reagan and gave him a *pro forma* letter of resignation (apparently only to be used for bargaining purposes), Reagan kept it and said that they would discuss the matter further the next day. Before he left the Oval Office, Haig requested that the resignation not be accepted until after the most recent Middle East crisis (due to the Israeli invasion of Lebanon) had subsided. The next day, during a meeting with his staff, Reagan proposed that Haig's resignation be postponed for several months, until after the congressional elections, or that at least the decision be deferred until after the weekend, when it could be thought through completely. Clark, Deaver, and Baker opposed

postponement of the decision, urging that it be settled once and for all, provided that George P. Shultz accepted the invitation to replace Haig, which could be announced simultaneously with the resignation. Reagan yielded to their advice. After obtaining Shultz's acceptance, the announcement of the State Department change was made that afternoon, June 25. Haig was allowed to continue his Middle East diplomacy until July 5 (when it was terminated even before Shultz's appointment was confirmed by the Senate).[25]

Another instance of collaboration between the national security assistant and the political aides occurred in the winter of 1983. In an effort to show U.S. flexibility in sensitive NATO decisions about Intermediate Nuclear Forces (INF) in Europe, Clark and Meese reportedly drafted an "open letter" from Reagan to be read by Vice President Bush during a speech in West Berlin. During the speech on January 31, Bush quoted the letter, reading, in part: "I have asked Vice President Bush . . . to propose to Soviet General Secretary [Yuri] Andropov that he and I meet wherever and whenever he wants in order to sign an agreement banning U.S. and Soviet intermediate range land-based nuclear missle weapons from the face of the earth."[26] The letter was well received by European leaders, with the caveat that a change in tone would need to be accompanied by a change in policy substance. Such a change was not anticipated by Clark and Meese. Their main objective was to influence European and U.S. public opinion without changing the administration's negotiating posture. The administration had hitherto insisted upon maintaining its "zero-zero" INF proposal, and the speech was consistent with that stance.[27]

THE DISCOMFORT OF TOO MANY IN THE INNER CIRCLE

Although every member of the White House "Big Four"—Clark, Meese, Deaver, and Baker—had close relations with Reagan, they did not always get along well with one another. In September 1982, reporter Howell Raines wrote that "second level" White House staffers "have been frustrated by the breakdown in communications among the four."[28]

By March 1983 friction between Clark and Baker, in particular, spilled into public view and had affected their communications.

Baker apparently thought that military spending should be cut and sought to persuade the president to show "flexibility" with the defense budget. Clark became irritated after repeatedly being told by Baker, as well as Deaver, that the administration's military buildup lacked wide public support. As one consequence, according to an anonymous aide, Clark became "rather stingy" in sharing information with the political assistants. Allegedly, he provided a copy of the president's "Star Wars" speech (the proposal to accelerate research on ballistic missile defense systems) to the other senior aides only a few hours before it was delivered. Later, the political aides complained that the proposal had not been well presented and that their inability to know the details in advance had made it difficult to reassure the public and Congress about the president's intentions. Baker was reportedly frustrated by Clark's "lack of political sensitivity."[29]

In addition, because of negative sentiment in Congress about military assistance to El Salvador, Baker and congressional liaison aide Kenneth M. Duberstein reportedly suggested that Reagan go to Capitol Hill to rally support for the proposed $110 million aid proposal. However, Clark insisted that the briefings be at the White House, and he prevailed.[30]

As with Allen, the political assistants eventually began criticizing Clark's performance. According to one White House official, Baker and Deaver felt that Clark was not "getting material to the President in a timely manner." Clark, on the other hand, reportedly disagreed with how Deaver handled the president's schedule and did not appreciate Baker altering foreign policy proposals for political reasons.[31]

On October 13, Reagan announced that Clark had been appointed secretary of interior and that Robert C. McFarlane would replace him as national security assistant. According to Cannon, senior administration officials indicated that Clark had asked to be moved from his White House post because of bitterness and strain among the staff, characterized as "persistent grinding friction." Apparently, relations between Clark and Deaver were so tense that they did not return each other's telephone calls. Both Deaver and Baker were said to be resentful of Clark's easy access to the president, especially since his private meetings with Reagan had increased as White House staff relationships soured. Evidently, the

friction had reached its zenith the preceding April after the administration lost an important vote on the defense budget in the Senate Budget Committee.[32]

But the influence of the political aides on Clark's move to the department of interior should not be overstated. Clark left on his own accord. He did not like the demanding nature of his NSC post nor work within the government in general.[33]

McFARLANE'S PERFORMANCE WITHOUT INNER-CIRCLE MEMBERSHIP

One major concern for administration conservatives was that Clark's departure might decrease their influence with Reagan. After Baker, who was perceived to be a moderate, made a bid for the NSC post, he was opposed not only by Clark but also by Meese, Secretary of Defense Weinberger, and CIA Director Casey. Since McFarlane did not possess the intimacy with Reagan that Clark had, Weinberger and Casey apparently felt that he might experience access restrictions similar to Allen's, and that Baker's influence would grow correspondingly. Reagan countered these concerns by assuring Weinberger and Casey that their views would be adequately channeled by McFarlane, who would have access equal to that of the other top White House aides.[34]

Nevertheless, because McFarlane lacked a personal relationship with Reagan, he was soon criticized by some "administration officials" (as they were called by reporters) as being less effective than Clark. In particular, it was felt that his lower White House stature contributed to his inability to mediate disputes between Weinberger and Shultz (similar to the inability of James Lay with Louis Johnson and Dean Acheson, which made some members of President Truman's White House staff think the NSC's enforcement ability was deficient). In an effort to promote his standing, McFarlane eventually appeared on several talk shows and gave background briefings to journalists.[35]

As the presidential election drew near, McFarlane, along with Shultz, argued that Reagan stick to his earlier stated conditions for an arms control summit with the Soviet Union—that it be carefully prepared and have a high chance of success—after the president was urged by Senate Majority Leader Howard H. Baker, Jr.,

and Senate Foreign Relations Committee Chairman Charles H. Percy to hold a summit meeting, regardless of the conditions. A statement to the two senators, which dismissed their proposal, had been cleared by Shultz and McFarlane, but not by presidential assistant James Baker III. Subsequently, a number of the political advisers agreed that the dismissal was, as one said, "not right, politically."[36] Before his news conference that week, it was decided that Reagan would make an "unspecific overture" to the Soviets about a summit. McFarlane and Shultz, as well as the political advisers, were apparently satisfied with that decision.[37]

Later that June, McFarlane was said to have "discretely complained" about the interference in his "domain" of the political advisers. Reportedly, Baker had been instrumental in the administration's support of an Australian initiative for a discussion by the Geneva-based multinational disarmament group about a comprehensive nuclear test ban, and the administration's agreement to discuss a ban on antisatellite weapons.[38]

CONCLUSION

President Reagan's relative lack of interest in his national security policy process at an early stage created insurmountable difficulties for Allen. Allen's performance was hindered by his lack of direct access to the president. Allen's "resignation" was reportedly influenced, in part, by Baker's and Deaver's dissatisfaction with the national security assistant's performance.

It took a longtime Reagan intimate, Clark, with the help of Secretary of Defense Weinberger, to get the president to shape up his national security policy process. Clark, who enjoyed direct access to Reagan, resumed daily intelligence briefings and became a potent force within the White House. On occasion, Clark's collaboration with other White House aides on foreign policy matters irritated Haig, who was sensitive to infringement on his prerogatives. Clark and Haig also clashed on numerous occasions. Evidently, Clark, Baker, and Deaver were instrumental in Haig's departure from the State Department.

Friction between Clark and political aides hindered the flow of information within the White House. Reportedly, Clark did not inform Baker and Deaver in a timely fashion about Reagan's "Star

Wars" speech because he resented their persistent reminders that the public might not support key aspects of the administration's massive defense expenditures.

By the time McFarlane replaced Clark, Reagan had developed an appreciation for an organized foreign policy process and for the importance of providing open access for his national security assistant. Even without an intimate relationship with the president, McFarlane enjoyed easy access to the Oval Office and did not hesitate to assert himself on national security matters. McFarlane, whose expertise in foreign and defense policy far surpassed both Allen's and Clark's, did not appreciate Baker and Deaver manipulating national security matters for domestic political reasons.

NOTES

1. Fred I. Greenstein, "The Need for an Early Appraisal of the Reagan Presidency," in Fred I. Greenstein, ed., *The Reagan Presidency: An Early Assessment* (Baltimore: Johns Hopkins University Press, 1983), pp. 1–22, especially p. 7.

2. I. M. Destler, "The Evolution of Reagan Foreign Policy," in ibid., pp. 122–123; Duncan L. Clarke, "Integrating Arms Control, Defense, and Foreign Policy in the Executive Branch of the U.S. Government," in *Decisionmaking for Arms Limitation*, eds. Hans Guenter Brauch and Duncan L. Clarke (Cambridge, Mass.: Ballinger, 1983), pp. 16–26; and Alexander M. Haig, Jr., *Caveat: Realism, Reagan and Foreign Policy* (New York: Macmillan, 1984), pp. 75–76.

3. Destler, "The Evolution of Reagan Foreign Policy," p. 120; Haig, *Caveat*, pp. 12, 58; Laurence I. Barrett, *Gambling with History: Ronald Reagan in the White House* (New York: Doubleday, 1983), p. 221; and Michael R. Gordan, "NSC: A Lower Profile?" *National Journal* 13 (25 April 1981): 688.

4. Elizabeth Bumiller, "The Powers and Puzzles of Richard Allen: The Disappearing 'Disappearing Act' of the National Security Adviser," *Washington Post*, 28 June 1981, p. H1. See also *New York Times*, 4 March 1981, p. A2; Frank Van Der Linden, *The Real Reagan* (New York: William Morrow, 1981), p. 251; and John Osborne, "White House Watch: Fun in the Junkyard," *The New Republic* 184 (14 February 1981): 12.

5. Destler, "The Evolution of Reagan Foreign Policy," p. 121. See also Clarke, "Integrating Arms Control, Defense, and Foreign Policy," p. 18; and Haig, *Caveat*, p. 85.

6. Destler, "The Evolution of Reagan Foreign Policy," p. 121; and Barrett, *Gambling with History*, pp. 226–227.

7. Mary McNeil, ed., *Reagan's First Year* (Washington, D.C.: Congressional Quarterly, 1982), p. 13; Ronald Brownstein and Nina Easton, *Reagan's Ruling Class: Portraits of the President's Top 100 Officials* (Washington, D.C.: Presidential Accountability Group, 1982), pp. 654–657; and Lou Cannon and Lee Lescaze, "Rocky Start in Handling Foreign Policy," *Washington Post*, 25 May 1981, p. A12.

8. In January 1985, Baker became secretary of the treasury and Donald R. Regan became White House chief of staff.

9. Destler, "The Evolution of Reagan Foreign Policy," p. 121; Barrett, *Gambling with History*, pp. 226–227; Greenstein, "The Need for an Early Appraisal," p. 17; and Brownstein and Easton, *Reagan's Ruling Class*, pp. 643–653.

10. Destler, "The Evolution of Reagan Foreign Policy," pp. 121–122; Brownstein and Easton, *Reagan's Ruling Class*, pp. 643, 647; Dom Bonafede, "That's Mike Deaver at the Hub of Ronald Reagan's Presidential World," *National Journal* 13 (August 1981): 1462; *Washington Post*, 24 May 1981, p. A2; and 26 May 1981, p. A1.

11. Osborne, "Fun in the Junkyard": 12; Haig, *Caveat*, p. 86; John Osborne, "White House Watch: Cleanup Time," *The New Republic* 184 (14 March 1981): 10.

12. Haig, *Caveat*, p. 188.

13. Barrett, *Gambling with History*, p. 231.

14. Cannon and Lescaze, "Rocky Start in Handling Foreign Policy," p. A1. See also Clarke, "Integrating Arms Control, Defense, and Foreign Policy," pp. 18–21.

15. Cannon and Lescaze, "Rocky Start in Handling Foreign Policy," p. A12; Barrett, *Gambling with History*, pp. 98, 231, 258; Hedrick Smith, "White House Hit a Last-Minute Snag on Canada Trip," *New York Times*, 11 March 1981, p. A11; Bumiller, "The Puzzles of Richard Allen," p. H4; and Edward T. Pound, "Allen Exonerated by Justice Department on Gifts and Financial Disclosure," *New York Times*, 24 December 1981, p. A1.

16. *Washington Post*, 24 May 1981, p. A2; 27 May 1981, p. A8; Haig, *Caveat*, pp. 76, 84; Brownstein and Easton, *Reagan's Ruling Class*, p. 664; John Osborne, "White House Watch: Haig and the System," *The New Republic* 184 (28 March 1984): 8; Clarke, "Integrating Arms Control, Defense, and Foreign Policy," p. 18; and Strobe Talbott, *Deadly Gambits: The Reagan Administration and the Stalemate in Nuclear Arms Control* (New York: Knopf, 1984), p. 11.

17. *Caveat*, p. 85. Emphasis in original. See also pp. 74–77. Another instance of Haig appealing to Meese because of Allen's inability to reach

Reagan is reported on p. 132. See also Barrett, *Gambling with History*, pp. 246, 312.

18. Clarke, "Integrating Arms Control, Defense, and Foreign Policy," p. 18; John E. Endicott, "The National Security Council," in John F. Reichart and Steven R. Sturm, eds., *American Defense Policy* (Baltimore: Johns Hopkins University Press, 1982), pp. 521–527, especially p. 526; Brownstein and Easton, *Reagan's Ruling Class*, p. 667; and *Washington Post*, 24 May 1981, p. A2; and 28 June 1981, p. H5.

19. Barrett, *Gambling with History*, p. 232. See also *New York Times*, 3 November 1981, p. A1; and 1 December 1981, p. A10.

20. Barrett, *Gambling with History*, pp. 233, 258; Brownstein and Easton, *Reagan's Ruling Class*, p. 666; and *New York Times*, 20 January 1982, p. A10.

21. Clark's increased stature is reflected in Reagan's statement on 12 January 1982, reprinted in Robert E. Hunter, *Presidential Control of Foreign Policy: Management or Mishap?* (New York: Praeger, 1982), p. 109. See also Dick Kirschen, "Clark Emerges as a Tough Manager, Not a Rival to the Secretary of State," *National Journal* 14 (17 July 1982): 1248; *Washington Post*, 2 January 1982, p. 1, 5 January 1982, p. 1, and 16 May 1983, p. A9; *New York Times*, 26 April 1982, p. 17; Barrett, *Gambling with History*, pp. 98–99, 234; Clarke, "Integrating Arms Control, Defense, and Foreign Policy," p. 21; and Brownstein and Easton, *Reagan's Ruling Class*, pp. 643, 667.

22. Quoted in Brownstein and Easton, *Reagan's Ruling Class*, p. 668.

23. Haig, *Caveat*, p. 307.

24. Destler, "The Evolution of Reagan Foreign Policy," p. 149; and Barrett, *Gambling with History*, p. 244.

25. Barrett, *Gambling with History*, pp. 237, 242–250; Haig, *Caveat*, pp. 317–352; and *New York Times*, 26 June 1982, p. A1.

26. Quoted in Talbott, *Deadly Gambits*, p. 175.

27. Ibid., pp. 175–176.

28. Howell Raines, "Speaking of the Breakup of 'the Team,' " *New York Times*, 6 September 1982, p. A18. See also *New York Times*, 29 November 1982, p. A19.

29. Steven R. Weisman, "Now, Talk of New Strains Among the Top Aides," *New York Times*, 31 March 1983, p. B12.

30. Ibid.

31. Ibid.

32. Lou Cannon and David Hoffman, "Reagan Adviser Clark Named to Succeed Watt: Decision Made Suddenly," *Washington Post*, 14 October 1983, pp. A1, A4; and *New York Times*, 31 March 1983, p. B12. Though Shultz clearly had become upset with Clark's increased role in foreign

policy substance by that time, it does not appear that his displeasure was a decisive reason for Clark's departure from the White House. "Clark Appointment Catches State Department Unawares," *New York Times*, 14 October 1983, pp. A1, A4; and Don Oberdorfer, "Shultz's Roar on Policy-Making Got Results," *Washington Post*, 23 October 1983, pp. A1, A6.

33. Lou Cannon, "Overtaxed, Clark Sought Interior Post," *Washington Post*, 15 October 1983, pp. A1, A6; and Barrett, *Gambling with History*, pp. 332–335.

34. Michael Getler, "McFarlane May Move Up," *Washington Post*, 14 October 1983, pp. A1, A6, A7; Lou Cannon and David Hoffman, "McFarlane Nomination Seen Near," *Washington Post*, 17 October 1983, pp. A1, A9 and 18 October 1983, pp. A1, A8; Stephen R. Wiesman, "McFarlane Called Choice of Reagan for Security Post," *New York Times*, 17 October 1983, pp. A1, A6; Lou Cannon, "Reagan Appoints McFarlane Adviser on U.S. Security," *Washington Post*, 18 October 1983, pp. A1, A8; and John M. Goshko, "Kirkpatrick Thought Clark Should Stay," *Washington Post*, 14 October 1983, pp. A1, A7.

35. *New York Times*, 10 January 1984, p. A18, 28 March 1984, p. B10; Lou Cannon and David Hoffman, "Revamped White House Staff Found to Be Still Flawed," *Washington Post*, 19 March 1984, pp. A1, A9; and Leslie Gelb, "McFarlane Carving His Niche," *New York Times*, 28 March 1984, p. B10.

36. David Hoffman, "Reagan Treads Delicate Line in Soviet Relations," *Washington Post*, 17 June 1984, pp. A1, A4.

37. Ibid., p. A4.

38. Rowland Evans and Robert Novak, " . . . With Security Complications," *Washington Post*, 27 June 1984, p. A15.

10

Conclusion

This analysis of thirty-seven years of interaction between the national security assistant and other senior White House aides defies hard-and-fast generalizations, let alone prescriptions. Much of the written record on this subject is replete with misinformation, omissions, and sometimes parochial or self-serving accounts of past experiences. This study marshaled available evidence and checked its accuracy by questioning former senior administration officials about the written record. Future researchers will add to and clarify some of these findings. Consequently, the general conclusions contained in this chapter must be viewed in that light.

INTRIGUE AND INFIGHTING

Rather than continuous, vitriolic backbiting and power struggle among senior presidential assistants, the general picture that emerges is one of usually cordial relations interspersed with periodic, often issue-oriented, friction. Much of what tension has existed between White House political aides (and, on rare occasions, the president) and the national security assistant relates directly to the assistant's public visibility. However, such public exposure does not in itself necessarily result in tension unless one or both of two additional factors are present: one, the national security assistant is a *popular* public figure, or, two, he performs a significant number of diplomatic functions. Although McGeorge Bundy was a foreign pol-

icy spokesman while he was national security assistant during the Kennedy and Johnson administrations, he was not a glamourous, popular public figure. It was inconceivable that he could upstage the young, handsome John Kennedy or the outgoing, backslapping Texan even if he had entertained such a thought (which he apparently did not do). Bundy's diplomatic activities were rather limited, especially in comparison to Henry Kissinger's, thereby minimizing the likelihood of friction with the State Department. Kissinger was popular during both the Nixon and Ford administrations. His appearances even at downtown Washington restaurants became "media events." President Nixon's staff might have leaked stories about Kissinger, Ford's staff unquestionably did so. These stories focused on Kissinger's disagreement with the president over foreign policy and were motivated generally by a desire to shift the public limelight back to the president.

Friction between staff members because of the national security assistant's public visibility is probably accentuated during a presidential election year. Haldeman wanted Kissinger to take the blame for Vietnam peace speculation when he felt Kissinger's "peace is at hand" statement made the administration appear opportunist. Moreover, Haldeman did not consider peace overtures to be a political asset.

Although public visibility opens the possibility that the national security assistant can be made a lightning rod for criticism directed at an unpopular policy, it is even more possible when the assistant is associated with such a policy because of his personal diplomacy. Furthermore, if the national security assistant's diplomacy becomes so extensive that he, not the president, is thought by some to be in control of foreign policy, White House aides will seek ways to demonstrate ultimate presidential control. Ford clearly wanted it known that he was in charge yet he did not want this to be revealed through unauthorized leaks to the press about his substantive differences with Kissinger over foreign policy. However, some of his aides leaked such stories anyway.

The struggle between the secretary of state and the national security assistant that results when the assistant makes public statements uncoordinated and inconsistent with the secretary's public stances—even though it is rarely, if ever, a healthy situation—does not necessarily result in intra–White House tension, even when

the struggle becomes an issue in Congress and among the foreign policy community. Zbigniew Brzezinski's disagreements with Cyrus Vance, which were controversial, did not result in background efforts by the White House staff to reduce Brzezinski's visibility (they did, however, seek momentarily to make Brzezinski's public statements consistent with Vance's). This is probably attributable to their perception that Vance's stances gradually lost public favor while Brzezinski's became increasingly popular.

Friction within the White House quite commonly does result, however, either from a specialized, rigidly compartmentalized staffing structure, from the pull between domestic *politics* and foreign *policy*, or both. Contrary to conventional wisdom, friction may be more related to the procedures and structures of staffing than to personalities. Most presidents will not tolerate personal, petty quarreling among staff members, especially if it catches the attention of the press or threatens to jeopardize policy formulation. Friction related to staff procedures and structures is different. Politically sensitive matters, like aspects of U.S.-Israel relations and the perennial trade-off between the defense budget and various domestic programs, tend to cause friction when the boundaries of staff responsibility are rigidly delineated. John Ehrlichman and Stuart Eisenstat, the principal aides for domestic policy during the Nixon and Carter administrations, clashed with Kissinger and Brzezinski: Ehrlichman and Kissinger over domestic discontent subsequent to the U.S. bombing of Cambodia; Eisenstat and Brzezinski over U.S.-Israel relations; and both sets of aides over the defense budget. Had boundaries of responsibility within the Nixon and Carter White Houses been more fluid, Ehrlichman and Eisenstat might have been more understanding of perceived military and diplomatic imperatives, and Kissinger and Brzezinski might have had a greater appreciation for the president's domestic political considerations.

Distinct from friction related to the aides' various responsibilities is that which results from the frequent pull between domestic politics and foreign policy. When the national security assistant is clearly supportive of a policy that political aides feel is hurting the president politically, there will usually, but not always, be friction. Political aide Bill Moyers, who opposed Johnson's Vietnam War policy for domestic political (as well as policy) reasons, did

not clash with Walt Rostow, who was then national security assistant and a strong supporter of the administration's position. Moyers and Rostow got along well on a *personal* level. Both aides probably realized that it was useful to have on the staff both an opponent and proponent of the administration's Vietnam policy as a lightning rod for criticism from the right and left.

However, instances of tension because of dissonance between politics and policy are numerous. Ehrlichman clashed with Kissinger during Nixon's 1969 European trip: Kissinger was interested in the diplomatic impact of meetings with foreign dignitaries while Ehrlichman was concerned about the trip's effect on U.S. public opinion. Some of Ford's aides wanted the president to make a dramatic response to allegations of past CIA misdeeds. They clashed with Kissinger, who felt that such a response would lead to disclosures of sensitive national security information. Brzezinski clashed with Carter's special Middle East negotiator, Robert Strauss. Brzezinski felt that Strauss, because of his reading of domestic politics, would not press the administration's position on West Bank settlements during his Middle East visit in August 1979. Reagan's second national security assistant, William Clark, had difficulty with political aides James Baker and Michael Deaver after they told him repeatedly that the public did not support the administration's massive military buildup. Robert McFarlane, who replaced Clark, did not appreciate Baker's involvement in arms control proposals that McFarlane felt were made merely for domestic political reasons.

In general, then, friction within the White House is likely when the national security assistant is a popular foreign policy spokesman and an active diplomatic operative. Friction is also likely over domestically sensitive issues when boundaries of responsibility within the White House are drawn sharply or when there is substantial discrepancy between perceived foreign policy imperatives and domestic political sentiment. When these conditions are absent, relations tend to be cordial and cooperative.

A national security assistant who continues over from a previous administration presents a unique case. Political aides might feel it would be politically beneficial for the president to criticize the policies of his predecessor, distance himself from them, or at least establish his own "independence," particularly from past

policies that have become contentious politically. In this case the national security assistant will probably seek to prevent or at least soften such criticism. However, it is likely that the political aides will resent this, as when Ford's speech-writing staff wanted the president to allude to the foreign policy "disarray" of the Nixon administration.

THE INTEGRATION OF FOREIGN POLICY WITH DOMESTIC POLITICS BY THE STAFF

Every president found it necessary to include domestic political advisers in foreign policy deliberations. Some only did so, however, after a major foreign policy embarrassment. For Kennedy, it was the Bay of Pigs incident in April 1961. For Carter, it was the announcement of plans for a joint U.S.-Soviet Middle East peace initiative in October 1977.

Except for the Truman administration, political advisers were invited to NSC meetings regularly, some participating more than others. But even when the political aides did not participate in formal policy deliberations, their counsel was sought in informal settings. Political aides participated in Johnson's Tuesday luncheons, Carter's Friday breakfasts, and during meetings of Kennedy's Executive Committee. Similarly, Staff Secretary Andrew Goodpaster invited political advisers to *ad hoc* Oval Office meetings with President Eisenhower. Political aide H. R. Haldeman attended many of Kissinger's meetings with Nixon.

The ultimate responsibility, however, for integrating foreign policy with domestic politics is the president's. But his aides have often pursued this on their own initiative. Some national security assistants assumed the responsibility to periodically notify political advisers about sensitive international developments—as did Truman's first national security assistant, Sidney Souers, with political adviser Clark Clifford. Others created institutionalized procedures to facilitate integration: such as inviting political advisers to NSC staff meetings, as did Bundy; having a weekly, confidential meeting among a few aides, as did Bundy and political aide Theodore Sorensen with Budget Director David Bell; or asking NSC staffers to send weekly reports and to work in other White House

offices on a part-time basis, as did George Christian, Johnson's fourth press secretary.

INFORMATION SHARING

Trust and mutual confidence are central to effective information sharing between the national security assistant and the political advisers. Since it is not possible, desirable, or necessary for every presidential aide to read all cable traffic and other pertinent information, the national security assistant and his staff must be relied upon by the political aides to keep them informed of sensitive developments. This places a major burden on the national security assistant in deciding what information to "hold tight" to reduce the probability of leaks.

When a political aide discovers that he was not informed about a matter for which he felt he had a legitimate need to know, his confidence in the timely transmittal of relevant information will be eroded or undermined altogether. George Reedy, while Johnson's press secretary, did not know about the administration's proposal for the Gulf of Tonkin Resolution until just before it was announced, and he had difficulty explaining it to the press immediately thereafter. Reedy, obviously, was understandably skeptical about *ad hoc* arrangements for information sharing.

On the other hand, the president puts the national security assistant in an awkward position—and may also jeopardize the conduct of foreign policy—if he promises a political aide access to *all* sensitive foreign policy information. Ron Nessen, Ford's press secretary, had a legitimate reason to protest when Brent Scowcroft withheld the report submitted to him by former President Nixon upon his return from the People's Republic of China in February 1976. Scowcroft knew that the administration would be liable to a Freedom of Information request and wanted the report kept secret since it contained sensitive information about U.S.-Chinese relations. Yet Ford had promised Nessen near-total access to information.

The national security assistant can decide not to share sensitive information with a political aide whom he thinks *wants* such information for *personal* reasons rather than *needs* such information for *presidential* reasons. But such a judgment will inevitably be

challenged and will probably cause resentment. Eisenstat, for instance, questioned the advisability of having his access to sensitive cables about the Middle East cut off from him by Brzezinski.

But, while unauthorized leaks are important considerations, so too are those considerations relating to the necessity of political aides understanding the diplomatic background of potentially explosive and domestically sensitive national security developments. If political aides are inadequately informed of these matters, their public explanations of the administration's stance will likely be inadequate. Furthermore, their perspectives and policy stances might be parochial—focusing excessively on domestic political considerations. Kissinger's extensive briefings of Haldeman and Ehrlichman about the U.S. bombing and subsequent ground invasion of Cambodia suggest that Kissinger was aware of the importance of this. Bundy displayed a similar awareness when, in October 1965, he sent Johnson a memorandum advising him how to handle his impending meeting with Vietnam War critic Pope Paul VI, a memorandum that was shared with political aides Moyers and Valenti.

INFLUENCE ON PRESIDENTIAL DECISION MAKING

The interaction of the national security assistant with other members of the White House staff has affected presidential decision making significantly. It has influenced key personnel changes, the scope of the national security assistant's responsibilities, and policy decisions.

Personnel Changes

Presidenial staff relationships affect personnel changes both inside and outside the White House. One former Nixon staffer was certain that Kissinger's reluctance to confront Haldeman on personnel changes in the winter of 1972 resulted in the "purge" of senior officials within the Arms Control and Disarmament Agency (ACDA). Haldeman (and others) thought these officials were too liberal. But Kissinger had relied on their analytical support and, in addition, their liberal stances made him appear to be advocating

centrist positions. Kissinger's failure to go to bat for these officials (for whatever reason) eventually returned to haunt him. Their successors, especially Fred Ikle and John Lehman, eventually allied with Secretary of Defense Donald Rumsfeld to thwart Kissinger's SALT II proposal.

The matter of personnel changes is a subject, like so many others, where personal relations can be decisive. Brzezinksi—whose relations with Hamilton Jordan, a senior Carter aide, were better than Kissinger's were with Haldeman—allied himself with Jordan in an effort to secure the appointment of George Seignious to replace Paul Warnke as ACDA director. Their advice prevailed over that given by Vance, who opposed Seignious's appointment. Similarly, before Clark's relations with Baker and Deaver soured, the three evidently had a hand in Secretary of State Alexander Haig's resignation and the appointment of George Shultz to replace him.

When political aides are dissatisfied with the performance of the national security assistant they might seek to get rid of him. Apparently, Baker and Deaver, among others, were instrumental in Richard Allen's resignation.

Scope of the National Security Assistant's Responsibilities

The breadth of the national security assistant's policy jurisdiction (and, for that matter, the jurisdiction of political aides) is affected by these interrelationships. Clifford was instrumental in Souers's assumption of responsibility for seeking presidential approval of NSC papers and for notifying departments and agencies responsible for implementing policy decisions. Sherman Adams and Jerry Persons, two of Eisenhower's political assistants, asked Robert Cutler and Gordan Gray, who served at various times as national security assistants, to preside over annual meetings of the Advertising Council so that they could monitor cabinet spokesmen and prevent them from disclosing sensitive national security information. Some members of Nixon's staff wanted Kissinger to "take the heat" for pre-election peace speculation in 1971 and recommended to Nixon that Kissinger hold his first live televised news conference. Several of Ford's political aides recommended (unsuccessfully) that Scowcroft become a visible foreign policy

spokesman as a counterweight to Secretary of State Kissinger's prominent media role.

Pressure within the White House to expand the national security assistant's stature and responsibilities tends to build when there are significant interdepartmental disputes. Some members of Truman's staff thought James Lay, who replaced Souers as national security assistant, needed more enforcement ability because the growing animosity between Secretary of Defense Louis Johnson and Secretary of State Dean Acheson made policy coordination difficult during the Korean War. Similarly, a number of Reagan's aides thought McFarlane's stature should be upgraded so that he would be better able to mediate disputes between Secretary of Defense Caspar Weinberger and Secretary of State Shultz. Of course, such role expansion is possible only when the national security assistant originally assumed a low profile.

When White House aides feel that a particular matter is not in any cabinet member's bureaucratic interest to support but should, nonetheless, be raised in an NSC or other high-level meeting, they might ask the national security assistant to introduce it. Hence, Bryce Harlow, one of Eisenhower's political assistants, asked Gray to recommend at an NSC meeting the establishment of a council for long-range defense planning.

Political aides may also seek to check or even downgrade the national security assistant's authority. In the Eisenhower White House, where aides were not supposed to challenge the advice of cabinet secretaries during policy meetings, Adams clearly thought it had been inappropriate for Cutler to voice his opinion about tariffs on British bicycles during an NSC meeting. Donald Rumsfeld, one of Ford's political advisers, reportedly proposed that only Ford, not Kissinger, conduct media briefings and that Kissinger be excluded from press photographs of the president and foreign leaders at the NATO conference in Brussels in May 1975. After Brzezinski, during his trip to the People's Republic of China in May 1978, made statements about the Soviet Union that diverged sharply from statements made prior to that time by Vance, several of Carter's political aides sought to ensure that Brzezinski's public statements were consistent with Vance's in the future (although this effort soon waned as they felt Brzezinski's stances were more popular than Vance's). Baker assured reporters that Haig re-

mained the Reagan administration's primary foreign policy official after it became known that Allen had opposed one of Haig's State Department nominations.

Policy Decisions

Finally, interactions among staff can influence policy decisions. This happened with great frequency during the Carter administration. Brzezinski allied himself with other White House aides, thereby increasing his influence relative to Vance's on decisions about U.S. response to the Soviet invasion of Afghanistan and to the hostage crisis in Iran. When this happens, cabinet secretaries will probably try to counteract it, perhaps by allying themselves with other members on the White House staff.[1] Vance, at least once, tried unsuccessfully to do this with Jordan and, on numerous occasions, did so successfully with presidential assistant Lloyd Cutler.

But the national security assistant has advantages here. His close proximity to and daily contact with the president allows him to be more in tune with the president's political concerns, not to mention the concerns of the political advisers. Brzezinski allied himself frequently with political aides Hamilton Jordan and Jody Powell by asserting that his advice would best serve Carter's political interests. Another advantage the national security assistant usually has over cabinet secretaries is a better understanding of the president's character and emotions. Knowing that Johnson had a hyperbolic personality, Moyers and Bundy advised Johnson not to make a veiled reference to a communist threat (for which there was no substantial proof) when he announced the landing of U.S. troops in the Dominican Republic in April 1965. Secretary of State Dean Rusk, on the other hand, not knowing Johnson as well as members of the White House staff, wanted the president to allude to such a threat. In his first announcement, Johnson did not mention communist involvement. But four days later, when he made reference to it in response to criticism about the intervention, he did in fact exaggerate as Moyers and Bundy had feared.

But White House staff interaction can work in reverse as well: national security assistants, at a cabinet secretary's urging, can prevent the president from doing something the political aides want him to do. After an appeal from Haig, Clark reportedly convinced

Reagan to allow the press to take photographs of his meeting with British Prime Minister Margaret Thatcher during the Falkland Islands War in June 1982. The political aides had wanted to downplay the U.S. tilt toward Great Britain. But Haig feared that not allowing photographs would be interpreted as U.S. sympathy for Argentina, thereby heightening the hopes of Argentine leaders, causing them to prolong the war.

Finally, staff unanimity or near-unanimity on policy questions does not necessarily carry the day with the president, nor are staff alliances permanent. Most of Kennedy's staff opposed live presidential press conferences, yet Kennedy held them anyway. And, although Lloyd Cutler usually sided with Vance in opposition to Brzezinski's advice, he sided with Brzezinski in advising Carter how to respond to the U.S. hostage crisis in Iran.

ACCESS TO THE PRESIDENT

Restrictions by a White House political assistant on the national security assistant's access to the president are rare. Only in the early Reagan administration did a political assistant exercise substantial, probably excessive, control over the national security assistant's access, and that affected only Allen. When this happens, executive branch officials will soon realize that sending memoranda to the president through the national security assistant is futile. Unless rectified or unless another acceptable communications channel is opened, this access restriction will likely create an explosive situation within the executive branch and, almost certainly, negative political fallout for the president. In response to the concerns of some of his cabinet officers, Reagan felt compelled to assure them that Clark, and later McFarlane, would have access to him.

The only other apparent access restriction was Kissinger's by Haldeman. But this occurred only twice: when Haldeman felt that Kissinger was getting involved in a matter outside his area of responsibility—the fate of Apollo 13 in April 1970; and when Haldeman believed it would have been premature for Kissinger to wake Nixon on the basis of unconfirmed evidence of Egyptian President Nasser's fatal heart attack in September of the same year.

Generally, instead of restricting access, the picture that emerges

from this analysis is that political aides enhance it. They act as middlemen facilitating communication between the national security assistant and the president. When the president is angry about something or has drawn himself into seclusion, a political aide might be the national security assistant's best means of getting through to the chief executive without ruffling feathers (a role played by Haldeman and by his replacement, Haig, for Kissinger). Also, when he is angry with or hesitant to confront the national security assistant on a given matter, the president might have another White House aide deliver his message (as did Valenti and Moyers with Bundy, and Haldeman and Ehrlichman with Kissinger).

Political aides have also served as a channel through which the national security assistant sent memoranda to the president. In only one case does it appear that memoranda may have been tampered with en route to the Oval Office. Rumsfeld reportedly asked James Connor, the cabinet secretary, to "balance" Kissinger's position papers before they reached Ford. However, one Ford staffer said that if this did in fact happen, it probably made little difference.

Only during the early Reagan administration was it necessary for senior officials outside the White House to appeal to another White House aide for access to the president because they had not been successful in going through the national security assistant. This occurred when the national security assistant's own access was restricted. Secretary of State Haig thus tried to reach Reagan through political adviser Edwin Meese.

When executive branch officials contact a political aide rather than the national security assistant on a foreign policy matter, it is likely that they are doing so not because the assistant has restricted their access, but because they think the political aide sympathizes with their position more than the assistant. This is more of an alliance than a "backdoor" access. During the Johnson administration, officials who agreed with Moyers's views on foreign policy made their Oval Office connection through him for persuasive, not merely communicative, purposes.

PRESCRIPTIONS FOR MANAGING STAFF IMPACT ON FOREIGN POLICY

Describing interactions among White House staff members is a difficult exercise. Identifying the influence of these actions on for-

eign policy is an imperfect enterprise. What follows here are qualified "prescriptions."

AT AN EARLY STAGE, THE PRESIDENT SHOULD INFORM HIS ENTIRE WHITE HOUSE STAFF ABOUT HIS PREFERENCES REGARDING THE FOREIGN POLICY PROCESS. POLICY-MAKING PROCEDURES SHOULD BE SUGGESTED TO AN INCOMING PRESIDENT BY HIS TRANSITION TEAM. THE RECOMMENDATIONS APPROVED BY THE PRESIDENT SHOULD BE IN WRITING AND CIRCULATED THROUGHOUT THE WHITE HOUSE AND AMONG CABINET SECRETARIES. If the entire staff does not know the president's preferences, certain aides could misinterpret the behavior of another aide who is merely following instructions. This misinterpretation could result in harmful staff friction. Furthermore, shared knowledge of commonly understood procedures can help presidential assistants keep each other in line and will provide cabinet secretaries with reasonably clear expectations of their prerogatives and responsibilities. Some constraints on staff behavior that might be imposed by the president—such as withholding the staff members' personal policy views during meetings with cabinet secretaries—may be difficult to follow. Compliance can be facilitated by intra-staff and cabinet monitoring.

AT LEAST ONE, MAYBE MORE, POLITICAL ADVISERS SHOULD BE INCLUDED IN FOREIGN POLICY DISCUSSIONS SO THAT POTENTIAL DOMESTIC REACTIONS ARE CONSIDERED ALONG WITH VARIOUS POLICY OPTIONS. CONVERSELY, THE NATIONAL SECURITY ASSISTANT, OR AT LEAST ONE NSC STAFF MEMBER, SHOULD ATTEND GENERAL WHITE HOUSE STAFF MEETINGS. If political advisers are insulated from the foreign policy-making process, it is likely that the administration will get itself into trouble domestically. There are instances, of course, when the perceived national interest will and must override domestic political considerations. But the home front ultimately determines foreign policy effectiveness and the distinction between domestic and foreign matters is frequently artificial.

THE PRESIDENT SHOULD NOT RELY EXCESSIVELY ON HIS WHITE HOUSE ADVISERS FOR COUNSEL ABOUT MID-STREAM FOREIGN POLICY PERSONNEL CHANGES, ESPECIALLY IF THOSE ADVISERS ARE NOT ACTIVELY INVOLVED IN PERTINENT ONGOING DIPLOMATIC ACTIVITIES. When the political advisers are not intimately aware of the international environment or of U.S. strategy, their counsel about personnel

changes, if followed, can upset months, even years, of diplomatic efforts. For example, Clark, Baker, and Deaver evidently convinced Reagan to ask for Haig's resignation on June 25, 1982, in the heat of the Middle East crisis triggered by the Israeli invasion of Lebanon even though both Reagan and Haig earlier had wanted to postpone the resignation. Haig's abrupt departure might have been one reason why the first Beirut settlement was not achieved until mid-August.

THE PRESIDENT SHOULD STRICTLY LIMIT THE PUBLIC SPOKESMANSHIP AND DIPLOMATIC RESPONSIBILITIES OF THE NATIONAL SECURITY ASSISTANT. Three interrelated hazards are associated with these responsibilities. First, a national security assistant in the public spotlight with extensive diplomatic responsibilities will be perceived as usurping the prerogatives of the secretary of state. Hence, an NSC–State Department rift may well result and become a political issue. Critics may then charge that the president cannot manage his foreign policy process. Second, if the assistant's visibility and diplomacy make him a popular figure with the general public, it is possible that the president's own popularity will be jeopardized, especially if the assistant's media presence causes the president to be seen as deficient in his command of foreign policy. Third, other White House aides will seek to downgrade the national security assistant if his popularity or an NSC-State rift are perceived to be hurting the president politically.[2] This can undermine the national security assistant's authority, thereby creating confusion throughout the national security policy process.

THE PRESIDENT SHOULD TREAT HIS STAFF AS GENERALISTS, SHOULD NOT ERECT RIGID BOUNDARIES OF RESPONSIBILITY AMONG THEM, AND SHOULD LET THE CABINET SECRETARIES—WHO ALREADY HAVE SPECIALIZED BUREAUCRATIC INTERESTS AND MISSIONS—DO MOST OF THE DISPUTING. It is debatable whether friction between the domestic and national security assistants has a positive net benefit. On the one hand, if they argue in the president's presence they will expose him to the pros and cons of policy questions (such as trade-offs between the defense budget and social programs). On the other hand, such friction can harm the aides' relationships in instances where harmony is essential (such as when a political aide serves as a communication link between the president and the national se-

curity assistant—as Valenti did for Bundy, and Ehrlichman and Haldeman did for Kissinger). Since cabinet secretaries will protect their bureaucratic turfs and because the NSC provides a forum in which they can argue in the president's presence, it would probably be best for the White House staff to focus on articulating and coordinating administration policies throughout the bureaucracy and monitoring policy implementation. These are critical functions that can and should absorb most of the staff's time. While the staff can never wholly insulate itself from inevitable interdepartmental disputes, it should, when possible, retain a certain distance from them.

NOTES

1. There are other routes available as well: to ally with other cabinet officials, leak stories to the press, complain to the president, or threaten to resign.

2. Bundy's cordial relations with both the Kennedy and Johnson staffs, in contrast to Kissinger's with the Nixon and Ford staffs, are telling in this regard. Bundy did not infringe on cabinet secretaries' prerogatives nor did he seek to upstage the president.

Selected Bibliography

BOOKS AND SCHOLARLY ARTICLES

Acheson, Dean. *Present at the Creation: My Years at the State Department.* New York: W. W. Norton, 1969.

Adams, Sherman. *Firsthand Report: The Story of the Eisenhower Administration.* New York: Harper and Brothers, 1961.

Allen, Robert S., and Shannon, William V. *The Truman Merry-Go-Round.* New York: Vanguard, 1950.

Allison, Graham T. *Essence of Decision: Explaining the Cuban Missile Crisis.* Boston: Little, Brown, 1971.

Amrine, Michael. *The Awesome Challenge: The Hundred Days of Lyndon Johnson.* New York: G. P. Putnam's Sons, 1964.

Anderson, Patrick. *The Presidents' Men: White House Assistants of Franklin D. Roosevelt, Harry S. Truman, Dwight D. Eisenhower, John F. Kennedy, and Lyndon B. Johnson.* Garden City, N.Y.: Doubleday, 1968.

Barber, James D. *The Presidential Character.* Englewood Cliffs, N.J.: Prentice-Hall, 1972.

Barrett, Laurence, I. *Gambling with History: Ronald Reagan in the White House.* New York: Doubleday, 1983.

Berman, Larry. *Planning a Tragedy: The Americanization of the War in Vietnam.* New York: W. W. Norton, 1982.

Brownstein, Ronald, and Easton, Nina. *Reagan's Ruling Class: Portraits of the President's Top 100 Officials.* Washington, D.C.: Presidential Accountability Group, 1982.

Brzezinski, Zbigniew. *Power and Principle: Memoirs of the National Security Adviser, 1977–1981.* New York: Farrar, Straus & Giroux, 1983.

Caraley, Demetrios. *The Politics of Military Unification: A Study of Conflict and the Policy Process*. New York: Columbia University Press, 1966.

Carter, Jimmy. *Keeping Faith: Memoirs of a President*. New York: Bantam, 1982.

Casserly, John J. *The Ford White House: The Diary of a Speechwriter*. Boulder, Colo.: Colorado Associated Press, 1977.

Christian, George. *The President Steps Down: A Personal Memoir of the Transfer of Power*. New York: Macmillan, 1970.

Clark, Keith C., and Legere, Laurence J., eds. *The President and the Management of National Security*. New York: Praeger, 1969.

Clarke, Duncan L. "Integrating Arms Control, Defense, and Foreign Policy in the Executive Branch of the U.S. Government." In *Decisionmaking for Arms Limitation*, edited by Hans Guenter Brauch and Duncan L. Clarke. Cambridge, Mass.: Ballinger, 1983.

Colby, William, and Forbath, Peter. *Honorable Men: My Life in the CIA*. New York: Simon and Schuster, 1978.

Collier, Peter, and Horowitz, David. *The Kennedys: An American Drama*. New York: Summit Books, 1984.

Colson, Charles W. *Born Again*. Old Tappan, N.J.: Chosen Books, 1976.

Cornwell, Elmer E., Jr. *Presidential Leadership of Public Opinion*. Bloomington: Indiana University Press, 1965.

Cutler, Robert. *No Time for Rest*. Boston: Little, Brown, 1966.

Destler, I. M. "The Evolution of Reagan Foreign Policy." In *The Reagan Presidency: An Early Assessment*, edited by Fred I. Greenstein. Baltimore: Johns Hopkins University Press, 1983.

———. "A Job That Doesn't Work." *Foreign Policy* (Spring 1980): 80–91.

———. "National Security Management: What Presidents Have Wrought." *Political Science Quarterly* 95 (Winter 1980–1981): 573–588.

———. *Presidents, Bureaucrats and Foreign Policy*. Princeton: Princeton University Press, 1974.

Donovan, Hedley. "Advising a President." In *The Virginia Papers on the Presidency*, edited by Kenneth Thompson. Vol. 6. Washington, D.C.: University Press of America, 1981.

Donovan, Robert J. *Eisenhower: The Inside Story*. New York: Harper and Brothers, 1956.

———. *Tumultuous Years: The Presidency of Harry S Truman*. New York: W. W. Norton, 1982.

Ehrlichman, John. *Witness to Power: The Nixon Years*. New York: Simon and Schuster, 1982.

Eisenhower, Dwight D. *The White House Years: Mandate for Change, 1953–1956*. Garden City, N.Y.: Doubleday, 1963.

————. *The White House Years: Waging Peace, 1956–1961*. Garden City, N.Y.: Doubleday, 1965.

Endicott, John E. "The National Security Council." In *American Defense Policy*, edited by John F. Reichart and Steven R. Sturm. Baltimore: Johns Hopkins University Press, 1982.

Ford, Gerald R. *A Time to Heal*. New York: Harper and Row, 1979.

Fuller, Helen. *Year of Trial: Kennedy's Crucial Decisions*. New York: Harcourt, Brace and World, 1962.

Gaubard, Stephen R. *Kissinger: Portrait of a Mind*. New York: W. W. Norton, 1974.

George, Alexander L. *Presidential Decisionmaking in Foreign Policy: The Effective Use of Information and Advice*. Boulder, Colo.: Westview, 1980.

Goldman, Eric F. *The Tragedy of Lyndon Johnson*. New York: Alfred A. Knopf, 1968.

Graff, Henry F. *The Tuesday Cabinet: Deliberation and Decision on Peace and War under Lyndon Johnson*. Englewood Cliffs, N.J.: Prentice-Hall, 1970.

Greenstein, Fred I. *The Hidden-Hand Presidency: Eisenhower as Leader*. New York: Basic Books, 1982.

————., ed. *The Reagan Presidency: An Early Assessment*. Baltimore: Johns Hopkins University Press, 1983.

Gully, Bill, and Reese, Mary Ellen. *Breaking Cover*. New York: Simon and Schuster, 1980.

Haig, Alexander M., Jr. *Caveat: Realism, Reagan and Foreign Policy*. New York: Macmillan, 1984.

Halberstam, David. *The Best and the Brightest*. New York: Fawcett Crest, 1972.

Haldeman, H. R., with DiMona, Joseph. *The Ends of Power*. New York: Times Books, 1978.

Hall, David K. "The 'Custodian-Manager' of the Policymaking Process." In *Report of the Commission on the Organization of the Government for the Conduct of Foreign Policy*. Appendix E. Vol. 2. Ch. XII. Washington, D.C.: Government Printing Office, 1975.

Hartmann, Robert T. *Palace Politics: An Inside Account of the Ford Years*. New York: McGraw-Hill, 1980.

Heath, Jim F. *Decade of Disillusionment: The Kennedy-Johnson Years*. Bloomington: Indiana University Press, 1975.

Heller, Francis H., ed. *The Truman White House*. Lawrence, Kans.: Regents Press of Kansas, 1980.

Hersh, Seymour M. *The Price of Power: Kissinger in the Nixon White House*. New York: Summit Books, 1983.

Hess, Stephen. *Organizing the Presidency*. Washington, D.C.: The Brookings Institution, 1976.

Hewlett, Richard, and Duncan, Francis. *Atomic Shield, 1947–1952*. University Park: Pennsylvania State University Press, 1969.

Hilsman, Roger. *To Move a Nation: The Politics of Foreign Policy in the Administration of John F. Kennedy*. Garden City, N.Y.: Doubleday, 1967.

Hoopes, Townsend. *The Limits of Intervention: An Inside Account of How the Johnson Policy of Escalation Was Reversed*. New York: David McKay, 1969.

Hoxie, R. Gordon. "Staffing the Ford and Carter Presidencies." In *Organizing and Staffing the Presidency*, edited by Bradley D. Nash. New York: Center for the Study of the Presidency, 1980.

Humphrey, David C. "Tuesday Lunch at the Johnson White House: A Preliminary Assessment." *Diplomatic History* 8 (Winter 1984): 81–101.

Hunter, Robert E. *Presidential Control of Foreign Policy: Management or Mishap?* New York: Praeger, 1982.

Jackson, Henry M., Jr., ed. *The National Security Council: Subcommittee Papers on Policy-Making at the Presidential Level*. New York: Praeger, 1965.

Janis, Irving L. *Victims of Groupthink: A Psychological Study of Foreign-Policy Decisions and Fiascoes*. Boston: Houghton Mifflin, 1972.

Johnson, Lyndon Baines. *The Vantage Point: Perspectives of the Presidency, 1963–1969*. New York: Holt, Rinehart and Winston, 1971.

Johnson, Richard Tanner. *Managing the White House: An Intimate Study of the Presidency*. New York: Harper and Row, 1974.

Jordan, Hamilton. *Crisis: The Last Year of the Carter Presidency*. New York: Berkley Books, 1983.

Kalb, Marvin, and Kalb, Bernard. *Kissinger*. Boston: Little, Brown, 1974.

Kearns, Doris. *Lyndon Johnson and the American Dream*. New York: Harper and Row, 1976.

Kissinger, Henry A. *White House Years*. Boston: Little, Brown, 1979.

———. *Years of Upheaval*. Boston: Little, Brown, 1982.

Klein, Herbert G. *Making It Perfectly Clear*. Garden City, N.Y.: Doubleday, 1980.

Lasky, Victor. *Jimmy Carter: The Man and the Myth*. New York: Richard Marek, 1979.

Lichtenstein, Nelson, ed. *Political Profiles: The Johnson Years*. New York: Facts on File, 1976.

———., ed. *Political Profiles: The Kennedy Years*. New York: Facts on File, 1976.

Lilienthal, David E. *The Atomic Energy Years, 1945–1950.* New York: Harper and Row, 1964.

McNeil, Mary, ed. *Reagan's First Year.* Washington, D.C.: Congressional Quarterly, 1982.

McPherson, Harry. *A Political Education.* Boston: Little, Brown, 1972.

Medved, Michael. *The Shadow Presidents.* New York: Times Books, 1979.

Millis, Walter, ed. *The Forrestal Diaries.* New York: Viking, 1951.

Morris, Roger. *Haig: The General's Progress.* New York: Playboy Press, 1982.

————. *Uncertain Greatness: Henry Kissinger and American Foreign Policy.* New York: Harper and Row, 1981.

Nessen, Ron. *It Sure Looks Different from the Inside.* New York: Playboy Press, 1978.

Neustadt, Richard E. "The Constraining of the President: The Presidency after Watergate." *British Journal of Political Science* 4 (October 1974): 383–397.

————. *Presidential Power.* New York: Wiley, 1960.

Nixon, Richard M. *RN: The Memoirs of Richard Nixon.* New York: Grosset and Dunlap, 1978.

O'Donnell, Kenneth P., and Powers, David F., with McCarthy, Joe. *"Johnny, We Hardly Know Ye": Memories of John Fitzgerald Kennedy.* Boston: Little, Brown, 1972.

Osborne, John. *The Fifth Year of the Nixon Watch.* New York: Liveright, 1974.

————. *The Fourth Year of the Nixon Watch.* New York: Liveright, 1973.

————. *The Third Year of the Nixon Watch.* New York: Liveright, 1972.

————. *White House Watch: The Ford Years.* Washington, D.C.: New Republic Books, 1977.

Paige, Glenn D. *The Korean Decision.* New York: The Free Press, 1968.

Peters, Charles. "What Happened to the American Public?" In *Politics and the Oval Office: Towards Presidential Governance,* edited by Arnold T. Meltsner. San Francisco: Institute for Contemporary Studies, 1981.

Prados, John. *The Soviet Estimate: U.S. Intelligence Analysis and Russian Military Strength.* New York: Dial Press, 1982.

Rather, Dan, and Gates, Gary Paul. *The Palace Guard.* New York: Harper and Row, 1974.

Reeves, Richard. *A Ford Not a Lincoln.* New York: Harcourt Brace Jovanovich, 1975.

Roberts, Charles W., ed. *Has the President Too Much Power?* New York: Harper's Magazine Press, 1973.

————. *LBJ's Inner Circle.* New York: Delacorte, 1965.

Rostow, W. W. *The Diffusion of Power: An Essay in Recent History.* New York: Macmillan, 1972.

Safire, William. *Before the Fall: An Inside View of the Pre-Watergate White House.* Garden City, N.Y.: Doubleday, 1975.

Salinger, Pierre. *With Kennedy.* Garden City, N.Y.: Doubleday, 1966.

Schell, John. *The Time of Illusion.* New York: Knopf, 1976.

Schlesinger, Arthur M., Jr. *Robert Kennedy and His Times.* Boston: Houghton Mifflin, 1978.

———. *A Thousand Days: John F. Kennedy in the White House.* Boston: Houghton Mifflin, 1965.

Schoenebaum, Eleanora W., ed. *Political Profiles: The Eisenhower Years.* New York: Facts on File, 1977.

———., ed. *Political Profiles: The Nixon/Ford Years.* New York: Facts on File, 1979.

———., ed. *Political Profiles: The Truman Years.* New York: Facts on File, 1978.

Shogan, Robert. *Promises to Keep: Carter's First Hundred Days.* New York: Thomas Y. Crowell, 1977.

Sidney, Hugh. *John F. Kennedy, President.* New York: Atheneum, 1963.

———. *A Very Personal Presidency: Lyndon Johnson in the White House.* New York: Atheneum, 1968.

Sorensen, Theodore, C. *Kennedy.* New York: Harper and Row, 1965.

———. *The Kennedy Legacy.* New York: Macmillan, 1969.

Souers, Sidney W. "Policy Formulation and National Security." *American Political Science Review* 43 (June 1949): 534–543.

Steinberg, Alfred. *The Man from Missouri: The Life and Times of Harry S Truman.* New York: G. P. Putnam's Sons, 1962.

Stevenson, Charles A. *The End of Nowhere.* Boston: Beacon Press, 1972.

Szulc, Tad. *The Illusion of Peace.* New York: Viking, 1978.

Talbott, Strobe. *Deadly Gambits: The Reagan Administration and the Stalemate in Nuclear Arms Control.* New York: Knopf, 1984.

Tanzer, Lester, ed. *The Kennedy Circle.* Washington, D.C.: Luce, 1961.

terHorst, Jerald F. *Gerald Ford and the Future of the Presidency.* New York: The Third Press, 1974.

Theoharis, Arthur G. *The Truman Presidency: The Origins of the Imperial Presidency and the National Security State.* New York: Earl M. Coleman Enterprises, 1979.

Tocqueville, Alexis de. *Democracy in America.* Vol. I. Reprint. New York: Vintage Books, 1945.

Truman, Margaret. *Harry S. Truman.* New York: Morrow, 1973.

Truman, Harry. *Memoirs. Volume Two: Years of Trial and Hope.* Garden City, N.Y.: Doubleday, 1956.

Valenti, Jack. *A Very Human President*. New York: W. W. Norton, 1975.
Vance, Cyrus. *Hard Choices: Critical Years in America's Foreign Policy*. New York: Simon and Schuster, 1983.
Van Der Linden, Frank. *The Real Reagan*. New York: William Morrow, 1981.
White, Theodore H. *Breach of Faith: The Fall of Richard Nixon*. New York: Atheneum, 1975.
White, William S. *The Responsibles*. New York: Harper and Row, 1971.
Wilmot, Chester. *The Struggle for Europe*. New York: Harper, 1952.
Wise, Sidney, and Schier, Richard F., eds. *The Presidential Office*. New York: Thomas Y. Crowell, 1968.
Woodward, Bob, and Bernstein, Carl. *The Final Days*. New York: Simon and Schuster, 1976.

POPULAR MAGAZINES AND NEWSPAPERS

Alsop, Joseph, and Alsop, Stewart. "How Foreign Policy Is Made." *The Saturday Evening Post* 221 (30 April 1949).
Alsop, Stewart. "Facts Hard and Soft." *Newsweek* (18 December 1972): 112.
Brandt, Raymond P. "Sidney Souers May Become Truman's Military Adviser." *St. Louis Post-Dispatch* (3 December 1948).
Bonafede, Dom. "How the White House Helps Carter Make Up His Mind." *National Journal* 10 (15 April 1978): 584–588.
———. "That's Mike Deaver at the Hub of Ronald Reagan's Presidential World." *National Journal* 13 (August 1981): 1462.
Boston Daily Globe, 6 September 1958.
Carter, Jimmy. "Making Foreign and Defense Policy: Openness, Coherence and Efficiency." *National Journal* 8 (23 October 1976): 1528–1529.
Fischer, John. "Mr. Truman's Politburo." *Harper's* 202 (June 1951): 29–36.
Gelb, Leslie H. "Muskie and Brzezinski: The Struggle Over Foreign Policy." *New York Times Magazine* (20 July 1980): 26.
Gordan, Michael R. "NSC: A Lower Profile?" *National Journal* 13 (25 April 1981): 688.
Halberstram, David. "The Very Expensive Education of McGeorge Bundy." *Harper's* 239 (July 1969): 21–41.
Hersey, John. "The President." *New York Times Magazine* (20 April 1975): 108–109.
Hyman, Sidney. "When Bundy Says. . . . " *New York Times Magazine* (2 December 1962): 132.

Kansas City Star, 6 May 1984.

Kilpatrick, Carroll. "Johnson's 'Little State Dept.' Fades." *Washington Post*. 2 April 1966, p. A6.

Kirschen, Dick. "Clark Emerges as a Tough Manager, Not a Rival to the Secretary of State." *National Journal* 14 (17 July 1982): 1244–1248.

Kraft, Joseph. "Kennedy's Working Staff." *Harper's* 225 (December 1962): 29–36.

"Last Chance for Tough Viet Agreement." *Human Events* (25 November 1972): 1.

Leaman, Lawrence. "Playing for Keeps: The Long Distance Race of Donald Rumsfeld." *Washingtonian* 12 (February 1977): 92–107.

Los Angeles Times, 19 October 1972.

Mathews, Tom, with Clift, Eleanor, and DeFrank, Thomas M. "Zeroing in on Zbig." *Newsweek* (30 January 1978): 49–50.

Morgan, Thomas B. "The Most Happy Fella in the White House." *Life* 63 (1 December 1967): 80–88.

New York Post, 17 December 1948.

New York Times, 17 June 1950; 9 May 1969; 31 December 1972; 29 June, 4 July 1974; 24 May, 17 December 1976; 13 May 1977; 29 April 1980; 4, 11 March, 3 November, 24 December 1981; 20 January, 26 April, 26 June, 6 September, 29 November 1982; 31 March, 14, 17 October 1983; 10 January, 28 March 1984.

Novak, Jeremiah. "The Trilateral Connection." *The Atlantic Monthly* (July 1977): 57–59.

"O.K., S.A.," *Time* (9 January 1956): 18–22.

Osborne, John. "White House Watch: After One Year." *The New Republic* 178 (11 February 1978): 10–12.

———. "White House Watch: At Jimmy's Place." *The New Republic* 177 (29 October 1977): 9.

———. "White House Watch: Carter's Summit." *The New Republic* 179 (30 September 1978): 16.

———. "White House Watch: Chasing Symbols." *The New Republic* 178 (21 January 1978): 6, 8–10.

———. "White House Watch: Cleanup Time." *The New Republic* 184 (14 March 1981): 8–10.

———. "White House Watch: Dumping Bert." *The New Republic* 177 (17 September 1977): 8–12.

———. "White House Watch: Fun in the Junkyard." *The New Republic* 184 (14 February 1981): 8–9, 12.

———. "White House Watch: Haig and the System." *The New Republic* 184 (28 March 1984): 6, 8–9.

———. "White House Watch: Moving On." *The New Republic* 181 (17 November 1979): 6, 8, 10.

———. "White House Watch: News from Cloud 9." *The New Republic* 179 (4 November 1978): 9–11.

———. "White House Watch: Ringing the Changes." *The New Republic* 176 (25 June 1977): 9–11.

———. "White House Watch: Tennis, Folks?" *The New Republic* 177 (26 November 1977): 11–12.

———. "White House Watch: Two Stories." *The New Republic* 181 (15 September 1979): 8–10.

———. "White House Watch: Under Pressure." *The New Republic* 178 (24 June 1978): 9–14.

The Reporter, 10 May 1949.

Safire, William. "Puppet as Prince." *Harper's* 250 (March 1975): 12–17.

Time, 9 January 1956; 8 June 1970.

"Transcript of President's News Conference on Foreign and Domestic Matters." *New York Times*. 1 April 1966, p. 18.

Washington Post, 25 May 1974; 8 February 1975; 24–27 May, 28 June 1981; 2, 5 January 1982; 16 May, 14, 15, 17, 18, 23 October 1983; 19 March, 17, 27 June 1984.

Washington Star, 28 September 1949.

"Who Runs America." *U.S. News and World Report* (16 April 1979): 33.

GOVERNMENT DOCUMENTS, UNPUBLISHED MEMORANDA AND MANUSCRIPTS

Abilene, Kans. Eisenhower Library. Cutler, Robert. Letter to Hon. Bryce Harlow. 26 June 1958. Bryce N. Harlow File. Moscow Exhibition. Box 6. Folder: National Security Council.

Abilene, Kans. Eisenhower Library. Goodpaster, Andrew J. Note to Mr. Hagerty. 15 May 1955. White House Office. Office of the Staff Secretary. Subject Series. White House Subseries, A67-50. Folder: Staff Secretary File, 1957–60.

Abilene, Kans. Eisenhower Library. Goodpaster, Andrew J. Memorandum for Mr. Hagerty. 12 November 1955. White House Office. Office of the Staff Secretary. Subject Series. White House Subseries. Folder: Staff Secretary File, 1955 (5).

Abilene, Kans. Eisenhower Library. Goodpaster, Andrew J. Note to General Persons. 7 October 1955. White House Office. Office of the Staff Secretary. Subject Series. White House Subseries, A67-49, 67-50. Box 7. Folder: Staff Secretary File (4).

Abilene, Kans. Eisenhower Library. Goodpaster, Andrew J. Memorandum for the Record. 23 April 1955. White House Office. Office of the Staff Secretary. Subject Series. White House Subseries, A67-49, 67-50. Box 1. Folder: Administrative Arrangements (1).

Abilene, Kans. Eisenhower Library. Goodpaster, Andrew J. Memorandum for the Record. 1 October 1955. White House Office. Office of the Staff Secretary. Subject Series. White House Subseries, A67-49, 67-50. Box 1. Folder: Administrative Arrangements (2).

Abilene, Kans. Eisenhower Library. Goodpaster, Andrew J. Memorandum for the Record. 1 October 1955. White House Office. Office of the Staff Secretary. Subject Series. White House Subseries, A67-49, 67-50. Box 1. Folder: Administrative Arrangements (2).

Abilene, Kans. Eisenhower Library. Gray, Gordan. Memorandum for Bryce N. Harlow. 16 December 1958. Records of Bryce N. Harlow, 1953–61, A67-56. Box 6. Folder: National Security Council, 1958.

Abilene, Kans. Eisenhower Library. Harlow, Bryce. Memorandum for Gordan Gray. 12 November 1958. Records of Bryce N. Harlow, 1953–61, A67-56. Box 6, Folder: National Security Council, 1958.

Abilene, Kans. Eisenhower Library. Jackson, William H. Memorandum for Sherman Adams. 11 September 1956. White House Office. Office of the Staff Secretary. Subject Series. White House Subseries. Folder: William H. Jackson (4).

Abilene, Kans. Eisenhower Library. McKee, Frederick C. Letter to Bryce N. Harlow. 19 September 1958. Records of Bryce N. Harlow, 1953–61, A67-56. Box 6. Folder: National Security Council, 1958.

Abilene, Kans. Eisenhower Library. Minnich, L. Arthur. Note. 27 March 1953. White House Office. Office of the Staff Secretary. L. Arthur Minnich Series, A67-49. Box 1.

Abilene, Kans. Eisenhower Library. Minnich, L. Arthur. Note. 1 July 1953. White House Office. Office of the Staff Secretary. L. Arthur Minnich Series, A67-49. Box 1. Folder: Staff Meetings (3).

Abilene, Kans. Eisenhower Library. Persons, Wilton B. Memorandum for Gordan Gray. 14 January 1960. Files of Special Assistant Relating to the Office of Coordinator of Government Public Service Advertising (James M. Lambie, Jr.). Box 55. Folder: Gordan Gray.

Austin, Tex. Johnson Library. [Bator, Francis M.] FMB. Memorandum to McG.B. [McGeorge Bundy]. 28 September 1965. National Security File. Name File: Bator Memos. Boxes 1, 2.

Austin, Tex. Johnson Library. Bundy, McGeorge. Memorandum for Mr. Moyers. 9 September 1965. National Security File. Aide File: Bundy. Box 4. Folder: Vol. 14, Sept. 1–22, 1965.

Austin, Tex. Johnson Library. Bundy, McGeorge. Memorandum for the
President. 11 June 1964. National Security File. Aide File: Bundy.
Memos for the President, 6/64–2/65. Box 2. Folder: Vol. 5, 6/1–
30/64.

Austin, Tex. Johnson Library. Bundy, McGeorge. Memorandum for the
President. 9 August 1964. National Security File. Aide File: Bundy.
Memos for the President 6/64–2/65. Folder: Vol. 6, 7/1 to 9/30,
1964.

Austin, Tex. Johnson Library. Bundy, McGeorge. Memorandum for the
President. 6 October 1964. National Security File. Aide File: Bundy.
Memos for the President. Box 2, 6/64–2/65. Folder: Vol. 7, 10/1
to 12/31, 1964.

Austin, Tex. Johnson Library. Bundy, McGeorge. Memorandum for the
President. 20 October 1964. National Security File. Aide File:
Bundy. Memos for the President, 6/64–2/65. Folder: Vol. 7, 10/7
to 12/31, 1964.

Austin, Tex. Johnson Library. Bundy, McGeorge. Memorandum for the
President. 2 February 1965. National Security File. Aide File: Bundy.
Memos for the President. Box 2. Folder: Vol. 8, 1/1 to 2/28, 1965.

Austin, Tex. Johnson Library. Bundy, McGeorge. Memorandum for the
President. 19 February 1966. National Security File. Aide File:
Bundy. Box 6. Folder: Vol. 20, February 5–28, 1966.

Austin, Tex. Johnson Library. Bundy, McGeorge. Memorandum for the
President. 28 April 1965. National Security File. Aide File: Bundy.
Memos for the President. Box 3. Folder: Vol. 10, April 15–May
31, 1965.

Austin, Tex. Johnson Library. Bundy, McGeorge. Memorandum for the
President. 3 October 1965. National Security File. Aide File: Bundy.
Memos for the President. Box 5. Folder: Vol. 15, Sept. 23–Oct.
14, 1965.

Austin, Tex. Johnson Library. Bundy, McGeorge. Memorandum to the
President. 26 January 1966. National Security File. Aide File: Bundy.
Box 6. Folder: Vol. 19, Jan. 19–Feb. 4, 1966.

Austin, Tex. Johnson Library. Bundy, McGeorge. Memorandum to Valenti for the President. 27 November 1964. National Security File.
Aide File: Bundy. Memos to the President, 6/64–2/65. Folder: Vol.
7, 10/1 to 12/31, 1964.

Austin, Tex. Johnson Library. Bundy, McGeorge. Memorandum to Mr.
Jack Valenti. 28 June 1965. National Security File. Aide File: Bundy.
Boxes 18, 19. Folder: Luncheons with the President, Vol. 1, Part
1.

Austin, Tex. Johnson Library. Busby, [Horace]. Note to "Mac." 11-10-

64. National Security File. Aide File: Bundy. Memos for the President. Box 2. Folder: Vol. 7, 10/1 to 12/31, 1964.

Austin, Tex. Johnson Library. Busby, Horace. Memorandum for Mr. Bundy. 9 October 1964. Aide File: Busby. Box 18 (1301). Folder: Memos for McGeorge Bundy.

Austin, Tex. Johnson Library. Cater, Douglass. Memorandum for McGeorge Bundy. 23 May 1964. National Security File. Aide File: Bundy. Boxes 18, 19. Folder: Meetings on Southeast Asia, Vol. 1.

Austin, Tex. Johnson Library. Moyers, Bill. Memorandum for Bromely Smith. 1 March 1966. National Security File. Name File: Moyers. Boxes 7, 8.

Austin, Tex. Johnson Library. Moyers, Bill. Memorandum for McGeorge Bundy. 22 December 1965. Papers of LBJ. Office Files of Bill Moyers. Box 6 (1341). Folder: Bundy Memos.

Austin, Tex. Johnson Library. Moyers, Bill. Memorandum to the President. 24 January 1966. National Security File. Aide File: Bundy. Box 6. Folder: Vol. 19, Jan. 19–Feb. 4, 1966.

Austin, Tex. Johnson Library. Moyers, Bill. Memorandum for Walt Rostow. 30 September 1966. National Security File. Name File: Moyers, Boxes 7, 8.

Austin, Tex. Johnson Library. Moyers, Bill. Note to "Mac." 8/19/65. National Security File. Aide File: Bundy. Box 4. Folder: Vol. 13, August 1965.

Austin, Tex. Johnson Library. Rostow W. W. Memorandum for the President. 17 January 1967. National Security File. Name File: Rostow. Boxes 7, 8.

Austin, Tex. Johnson Library. Rostow, W. W. Memorandum for the President. 24 July 1968. National Security File. Name File: Rostow. Boxes 7, 8.

Boston, Mass. Kennedy Library. Arthur M. Schlesinger, Jr. Papers. Subject Files, 1961–1964 Boxes 1-24.

Boston, Mass. Kennedy Library. Bundy, McGeorge. Memorandum to Mr. Schlesinger. 11 April 1961. Arthur M. Schlesinger, Jr. Papers. Subject Files, 1961–1964. Box 5. Folder: Cuba 4/3/61–4/23/61.

Boston, Mass. Kennedy Library. Bundy, McGeorge. Memorandum for Mr. Arthur Schlesinger. 18 October 1961. Arthur M. Schlesinger, Jr. Papers. Subject Files, 1961–64. Box 3B. Folder: British Guiana 4/28/61–10/30/61.

Boston, Mass. Kennedy Library. Bundy, McGeorge. Memorandum to Mr. Sorensen. 8 March 1963. Papers of President Kennedy. National Security Files. Meetings and Memoranda. Box 327. Folder: Staff Memoranda, Theodore Sorensen, 1961–63.

Boston, Mass. Kennedy Library. Meeker, Leonard C. Memorandum of October 19, 1962. Meeting of the Executive Committee of the National Security Council. Arthur M. Schlesinger, Jr. Papers. Box 5.

Boston, Mass. Kennedy Library. O'Brien, Larry. Memoranda for McGeorge Bundy. 5 March 1962. Papers of President Kennedy. National Security Files. Box 327. Folder: Staff Memoranda, Maxwell Taylor, 1/62–4/62.

Boston, Mass. Kennedy Library. Memoranda of Authur M. Schlesinger, Jr. Papers of President Kennedy. National Security Files. Meetings and Memoranda. Box 327.

Boston, Mass. Kennedy Library. Sorensen, Theodore C. Confidential letter to McGeorge Bundy. 5 March 1963. Papers of President Kennedy. National Security Files. Meetings and Memoranda. Box 327. Folder: Staff Memoranda, Theodore Sorensen, 1961–63.

Boston, Mass. Kennedy Library. Sorensen, Theodore C. Memorandum for McGeorge Bundy. 6 January 1963. Box 327. Folder: Staff Memoranda, Theordore Sorensen, State of the Union Message, 1963.

Boston, Mass. Kennedy Library. Sorensen, Theodore C. Memorandum for the President. 27 October 1962. Papers of President Kennedy. National Security Files. Meetings and Memoranda. Box 327. Folder: Staff Memoranda, Theodore Sorensen, 1961–63.

Hall, David K. "Implementing Multiple Advocacy in the National Security Council, 1947–1980." Ph.D. diss., Stanford University, 1982.

————. "The National Security Assistant as Policy Spokesman, 1947–1981." Paper prepared for the American Political Science Association Convention, New York, 3 September 1981.

Independence, Mo. Truman Library. Acheson, Dean. Memorandum for James S. Lay. 7 February 1950. Papers of George M. Elsey. Subject File. Box 88. Folder: National Defense–Atomic Energy, 1950.

Independence, Mo. Truman Library. Elsey, George M. Memorandum [and Note attached] for Dr. Wayne Grover. 11 January 1950. Papers of George M. Elsey. Subject File. Box 88. Folder: National Defense–Atomic Energy, 1950.

Independence, Mo. Truman Library. Elsey, George M. Memorandum to James S. Lay. 17 April 1951. Papers of George M. Elsey.

Independence, Mo. Truman Library. Elsey, George M. Memorandum for Mr. Lay. 21 February 1951. Papers of George M. Elsey. Subject File. Box 89. Folder: National Defense–Defense Mobilization.

Independence, Mo. Truman Library. Elsey, George M. Memorandum for the President. 8 February 1950. Papers of George M. Elsey.

Subject File. Box 88. Folder: National Defense–Atomic Energy, 1950.

Independence, Mo. Truman Library. Elsey, George M. Memorandum for General Roberts. 4 December 1951. Papers of George M. Elsey. Subject File. Box 89. Folder: National Defense–National Security Council.

Independence, Mo. Truman Library. Elsey, George M. Notes regarding White House press release. 23 September 1949. Papers of George M. Elsey. Box 88. Folder: National Defense–Atomic Energy–Announcement of Russian Atomic Bomb.

Independence, Mo. Truman Library. Johnson, Louis. Memorandum for James S. Lay. 1 February 1950. Papers of George M. Elsey. Subject File. Box 88. Folder: National Defense–Atomic Energy, 1950.

Independence, Mo. Truman Library. Kung, H. H. [New York City Head of the Bank of China], Letter to Sidney W. Souers. 12 March 1948. Papers of Sidney W. Souers. Box 1.

Independence, Mo. Truman Library. Lay, James S. Memorandum for George M. Elsey. 7 February 1950. Papers of George M. Elsey. Subject File. Box 88. Folder: National Defense–Atomic Energy, 1950.

Independence, Mo. Truman Library. Memorandum for the Executive Secretary. National Security Council. Papers of Clark M. Clifford. Subject File. Box 11. Folder: National Military Establishment–Security Council.

Independence, Mo. Truman Library. Neustadt, Richard E. "Notes on the White House Staff Under President Truman." Essay written for the Public Administration Clearinghouse. June 1953.

Independence, Mo. Truman Library. NSC Action 123. "Record of Actions Taken by the National Security Council, 1947–1948." 6 October 1948. Papers of Harry S Truman. President's Secretary's Files. Subject File. National Security Council. Box 191.

Independence, Mo. Truman Library. Pike, Sumner T. Memorandum for James S. Lay. 7 February 1950. Papers of George M. Elsey. Subject File. Box 88. Folder: National Defense–Atomic Energy, 1950.

Independence, Mo. Truman Library. Souers, Sidney W. Note regarding receipt of "1 TOP SECRET document" for Mr. Clark M. Clifford. 11 March 1948. Papers of Clark M. Clifford. Subject File. Box 11.

Independence, Mo. Truman Library. Souers, Sidney W. Letter to H. H. Kung. 16 March 1948. Papers of Sidney W. Souers. Box 1.

Independence, Mo. Truman Library. Souers, Sidney W. Memorandum

for Mr. Clark M. Clifford. 22 April 1949. Papers of Clark M. Clifford. Subject File. Box 11.

Independence, Mo. Truman Library. Souers, Sidney W. Memorandum for Edward G. Miller, Jr. 20 December 1949. Papers of Sidney W. Souers.

Independence, Mo. Truman Library. Springarn, Stephen J. Memorandum for Clark M. Clifford. 21 September 1948. Papers of Harry S Truman. Official File 10-B.

Independence, Mo. Truman Library. Springarn, Stephen J. Memorandum for Mr. Clifford. 11 April 1949. Papers of Clark M. Clifford. Box 11.

Independence, Mo. Truman Library. Springarn, Stephen J. Memorandum for Mr. Clifford. 22 April 1949. Papers of Clark M. Clifford. Subject File. Box 11.

National Archives and Records Service, General Services Administration, *Historical Materials in the Dwight D. Eisenhower Library*, Abilene, Kans., 1981.

Solliday, Michael. "The Special Assistant to the President for National Security Affairs and the National Security Council: A Comparative Study of Presidential Decision-Making." Ph.D. diss., Southern Illinois University, 1975.

U.S. Congress. House. Committee on Appropriations. *Hearings on Department of Defense Appropriations for 1953*. Pt. 1. Hearings. Washington, D.C.: U.S. Government Printing Office, 1952.

U.S. Congress. Senate. Committee on Foreign Relations. *The National Security Adviser: Role and Accountability*. Hearings. Washington, D.C.: U.S. Government Printing Office, 1980.

U.S. Congress. Senate. Subcommittee on National Policy Machinery of the Committee on Government Operations. *Organizing for National Security*. Pt. 1. Hearings. Washington, D.C.: U.S. Government Printing Office, 1961.

U.S. *Statutes at Large*. 80th Cong., 1st sess. Vol. 61. Pt. 1. "National Security Act of 1947." Washington, D.C.: U.S. Government Printing Office, 1948.

U.S. Department of State. *Foreign Relations of the United States, 1949: Volume I*. Washington, D.C.: U.S. Government Printing Office, 1976.

Washington, D.C., National Archives. Minutes of the 1st through 128th Meeting of the National Security Council, 26 September 1947 to 9 January 1953.

ORAL HISTORIES

Abilene, Kans., Eisenhower Library

Adams, Sherman, 12 April 1967
Eisenhower, Dwight D., 20 June 1967
Gray, Gordan, 10 October 1967

Austin, Tex., Johnson Library

Cater, S. Douglass, Jr., 8 May 1969

Boston, Mass., Kennedy Library

Lisagor, Peter, 22 April 1966
Sorensen, Theodore C., 6, 15 April 1964

Independence, Mo., Truman Library

Clifford, Clark M., 16 March 1972
Elsey, George M., 9 March 1965 and 7 July 1970
Murphy, Charles S., 15 July 1969 and 19 May 1970

INTERVIEWS

Zbigniew Brzezinski, 2 November 1984
McGeorge Bundy, 14 July 1983
S. Douglass Cater, Jr., 8 November 1984
George E. Christian, Jr., 9 November 1984
Clark M. Clifford, 22 August 1984
Lloyd N. Cutler, 5 November 1984
Ralph A. Dungan, 3 October 1984
John Ehrlichman, 3 August 1983 and 15 May 1984
John S. D. Eisenhower, 25 July 1983
Stuart E. Eisenstat, 5 November 1984
George M. Elsey, 24 August and 24 September 1984
Frank Gannon, 10 September 1984
Leonard Garment, 2 October 1984
Andrew J. Goodpaster, 11 July 1983
Bryce N. Harlow, 7 September 1984

Karl G. Harr, 30 June 1983
Stephen H. Hess, 14 August 1984
Carl Kaysen, 3 October 1984
Winston Lord, 27 September 1984
Henry C. McPherson, Jr., 9 November 1984
L. Arthur Minnich, 27 August 1984
Charles W. Murphy, 14 August 1984
Robert Pastor, 29 October 1984
Bradley Patterson, 29 June 1983
William B. Quandt, 15 October 1984
George E. Reedy, 4 November 1984
Walt W. Rostow, 25 October 1984 and 8 January 1985
Donald Rumsfeld, 13 July 1983
Pierre E. G. Salinger, 27 October 1984
Jerrold Schector, 17 October 1984
Brent Scowcroft, 17 October 1984
Theodore C. Sorensen, 18 October 1984
Elmer B. Staats, 27 August 1984
David H. Stowe, 15 August 1984
Paul A. Theis, 3 October 1984
Jack Watson, 12 October 1984
Lee C. White, 5 October 1984

Index

About the Author

JOSEPH G. BOCK is a staff member at the BDM Corporation, a professional and technical services company, and is also a State Representative in the Missouri General Assembly. He has written or coauthored articles for *Signal, Presidential Studies Quarterly,* and *Defense and Foreign Policy.* He has also contributed to works on American politics, and has presented papers at the Conference on the Role of Government in the United States, and the Southeast Conference Association for Asian Studies.